MODS & B

Lancashire's Rock 'n' Roll Summer

Colin Evans

Max Books

First published in the UK in 2009 by Max Books

A CIP catalogue record for this title is available from the British Library

ISBN: 978-0-9562224-0-4

Typeset by Andrew Searle
Cover design: James Brierley

Printed and bound by CPI Anthony Rowe

MAX BOOKS
4 The Willows, Manor Avenue
Sale, Cheshire, M33 4NA
Tel: 0161 973 5259
Email: maxcricket@btinternet.com

Most photographs appear by kind permission of the Manchester Evening News, Lancashire County Cricket Club, and the Keith Hayhurst Archive. The photograph of Sonny Ramadhin is courtesy of PA Photos. The provenance of certain photographs is unknown and every effort has been made to trace copyright holders and the publishers will be pleased to make good any omissions brought to their attention.

PREFACE

Dear Reader - I wrote this book mainly to prove that, after 40 years or so of writing short pieces of garbage for the newspapers, I could discipline myself to compose a much longer one. What's it all about? Basically, the summer of 1965, what it meant to English cricket, particularly Lancashire and their batsman David Green who, in a season when runs were hard to get, made history by scoring over 2000 without once hitting a century. And what it meant to me, a 17 year-old launching his career in sports journalism while doubling up as a pseudo teenage rebel.

I tried hard to stay focused on those themes but, inevitably, wandered to unscheduled destinations as though flashing my senior citizen's travel pass at every passing bus. And so, as well as a detailed look at Lancashire's matches, Green's career, and the cricketing issues of that era, the ride took me through a changing landscape and a number of time zones. As a result, I bumped into sports stars like Duncan Edwards, George Best, Malcolm Allison, Alex Higgins and Eric Cantona.

But, though wet and chilly, it was the summer of '65 which lit up this diverse journey. Cricket, Mods and Rockers, the Vietnam war, Manchester's club scene, the civil rights movement, drugs, sex (well, just a little bit), rock 'n' roll. Digging life - y'know, man, what we were all into. Weren't we?....

Colin Evans, 2009

ACKNOWLEDGEMENTS

David Green's razor sharp memory was a major source for this book and for many years I was a member of the cricket writing corps who appreciate his knowledge, sense of humour, and zest for life. Many thanks, David.

I also have to thank my Managing Editor Andrew Searle, for his enthusiasm and ability to take obstacles in his stride; the Rev Malcolm Lorimer who urged me to publish; Ken Grime, Nicky Burchill, Paul Welsby, Stephen Thorpe, Chris Brierley, and Karen Alexander, all of whom provided research, material and advice. Other sources are mentioned in the book and I thank them all.

As one theme of this book is sports journalism, I want to acknowledge all former colleagues for their friendship and tolerance, particularly Stan Miller who taught me what freelance journalism was all about and who provided some unforgettable moments in the Old Trafford Press Box.

I am also deeply in debt to:

All at Lancashire County Cricket Club who put up with me for over 30 years;
All at the Manchester Evening News who put up with me for over 30 years;
All my family and friends who have put up with me for over 60 years.

Of the numerous publications I referred to, the following stand out and I wish to fully acknowledge them, their authors, editors and contributors: Wisden Cricketers' Almanack, The Wisden Cricketer, Manchester Evening News, Playfair Cricket Annual, Central 1179 (Phil Scott and Keith Rylatt and Bee Cool Publishing Ltd), Lancashire County Cricket Club Year Book, Lancashire Cricket Annual, From The Stretford End (Brian Bearshaw), David Lloyd The Autobiography, Bowled Statham (Tony Derlien), Lancashire Cricket At The Top (Vernon Addison and Brian Bearshaw). Others are mentioned at relevant stages of the book.

If there are any omissions in the above lists, I apologise sincerely. And despite all the help I received from so many people, this book would not have been written without the constant encouragement and belief of my wife, Fi.

Front cover: Mods and their scooters, and Harry Pilling one of the stars of the 1965 summer. Pictures courtesy of the Manchester Evening News.

Cover design: James Brierley.

To Fi

"Whilst the absence of Test Matches tended to give the Old Trafford scene an unaccustomed touch of dullness, the summer, in spite of the weather, had its compensations in the uprising of David Green into an opening batsman with aggressive qualities second to none..."

Lancashire County Cricket Year Book

"Evans, in time, may prove a useful member of staff, and I recommend that, following his six months period as a probationary reporter, he is offered an indentureship. However, I do have some concerns. I believe he keeps disreputable company...."

Internal memo, Warrington Guardian Newspaper Series

It was in 1965 that David Green made cricketing history by becoming the only batsman to score 2000 or more first-class runs without once making a century. The summer was chilly and wet, the pitches suited seam bowling rather than Green's favoured style of stroke play, but his remarkable consistency and stamina enabled him to play in 34 Championship and other first-class matches, allowing him to stack up the runs. Evans was a Lancashire fan and a rookie hack on his local paper. That season he covered his first cricket match, a Manchester Association fixture to start a long, undistinguished career in sports writing. But it wasn't just the cricket which made the summer of '65 stick in his memory...

ONE

SOMETHING happened that summer. As though the life of the world skipped a heartbeat. Everything got faster, more intense. Some of us went too quickly, others were left behind bemused, some merely stayed where they were. The gap grew into a chasm and part of the world which we had all known and had so easily accepted slipped into the void. Much later, perhaps, we were to look back with regret at that which was lost, but then we didn't care, because there was so much new stuff around. Dylan had spoken, the times were changing, and we were in the vanguard of this great social revolution. Hell, they were close to landing a man on the moon, and you could legally bomb down the new motorways at 100 mph plus, if you had a Jag. Life in the fast lane. We loved it. Slowcoaches sneeringly overtaken, tradition crumpled up and tossed to one side like a lost betting slip.

Yet hide-bound county cricket, the slowest and the most traditional, hung on by its fingertips. I don't know how. Perhaps because it was so unthreatening and few, beyond those directly involved, bothered with it. While traffic buzzed down the unregulated M6 and M1 (the 70 mph limit wasn't imposed until December 1965), cricket trundled along England's byways, stopping off to play a game here, another there, staying quietly indoors if it rained - and that season it rained a lot. For David Green and his Lancashire team-mates it was cricket, cricket, cricket, day after day of it from May to September with little reward other than a reasonable salary and for little reason except their love of the game. No England stardom. No roar of the crowd.

Green played 28 Championship matches, each scheduled to last three days, and six other games of similar duration, a punishing timetable taking into account travelling between fixtures. The end of one match, say in Manchester, might be followed by the start of the next only 18 hours later and 200 miles away in London, then another in Taunton, leaving little time to think and reflect on the Vietnam war, the space race, or the great cultural reformation of the Swinging Sixties which my old man thought could easily be sorted with a few kicks up the backside and a couple of years of National Service. "Mods and Rockers?! Bloody long haired louts, the lot of 'em. And don't tell me that's music. That's just bloody noise, that is."

My Generation. We were changing the world, and didn't we know it. Pumped up with self-importance, shouting *our* freedom, playing *our* music, and popping *our* pills we lived for now, for kicks, and wanted to move so fast that we would always be a blur on the horizon. Summer '65 was scooter rides to Blackpool, hitch-hiking to London, sleeping on the beach at Brighton, all-night dance sessions in the Manchester clubs, and crazy booze and Benzedrine fuelled parties in strangers' houses. It didn't last long. Some progressed to Flower Power and alternative lifestyles, but somehow psychedelia and LSD was a step too far for most of us. Eventually we settled for the delights of small town life. Marriage, work, kids, divorce, redundancy, the pub, memories. That summer, though, was different.

Sociologists have since argued about the value of the Swinging Sixties. An extreme view is that it was the end of civilization. We became more materialistic, more self-indulgent, and more intent on trivia than cultural self-improvement.

Christopher Booker, for instance, said 1965 was the pivotal year of an era in which people were unable to cope with the post-war economic boom. "By 1967-68 many were beginning to feel ...that in the previous 10 years they had come through a shattering experience."

Bernard Levin claimed that the 'stones beneath Britain's feet had shifted.'

"...as she walked ahead with her once purposeful stride she began to stumble, then fall down. Eventually she had fallen down so often that she was not only covered in mud but the laughing stock of passers by."

A more sympathetic stock-taking of the Sixties highlighted massive progress. American scientists, in 1965, had produced riveting new evidence to back The Big Bang theory of creation, and, in Britain, we were experiencing The Big Bang of a new cultural universe. Sparsely researched particles of materialism, idealism, sexual freedom, social mobility and artistic innovation were fired through an accelerator, colliding and sparking to produce a new type of life. No doubt there was some 'dark matter' in the mix, too. Something unknown, possibly dangerous. But, overall, it was an experiment well worth the risk.

For me, the Sixties was all about 1965, and particularly that summer. We felt we could do anything. Well, almost anything. There were some inhibiting factors. Like a job. Mine was as a reporter at the sleepy local newspaper, and while at night and during the weekend I kept 'disreputable company', I also had to mingle daily with the high and mighty of our little, leafy part of Cheshire. And to write about cricket.

One Saturday afternoon in late April, surprisingly warm and sunny, I slouched up to the local club, armed with chewed off biro, a 'Reporter's Notebook' stained with coffee spills, and four pints of bitter consumed at a fairly casual 'summer is here' pace in the Lion. My first match working as a stringer for the Manchester Evening News Pink, the weekend sports edition.

Not a big order, it's true, 50 words and scoreboard to be phoned to the copy room at 3.20pm, with a 25 words 'add' and score update at tea, 3s 9d for the lot. But still, it was a start, the threshold of a career.

The big balding bloke filling the doorway of the green painted, wooden pavilion looked me up and down and said: "You can't come in here, Sonny Jim. This is for players and officials only." I didn't argue. His outstretched arms pushed against each side of the framework like Samson and the pillars. Only without the hair. I went up to the local businessman I knew to be the club captain, lolling back in a deckchair on the veranda, and said: "I'm covering the game for the Evening News, can you give me the team?"

"No."

"Why?"

"Because I don't like the Evening News, that's why."

Those rebuffs proved to be excellent experience for the next 40 years!

*****

YOU can like county cricket, enjoy it, think it's a great day out, but you can't *love* it unless you have been to a county championship match. Attended, endured, each day, all day. It's then that you soak up all its juices and emerge a differently flavoured human being. I'm not saying it makes you a better human being, just a different one. Especially when you've watched the rain teem down hour after hour, heard innumerable announcements that the umpires will inspect the pitch again if and when the weather improves (in the meantime they will put their feet up and have another cuppa while you drain the dregs of your flask because the last tea bar in the ground closed an hour ago), and when you realise that you have wasted several days of your life, perhaps along with hundreds of pounds in hotel, travel and other costs - that's when you know you love cricket. Cricket might not love you but, nonetheless, you embrace it and refuse to let it go, huddled together in a damp, chilly stand with a few other optimistic souls, keeping faith, until you see a couple of players, dressed in their civvies, dragging their gear towards the car park, and you know it's all over even though the man on the tannoy cheerfully announces: "The umpires will continue to monitor the situation..."

In the mid 1960s the number of fans who loved county cricket had fallen dramatically. One report glumly noted: "Attendances are causing serious concern. In 1947 the number who paid for admission totalled 2,200,910. In 1965 it was 659,560." It was the lowest ever recorded.

While no-one had expected the surge of the immediate post-war years to continue, neither had anyone believed the decline would be so steep. One solution was Sunday cricket, following Australia's lead. The Sunday trading laws prohibited payment at the turnstile, but money could be made via other channels, including car parking. Some Sunday friendlies were televised, and it was proposed that 12 county matches would include Sunday play in 1966. Three years later came the birth of the Sunday League.

But in '65 the game seemed on the road to nowhere. Or, at least, at a dangerous crossroads: archaic administration, poor spectator facilities, dire weather, dreadful pitches which made batting a lottery. It could be exciting if you thrived on the clatter of wickets tumbling, daft declarations to get a result, and last-gasp finishes but, for me and my mates, the entertainment value was zilch.

As chippy grammar school kids, nurtured on cricket as a game and as a beneficial philosophy for life, we had watched Lancashire at Old Trafford as much as possible, catching the old steam puffer from our town to Altrincham, switching to the electric train service, jumping out at the Warwick Road station next to the ground, and reluctantly paying a junior admission fee after unsuccessfully trying to get in free by climbing over the perimeter wall. But now, as part of a wider group, some of whom had started work at 15, we were into something with a little more adrenaline. Drink, drugs, Blues, women. Digging life, man. Far out - well, as far out as you could get in a small, semi-rural town where the Conservative MP had the biggest majority in the country and gooseberry shows were held in high esteem. They grew them big, green and hairy - the goosegogs not the MPs - on the allotments, placed them lovingly in velvet lined boxes to be weighed at the Drovers' Arms and suchlike venues, lifted them out delicately, like an archaeologist handling a rare Egyptian artefact or a butcher dangling a pair of lamb's bollocks, and weighed them on the miniature scales. "Twenty two pennyweight! - first prize to Tom Stubbs." And Tom would glow proudly, while his big rival Jack Warburton would smile grimly and whisper to his missus: "I'll beat the bastard next time."

As for the Parliamentary constituency, our representative was one of several retired Lt. Cols. who controlled large estates in the area. This one also had a Sir attached to his double-barrelled moniker, a Hall which included a full-scale theatre for his family to stage Noel Coward and Oscar Wilde plays, a fjord or two in Norway where he fished for salmon, and a hearty, gung-ho approach which went down well enough until he fell asleep at a Young Conservatives AGM, resisting nudges from his companions on the top table until, finally, heroically, he jerked himself upright, pounded the table with his fists, and loudly grunted: "Hear, hear! Hear, hear!" Only then did he take in the rather embarrassed silence - the meeting had been closed several seconds earlier.

A few people were ready to haul cricket screaming and kicking into a new era. It could be that many more within the game felt the need for change, but were either powerless or too wary to try. There was certainly unrest at Old Trafford and it had come to a head late in 1964 when four players were sacked. The members had had enough, mounting a rebellion at the way the club was handled, resulting in the committee being kicked out at a special general meeting. One of the dissidents (he refused to be tagged a 'rebel') was Cedric Rhoades, a local businessman, who was to become the club's chairman for 18 years and it was during his regime that, after a lengthy spell in the doldrums, Lancashire regained its pride and passion, mainly through achievements in the speeded up version of the game, one-day cricket.

But Rhoades and his go-ahead colleagues had only just won committee places when the 1965 season began, there had to be a transitional period before they could exert real power, and it was to be another four years before he took the helm as chairman. Nationally, the first one-day competition, the Gillette Cup, had been introduced in 1963 and that, coupled with the events in Manchester, offered a ray of hope to those who believed cricket had to throw off its chains. But radical reform was still a distance away.

Basically, Lancashire's county cricket consisted of the four months long championship of 28 three day fixtures, and other first-class games against the touring sides - in 1965 New Zealand and South Africa - and Oxford University. Players might also be picked for representative teams, MCC or TN Pearce's XI for instance, as well as England. Sundays were still rest days, otherwise it was a summer long test of endurance. For me, too.

Weekends were particularly exhausting. If it wasn't a party, or a quick hitch down south, it was an all-nighter at the Twisted Wheel or one of the other venues in Manchester's burgeoning club scene. One was called Heaven and Hell. The ground floor was Heaven, and that was rough enough with a dimly lit stage and a refreshment bar. The cellar was Hell, with no lights and refreshments of your own making. Mods from all over the country visited The Wheel. But the North Manchester crew was the most obvious. They wore sharp Italian suits and razored hair-cuts, rode scooters piled high with wing mirrors, and parked in neat rows along Brazennose Street. *Knew about stuff.* Had jobs in town. Strutted. Flaunted. There was a hierarchy. The pack leaders were known as Faces. Below them were the High Numbers, then the Numbers and the Tickets. From the Cheshire backwoods, and only dipping our toes into the Mod life, we looked dull in comparison. Had the hair OK, razored and backcombed, but the clothes, leather jacket and Levis, deliberately shrunk and faded by sitting in the bath with them on, lacked the original Mod style, indeed, carried a whiff of Rocker, the leather-clad character who dosed on rock 'n' roll and motor bike fumes. Ringo Starr coined the term 'Mockers'. It didn't matter. As we told our parents and bragged among ourselves: "We're where it's at."

Self expression was the theme, self-indulgence the key. So while Operation Rolling Thunder got under way in Vietnam, while Martin Luther King upped the stakes in the race struggle, and while my Dad roared: "Is this what we fought the war for?!" we shrugged on our ex-USA combat jackets, decorated with machine gun bullet holes, and snapped up from the Army and Navy Stores in Altrincham via Korea for a mere £2 10s. Across the back of these green jackets we scrawled black marker pen slogans like CND, Fidel Rules, Stones, and, under the collar, because blasphemy was an issue, Sex is God.

And so, suitably attired, we roared down our hometown roads on our snazzy Italian jobs, eliciting disgusted looks from the older housewives as they gossiped at the front gates, and maybe a wistful glance or two from some of the younger ones, who as teenagers had screamed at Elvis and Little Richard and were settled down now with Ronnie or Kenny - back in civvies after National Service - and had a couple of kiddies and a new hi-fi, but still, sometimes, had the yearning to scream again, maybe from the pillion seat of a 150cc Lambretta scooter. And, given half a chance, we would have said: "C'mon luv, fancy a ride?" And, of course, they would have snorted their refusal: "Cheeky young bugger" because, after all, their men were men and we were just boys, playing at it.

To be a Mod - a Face, not the halfway cut like me - you required:

Italian scooter with 12 wing mirrors;
Italian designed suit, preferably mohair;
Fur trimmed fish-tail Parka;
Trendy barber - the best in Manchester were on St Peter's Street and Deansgate;
Deep regard for soul music;
Ability to look cool while dancing like a dervish.

To be a Rocker, you needed:

Decent English motorbike, say 250cc BSA;
Lots of grease (for hair and bike);
Metal encrusted leather jacket;
Spare chains and spanners (for repairs and self defence);
Ability to look cool while doing the ton.

Fashion-wise, neither Mods nor Rockers could touch the 1950s Teddy Boys, and one or two were still knocking about - minimum requirements:

Crepe soled shoes known as brothel creepers;
Drainpipe trousers with cute little turn-ups;

Edwardian style thigh length dress jacket;
Massive quiff and thigh length sideburns;
XL size jar Brylcreem (as advertised in The Cricketer).

You were voted Top of the Teds if you also sported:

Narrowed eyes a la James Dean;
Set of size 12 fishhooks (pinned into lapels to deter opponents from decking you with a Glasgow kiss);
Ability to shrug Edwardian style jacket back over shoulders while fully buttoned thereby turning it into a straitjacket;
Ability to swagger down the road with pinioned arms.

*****

DAVID Green had first played for Lancashire as an amateur and while still studying at Oxford. Tall, solidly built, he followed in his dad's footsteps by playing rugby union for Sale and liked to give things a bash. Opposing forwards, a cricket ball, a pint of ale, and fools, some of whom he found in the Old Trafford committee room.

His whirlwind batting often created ripples of excitement in the stands, but sometimes exasperated the county coach. About the same time that I was making my cricket reporting debut for the Manchester Evening News Pink, he was appearing for the MCC in the annual season's curtain-raiser at Lord's against Yorkshire. In London, it was wet. Five hours were lost on the first day, spoiling it as a truly competitive game, but one of the highlights was the MCC's opening stand between Green and Middlesex's Mike Brearley, which put on 62 against the new ball attack of Fred Trueman and Tony Nicholson. Green made 39, only to be trapped lbw by Ray Illingworth's off-spin - Brearley, the 1964 Young Cricketer Of The Year, who had clattered Trueman for three successive fours in his first over, carried his bat for 90.

MCC were captained by the tall, elegant England star Ted Dexter who, six months previously, had stood for the Conservatives in the General Election at Cardiff, only to be crushed by Labour's Jim Callaghan.

"I remember before the game walking to the nets with E R Dexter," Green recalled. "He looked at my bat and said: 'So that's the Thunderblade,' which I took as a way of saying that he had heard of my reputation for giving the ball a bit of welly. It made me feel good. I'll never forget that."

Dexter's season fell apart in more horrifying fashion than his political career, when, pushing his car which had run out of petrol, he broke his leg and missed the summer series with South Africa.

Green was named in a MCC side of 'Test possibles' for the next game the same week against Surrey. Led by the already established Colin Cowdrey, the hopefuls included Alan Jones, Keith Fletcher, Colin Milburn, Barry Knight, David Allen, Alan Knott, Robin Hobbs, Derek Underwood and John Dye. Again rain ruined it, and Green, only able to make a couple, never had a real hope after that of forcing his way into the England side.

"It didn't enter my mind," he admitted. "England were so strong in batting, and I wasn't good enough. I was an opener - look at the some of the others who opened in those first two matches, Geoff Boycott, Jack Hampshire, Brearley, and John Edrich. Then there was Bob Barber, who had left Lancashire a few years earlier and had done so well at Warwickshire."

And yet Brearley's form faded, the highly promising Hampshire lacked consistency, Barber's top score in the six Tests against New Zealand and South Africa was 56, while Boycott's slow scoring earned severe criticism after the second Test against South Africa and he was dropped for the final game.

Edrich was the outstanding success. He won the first to 1000 runs race by June 17 and took only a month more to make it 2000, having a run of 139, 121 not out, 205 no, 55, 96, 188, 92, 105 no, and 310 no (against New Zealand), a total of 1311 runs in nine consecutive innings. This sequence, it was said in Playfair Monthly, 'has earned him immortality. It has also produced exceptional joy in the general area of Kennington where a great deal of bitterness still rankles as Brearley was preferred to Edrich for the South African tour last winter. In the grim and sordid weather of 1965, Edrich has performed a miracle...'

Edrich, however, was felled by a ball from South Africa's Peter Pollock at Lord's and, though he came back for Surrey, it kept him out of the Test side for the rest of the season.

Barber and Boycott formed England's opening partnership for most of the summer, and they did well enough as a pair with a series of half century partnerships, although a combined tally of 247 runs from 10 knocks against the powerful Springbok attack wasn't that impressive, even taking into account the quality of Peter Pollock's pace bowling.

Pollock broke their partnership at 0 and 1 in the vital second Test at Trent Bridge, pushing South Africa towards their first Test victory in England for 10 years. Green accepts he probably would not have done any better. Perhaps his attacking instincts might have brought quick runs, and his defence was 'decent', but patience wasn't his finest virtue. "I'd hit a bad ball for four, but then I'd want to treat the next delivery the same way."

So Green drove away from Lord's late on Tuesday afternoon, May 4, to link up with his Lancashire brethren who were playing at Taunton against Somerset the next morning. It remained damp, cloudy and cool.

*****

1965 saw the early development of one of the most influential personalities in Lancashire's history. Cedric Rhoades had led a coup at the end of the previous season in which the Old Trafford committee had resigned en bloc on a vote of no confidence. Rhoades and several of his supporters were elected onto a new committee and he was to transform the club as its chairman over almost two decades.

Clever, dynamic, he loved history, read Gibbons' Decline and Fall of the Roman Empire, and had risen from office boy to owner of a Manchester textile firm. He proved to be a forward-looking cricket Caesar, advocating more government cash for sport, more encouragement of school cricket, and for Lancashire to be financially independent. He even suggested a Big City League. Most of all he wanted success on the field and promised longer contracts and better pay deals for the players.

"I want to make Lancashire the Real Madrid of cricket," he said. For the first half of his regime, he looked capable of achieving his dream. Lancashire won a glut of one-day trophies, improvements were made to the ground, and the club was run on more business-like lines. But the dream faded and Rhoades metamorphosed from admired hands-on chairman to feared autocrat. He loved the power, and stayed far too long. It ended on the most bitter note after a poor 1986 campaign which cost manager Jack Bond and coach Peter Lever their jobs. At the AGM Rhoades came under pressure from a member, primed beforehand, who asked why the committee had appointed Clive Lloyd as their captain for the 1986 season, knowing that he would be unavailable for many championship games. Rhoades told the meeting that Jack Bond had recommended Lloyd as captain. Bond publicly refuted that when I interviewed him the next day, and, eventually, Rhoades resigned. He had devoted much of his life and most of his energy to the club.

I remember him ringing me late one morning to say: "I've just clinched a ground advertising deal worth £100,000 plus" - big money in those days. Hearing a whooshing noise in the background, I asked him where he was ringing from: "Euston station, got to go now or I'll miss the train back and I've got a meeting I can't afford to miss at 4 o'clock." Self publicist, certainly. I don't think he enjoyed anything more than standing in front of a packed AGM, dispelling members' anxieties and criticisms with a few pithy words, or a dramatic statement that Lancashire were to make a big signing. He calmed several potential storms that way.

Whatever the flaws, he was a chairman who got things done, and, mainly through his prodding, poking and demanding, Lancashire's sleeping giant awoke. Sadly, the exit of Bond and Lever, immediately after the 1986 Gillette

Cup final defeat by Sussex, heralded a decline and already under pressure from a group of members demanding change, he pressed the self destruct button at the AGM.

"Eighteen years... they don't know what I've put into this club," he said. Maybe he had only himself to blame for his acrimonious departure, but the saddest aspect was that subsequently he rarely visited the ground that he had so loved.

*****

BRIAN Statham had been appointed Lancashire's captain for 1965 at the ripe age of 34 and after a bizarre see-saw sequence of events. Shenanigans? Yes, with knobs on.

Statham, who had joined the club in 1951 and was now recognised as one of its all-time greats, was not Lancashire's automatic choice to replace the Australian Ken Grieves, who had been unceremoniously kicked out at the end of 1964. No, there were question marks against 'George' when it came to the captaincy. Wonderful bowler, loyal to the marrow, hugely respected by all and sundry, but could he cut it as the boss? Was he tough enough? Many in the committee room thought not. Or that the responsibilities of the job would affect his bowling. So, first, they looked elsewhere.

Now, although there was a newly constructed general committee following the rebellion, the cricket committee retained several of the old guard. And Lancashire, as a club, didn't have a great pedigree in picking captains. They left it too late in Cyril Washbrook's case, then, in 1960, gave it to Bob Barber, who as an amateur player - a 'gentleman' - was told in no uncertain terms that he had to keep a gap between him and the rest of the squad. Colonel Leonard Green, who had led Lancashire to three Championship triumphs in the 1920s, took Barber to one side and said: "Bob, you will have a problem as captain if you stay at the same hotel as the players. We are strongly advising you to stay at a different one." Barber took the advice, reluctantly, but it didn't work.

Young and comparatively inexperienced, he had problems with man-management. Peter Marner was sent home from a game against Kent at Folkestone because he ignored a committee order to wear his blazer at lunch and Jack Dyson, the former Manchester City star who had figured in the FA Cup win over Birmingham in 1956, was disciplined for a 'serious breach of discipline and an act of insubordination and insolence to the captain'.

In 1962, after Barber had joined Warwickshire, came the craziest choice of all - Joe Blackledge, who had captained Lancashire's 2nd X1 for a couple of years, and the Northern League club Chorley, but had never even played county cricket. It signalled the worst season in their then 98-year history and Old Trafford crowds slumped accordingly with only 65,000 paying to watch

48 days cricket. For such a big and proud club, this was rock-bottom. Or it would have been if things hadn't deteriorated!

Grieves took over, with Washbrook as manager, and did well enough with marginal improvement in the Championship and successive semis in the recently introduced Gillette Cup, but the second of these, in 1964, provoked a massive row. Lancashire, chasing a victory target of 295 from their 65 overs (as it was in those days), made a bright start of 67 in 12 overs thanks to Green's belligerence. Too bright for Warwickshire's liking. Scared stiff, they resorted to an ultra defensive field, the first time such tactics had been used in this new fangled game, and Lancashire gave it up with Geoff Clayton blocking it out, studiously ignoring the howls of protest from angry, bewildered fans to finish with an unbeaten 19 from 20 overs. It descended into a near riot, Lancashire finishing well short on 209-7.

Green explained: "Warwickshire were frightened. They'd made a really big total, but got the wind up when we started so well and they just placed two rings of fielders around us. We had never seen anything like it before. The feeling in our dressing-room was that it was unsportsmanlike, they were refusing to play the game.

"When Chimpy (Clayton) went out to bat he was angry. We all were. I can't remember exactly what was said, whether he told us what he intended to do. He might easily have said something like: 'If that's the way they want it, that's what they'll get.' Just pure frustration. And the fact that we had slipped well behind the rate, and had lost wickets. But we weren't surprised when Chimpy began to block it.

"We could hear the shouts getting louder from the crowd, and the chairman came into the dressing-room, obviously concerned, and asked Grieves what the hell was going on. I have to say this was a chairman who knew sweet FA about cricket. The captain explained as best he could, and the chairman replied: 'But why doesn't he hit it just hard enough to go in between the two rings of fielders, then he could get a run.' Well, of course, chairman, we hadn't thought of that. We'll just hit it between the two rings of fielders! Pillock.

"Anyway, the debate ended when Grieves got up and said, rather forcibly, that he'd had enough, and was going on to the balcony to call them in. In other words to stop the match there and then, forfeit the result. He was serious. He would have done it. God knows what would have happened. The chairman retreated, but I suspect that it might have had something to do with the committee sacking Grieves as the captain at the end of the season!" Clayton suffered the brunt of the criticism, but there remained a feeling that he was a fall guy.

Washbrook had made his Lancashire debut in the Championship-winning side of 1934. The manager was one of the most respected figures in the game, not universally liked - "I could be a bastard when it came to it" - but regarded as the most professional of all professionals. He found the attitude and behaviour of some players impossible to reconcile with his ethos and, without naming individuals, he stamped out a condemnatory end of season report.

As well as the Gillette Cup fiasco, there were complaints from several counties about Lancashire's behaviour - bad language and 'rude' gestures were mentioned. Grieves had the captaincy taken from him and, not having heard anything else from the committee, simply went into league cricket. Clayton, of course, was pushed quickly through the exit door, and Marner and Dyson were also sacked. Lancashire, at that point, had no captain, hardly enough for a decent team, and even had to look for a new secretary when Geoffrey Howard quit. The loss of this amiable, highly efficient figure was as damning as the departure of any player. He didn't want to leave Lancashire, but felt he had no choice, his position constantly undermined by the interference of a former secretary, Rupert Howard (no relation), who had been appointed chairman of the match committee in 1963. Geoffrey Howard was so popular that some staff were in tears when he announced his move to The Oval.

No wonder the members revolted. Yet, despite the overturning of the general committee, lessons were still to be learned. Echoes of the bad old days reverberated through Old Trafford when they set about choosing the 1965 skipper. Statham was an obvious candidate, although the previous hierarchy plainly had not thought so, for after being forced to resign en bloc but before new elections had taken place, they had placed an advert, under a box number, in The Times. It read: 'A first class county cricket club invites applications from persons with first class cricket experience for the position of captain of the county X1.'

Grieves described it as 'an insult to Brian Statham' and there were more protests from brassed-off supporters. Yet Lancashire refused to bow to public opinion. Questions remained over Statham's suitability, so they courted Warwickshire's AC Smith. Until he laid down conditions:

1: That Statham and Pullar (Lancashire's ex England batsman) accept me wholeheartedly;
2: No team manager;
3: The captain not to be outvoted by the selection committee;
4: Three years contract.

'Over confident' was what one committee man thought of that. The vote to appoint him was split 4-4. The chairman, Dick Bowman, used his casting vote to eliminate Smith from the discussions. Which left Statham a clear run. Well, not exactly. Lancashire had two-timed everyone by also talking about the captaincy with Freddie Millett. Hmmm… Millett was fairly well known in sporting circles as the captain of Cheshire in the Minor Counties, and had earned credit for the way he had led his side against Surrey in a Gillette Cup tie the previous summer. But captain of Lancashire?…they had to be joking! But he very nearly got it. The vote went 4-3 in favour of Statham, possibly because he had 69 more Test caps than his rival!

"I believe Statham has good reason to feel that he has not been treated too well," confessed one of the committee. Millett wasn't too happy, either. Entirely innocent in this sorry tale, he had been led to think that the job was his. You could deduce from all this that Lancashire were in the mire at the start of 1965, and you'd be right.

Green, though, wasn't particularly anxious. "We knew what had gone on and could hardly believe they'd got rid of players just like that. Chimpy and Porky (Peter Marner) were good players. I had a lot of respect for them. Grieves had been outstanding. Before that Barber had moved to Edgbaston and Roy Collins had quit. The team that I had started with in 1959 had melted away. We were left with not a lot. But this was a new season. You looked forward to it. I was playing cricket for a living. I could have had a proper job after Uni, a career of some sort, but, tell you the truth, I never really liked 'work' in that sort of way. No, cricket would do very nicely for me. Good money, around £2000 a year all in - other poor sods were slogging their guts out for £10 a week in those days - and the social life was, let's say, memorable, if I could remember all of it. I couldn't have asked for more, really."

*****

£10 a week!…gimme some of that. Starting rate for budding Hannen Swaffers at the newspaper was £6 15s weekly, and 2s 6d of that went on buying a new typewriter after months of hammering out the copy on a First World War correspondent's Imperial, which folded up so neatly you could almost stick it in your pocket but had the disadvantage of an over-used, smaller than average ribbon spool not in production since around 1919. With no replacement available, the ribbon was soon punctuated with holes. A slightly chipped 't' key tended to aggravate the problem. Therefore much of my copy was illegible as well as illiterate.

When The Editor asked me if I fancied an Olivetti, I said: "Yes, that would be great," thinking he was talking about a new Italian scooter that I'd not heard about. Next day a gleaming blue portable typewriter was on my desk with a terse note, ordering me to pay for it at half a crown a week: 'This will be deducted automatically from your wages.' I would have taken it with me on my cricket reporting debut that April if not for having to cart it into the pub first, risking a volley of taunts from the lads, most of whom had quickly hardening hands from the building trade and who referred to me sneeringly as the pen pusher. Still, like Green, I reckoned the summer of 1965 was opening out in front of me, full of promise.

TWO

MAY 1 1965: FA Cup Final day with the Liverpool-Leeds United clash going into extra-time at Wembley and the nation's soccer lovers glued to the box. But in our town the main attraction was the annual Festival, a pretty procession of hundreds of kids in fancy dress, horse-drawn tableaux featuring The Old Woman in the Shoe and Little Bo Peep and such, brass and silver bands, morris dancers, all led by my pal Ken giving a bravado performance as the pagan character Jack in the Green, who traditionally ushers in the spring.

Ken had ushered it in by downing a gallon of bitter before the start of the procession and, affected by the heat, the beer, and the heavy bush-like costume which covered him from head to toe, he rolled from kerb to kerb, gave a pagan belch and fell over. Good fun, but I would have preferred to have watched Norman 'bite yer legs' Hunter digging at the heels of Ian St John at Wembley, and Leeds' winger Albert Johansson making history by being the first black footballer to appear in the final. It had taken 92 years.

Johansson didn't have a great final. Gifted but inconsistent, he slipped out of soccer and into alcoholism and died in a high rise flat in Leeds in 1995. George Best mourned him, saying: "He was a brave man to actually go on the pitch in the first place. A nice man as well, which is more important than anything."

Black sportsmen/women had to battle long and hard for recognition in the UK. Back in 1939 there was outrage in the Lancashire dressing room over a suggestion to sign the great West Indian all-rounder Learie Constantine, then playing in league cricket.

Lancashire's all-rounder Len Hopwood recalled many years later: "….the thought of a coloured chap playing for Lancashire was ludicrous. We were clannish in those less enlightened days. We wanted none of Constantine. We would refuse to play. In all fairness I must say we had nothing against him personally. He was, in fact, very popular with us. There was no personal vendetta. But the thought of a black man taking the place of a white man in our side was anathema."

Nothing personal, just out and out racism, although Hopwood has to be admired for his honesty. Constantine, set to become a leading anti-racism campaigner, never played for Lancashire. Yet he had a surprisingly indulgent approach to racism within cricket, writing in the mid 1930s: "There have been incidents, mostly hushed up by us all - rivalries and vendettas that owed a lot of their sharpness and quite a bit of fun to colour. Sportsmen mostly have big hearts and we are quick to be kind, slow to be cruel…On the whole I have no complaints."

Attitudes at Old Trafford had softened by 1965 when the West Indian Sonny Ramadhin, who had linked up with Alf Valentine to demonise the England batsmen in 1950, was on the Red Rose staff and the signings of Farokh Engineer and Clive Lloyd were around the corner. And yet I suspect some of the old issues were simmering below the surface when Lancashire failed to give Big Clive the captaincy until 1981. By then he had been playing championship cricket for 12 years, and had established himself as the West Indies' longest reigning and most successful captain. Why did he have to wait so long for the Lancashire job? Lloyd is nowadays reluctant to stir up past troubles, but this has relevance and so I quote from his autobiography. Speaking of the decision to make David Lloyd the successor to Jack Bond in 1974, he said: "I admit I was aggrieved. I felt that the players wanted me. The secretary, Jack Wood, revealed that I had overwhelming support in a straw poll taken among them. So why was I passed over? Was there some racial consideration, or was it just that the committee wanted a Lancastrian in the post? I hoped it was the latter."

In 2003 he told me: "I was at my peak then, full of enthusiasm, and I know that if I'd had six years in the job I could have built a wonderful side. We would have won the championship. Just imagine Andy Roberts bowling with Peter Lever, Peter Lee and Ken Shuttleworth. It was a missed opportunity. We could have had that calibre of player. That's what I could have done for the club."

Michael Holding played a handful of games for Lancashire, and Colin Croft had a couple of seasons, but that was after Lever and Shuttleworth had departed, and, in any event, Croft rarely reproduced his Test form at county level. Basically, Lancashire missed out on Lloyd's Caribbean pace battery.

Sadly, Ramadhin was to make only three championship appearances in 1965 after a highly successful first season the previous year. Despite doubts over his action - "He will be watched carefully and steps taken accordingly", a pre-season committee report said - he would have played a key role but found the six days a week commitment too much and asked to be released from his three year contract. Lancashire might have had another West Indian, who offered to play for them when his university term ended. But, because he would not be available all season, the cricket committee said no. Otherwise the West Indies star Deryk Murray would have preceded Engineer as the club's first overseas wicketkeeper. With Geoff Clayton finding new employment at Somerset, Lancashire, instead, relied on Keith Goodwin, who was good behind the stumps but was a tail-end bat who, that summer, amassed 117 runs from 40 innings.

Murray, meanwhile, prospered at Cambridge University with Wisden noting him as "an attractive stroke player but also a batsman of considerable all round skill." Against the champions Worcestershire, Murray scored a remarkable century, making 108 out of a second innings total of 168, his last 60 runs coming in a last wicket stand of 70 with S G Russell. On the same day Goodwin was bowled for a duck by Middlesex's John Price.

This is not to criticise Goodwin, as such. He wasn't expected to make many runs and, in three day cricket, 'nine, 10, Jack' weren't encouraged to hang around at the crease. Statham, for instance, was once enjoying a little knock late in a day's play when Washbrook, then the captain, sent out a terse message: "Tell that silly bugger to get out now - he's got to bowl for the last half hour!" Statham had just hammered 62 in 31 minutes with two sixes and 12 fours!

But the wicketkeeping situation had strained Lancashire - to the extent that they had even offered Yorkshire's second X1 player Geoffrey Hodgson a three year deal at 'a minimum £700 a year'. Eventually Hodgson played just one first-class game and left at the end of the season. In that context, it's hard to understand how they could have rejected Murray, even for half the season, and, in fact, within three seasons Goodwin had to make way for Engineer, although he proved a loyal and popular team man, staying with the club for the rest of his career, a decision he later regretted having turned down offers from four other counties.

Jim Cumbes, who became the club's Chief Executive but was then a fast bowler in Lancashire's second XI, remembered Goodwin as "a smashing bloke and a good keeper. He tended to look after the young players, me included, and always had a special word for the quickies he kept to."

Some of the cricket committee's decisions smacked of pure arrogance. However, it was manager Washbrook who had advocated the purge of late 1964. Clayton's antics in the Gillette Cup tie with Warwickshire were incomprehensible to a man who had given his all in the name of Lancashire and England cricket. In his stern, rather unforgiving, gaze there were plenty of other dressing-room problems, and he advocated immediate action in his damning end of season inquest. While the report was kept secret, he referred to it during a lengthy interview a few years before his death in 1999 at the age of 84.

"I was amazed to discover complete changes of attitude and outlook by Lancashire players in the interval of five seasons since I played," he said. "Drastic action had to be taken if Lancashire cricket was to be restored. There were certain undesirable elements that had to be removed... gambling on dogs and horses went on secretly, particularly at Old Trafford. Some players were responsible for selfish performances with scant regard for team spirit. This had to be tackled or it would have permeated through the entire staff."

Washbrook, who packed in as manager at the end of 1964, left the cricket committee an alternative, import players or bank on the promising home-grown junior staff to come through. His preference was the latter, and they agreed. Although borne of desperation, this proved a wise choice. 1965 could be seen as a watershed for Lancashire, leading towards one of the most successful eras in the club's history. But much of the resentment and chaos of the previous five years could have been avoided with more care, and just a little compromise. There could, and should, have been a smoother transition, with older players gradually making way for the younger upstarts. Instead, Lancashire cricket had suffered badly and, as the new skipper, Statham faced a formidable challenge to revive the county's pride.

*****

THE cricket and soccer seasons only just overlapped. Manchester United were the League champions and it was time for the Cup Final, the Home Internationals, between England, Scotland, Wales and Northern Ireland, and end of season tours. England drew 2-2 with Scotland, Bobby Charlton, Jimmy Greaves, Denis Law and Ian St John all on the score sheet. Alf Ramsey's side then beat West Germany and Hungary 1-0, and held Yugoslavia 1-1, with Alan Ball making his debut. "It is the proudest moment of my life - I would willingly play for nothing," said the little midfielder.

They beat Sweden 2-1, Nobby Stiles using a replacement set of contact lenses which had been flown out to him after he had lost the original set. All was going well in the build up to the 1966 World Cup. Ireland also had reason to be pleased. Looking for a new manager, the team for the Dalymount Park game with Spain was chosen by 'committee' - and they won 1-0.

Although, in newspaper reports, team line-ups were still given as 1-11 rather than in formation, football was changing quickly. Sir Stan Matthews had retired a few months earlier at the age of 50, the first substitute waited impatiently in the dug-out, and George Best, with his long, dark locks, good looks and dazzling footwork was taking the game by storm.

My first decent pair of football boots, replacing the ones with nailed studs, were 'Stanley Matthews Continentals', bought for £2 from the Co-Op, and, in one of my early soccer books, there is a much thumbed picture line of Matthews jinking past the Scotland full-back Willie Haddock, accelerating to the by-line and pulling back a perfect pass for Nat Lofthouse to score.

Stan, 'The Wizard Of The Dribble', was regarded world-wide as a gentleman, an ambassador for the sport, who was never booked in almost 700 league matches. I saw him play once at Old Trafford late in his Blackpool career, and was disgusted when he tripped over the full-back's (Ian Greaves, I think) innocently outstretched boot, fell headlong into the area and claimed a penalty. With hindsight, I accept he thought he had been deliberately fouled, it just didn't look good at the time.

Makes you wonder whether the same judgement can be applied in the case of our modern players. The answer is no. They dive, simple as that. Anyway, we booed Matthews roundly and, as there was no video replay to prove it one way or the other, we knew we were right. Funny thing, booing, initiated by the ancient Greeks who considered it a civic duty to vent their disapproval at poor performances, and later taken up by the Romans. Now such disapproval is accompanied by an Anglo Saxon scream of fury so I'm glad Matthews was of a long past era. I would have hated to hear the fans bawling: "You fucking wanker!" at him. He would not have deserved that. Teetotaller and vegetarian, he attributed his longevity to living properly, simply taking care of himself. He stood at an open window three times daily to go through a deep breathing exercise.

Best, in comparison, glittered all too briefly. Matthews, Best, Cristiano Ronaldo - how do you compare players from such different times? Would Best have prospered in 2008? I think so. Smooth table top pitches, easier to control ball, the crackdown on tackling from behind - all would have suited him down to the ground. Let's zap Ronaldo back to 1965. Hunter and Billy Bremner snapping away at his ankles, little protection from the ref, a mud heap of a pitch. I'm not so sure of the outcome. The Irishman had to cope with all that and had the character as well as the skill to deal with it.

I'm biased, of course. For me, Best was the greatest. It's just that, unlike Matthews, he preferred breathing deeply in a smoky bar or in a bedroom rather than at an open window. George had shares in a city centre establishment vulgarly named after a woman of ill repute, and when he called time on his soccer career to concentrate on the 'better' things in life, the Manchester Evening News soccer writer David Meek adroitly wrote: "Slack Alice has finally got her man."

Another thing which endeared Best to me was that he liked cricket. In fact, he played in a 1965 Sunday charity match at Old Trafford, opening the batting with Jack Crompton, the United coach who also helped with Lancashire's pre-season fitness work. There is a picture of them striding out side by side, towards the middle. I don't know how many Besty got, but I bet he played some lavish shots.

Nat Lofthouse, incidentally, was, for many years, a footballing villain, as far as I was concerned because of the foul on United goalkeeper Harry Gregg which gave Bolton the first goal in their 2-0 FA Cup Final win in 1958. Lofthouse jumped into Gregg, who dropped the ball which rolled over the line - a foul, even in the days when soccer was a contact sport and even though the ref saw nothing wrong with it.

Lofthouse, a fearless centre-forward who would take it as well as give it, was known throughout Europe as The Lion of Vienna following an international when he raced half the length of the pitch to score, colliding with the Austrian keeper as he did so. In another game he had his shirt ripped off by a Spanish defender but still got the ball in the net. But, for many years, despite his reputation for courtesy and sportsmanship, I could never warm to him because of that Cup Final incident. Until he became President of Bolton, and instead of watching their last game of the season which they had to win to stave off relegation from the Premiership, he stuck to a long-held agreement to attend a Lancashire Sunday League match at Old Trafford.

Honouring such an arrangement in those circumstances took some guts but he explained: "A promise is a promise." On hearing the Bolton result midway through the afternoon, I left the Old Trafford Press Box, went up to the committee's Lancaster Suite and got a message to Nat, requesting an interview. He agreed immediately. Tanned, dressed neatly in a light grey suit, he came off the balcony looking like a Saga advert for healthy living, and I knew from the broad smile that he hadn't heard.

"I just wanted a comment from you, Nat, concerning the Bolton result."

"Oh," the smile slipping a little. "What's happened?"

"I'm afraid you are down."

And tears welled into the eyes of Nat Lofthouse. But only for a few moments, and recovering his poise, he gave me a first-class interview. The Lion of Vienna - yes, I'll go with that.

*****

The FA Cup Final and cricket had to be pushed to one side for my town's May Day Festival. As the local reporter I had to accompany one of the newspaper's 'snappers', whose task was to fill that week's special edition with hundreds of pretty photos. I noted the who, why and where in order to write lots of witty captions. Like the one for the lovely image of the shyly smiling nine year old bride and groom. 'All smiles at The Village Wedding - but how long before the rot sets in?' Thankfully, that one didn't get into print. Later the Festival Committee, worried that attendances were falling, decided that there was too much competition from the FA Cup Final, and that a change of date was necessary. So they wrote to the FA demanding that they put back the Wembley showpiece a week. It made sense, of course it did! Didn't the Lancaster Gate hot shots realise that their silly little football match was ruining our big day?!

*****

IT was the Wednesday after Cup Final day that Lancashire began their county campaign. David Green, given Lancashire's vice-captaincy and looked upon as a future leader, had arrived from MCC duty at Lord's and headed up a weak batting line-up which was duly demolished for a grand total of 211 from both innings. Ken Palmer (7-48) and left-armer Fred Rumsey did most of the damage. Lancashire were obviously a tad rusty, falling in a heap from 56-0 and 76-1 to 96 all out, Palmer enjoying a spell of 4-0 in 12 balls. Only Green resisted, scoring 43, including a six and seven fours, and 42, and their other consolation was the bowling of Statham and his new ball partner Ken Higgs, who claimed first innings figures of 30-7-55-5.

"Fine bowler, Higgs," said Green. "But he had struggled the previous season until we played Northants and Cyril Washbrook, the manager, asked for some advice from the Northants' scorer Jack Mercer who had been a good bowler himself. Jack had a good look at Higgs and immediately identified the problem - he wasn't 'finishing' his action properly. When I asked Higgs what he was going to do about it, he said: 'It's simple, Jack says I've got to show the batsman my arse.' It was sound advice, because he had a great season in 1965. 'Washy' wasn't adverse to asking people for help in that way, people he respected."

Higgs had joined Lancashire in 1958 but before that Statham often lacked a proper new ball partner, sometimes opening the bowling with left-arm spinner Malcolm Hilton. "He got through his over in less than two minutes," recalled Statham. "It didn't give me much of a rest! It was a big problem in those days. We got close to the Championship a couple of times and I think we could have won it with someone to work with me. We were handicapped."

Somerset cruised to a nine wicket win in that opening game, with Clayton enjoying the success against his former club. Not that he had much to do, most of Lancashire's batsmen were clean bowled or lbw in, what appears by reference to the scorecard, to be a sorry display. Green offered a different perspective: "First match. Not exactly the strongest batting you would see in the Championship. And Palmer bowling well. To be honest, we weren't too upset. The club had been in turmoil, it wasn't as though great things were anticipated. Most thought that if we could win a few games, that would be a step up the ladder. There wasn't any daft talk of challenging for the Championship or anything like that. And there were still 27 games left. A lot of cricket."

Lancashire's top six at Taunton was Green, Duncan Worsley, Geoff Pullar, Jack Bond, Bob Entwistle, and Mick Beddow, who also played rugby league for St Helens. Compare that to Yorkshire: Boycott, Hampshire, Padgett, Close, Sharpe and Illingworth. Fred Trueman, who was rated as a batsman and did something that Green couldn't achieve that year - score a century - had to bat at number nine. Surrey had: Stewart, Edrich, Storey, Barrington, Willett, Tindall. Worcestershire, the reigning champs: Horton, Fearnley, Headley, Graveney, D'Oliveira, Richardson. Those of you who recognise the names, or just some of them and therefore the strength of those units, will sympathise with Lancashire whose only Test batsman, Pullar, was past his best, although still, overall, a prolific scorer. Green, who wasn't to become a captain, and Bond, who was, were recognised for talent and experience, but others were distinctly average. The situation improved as the summer wore on and younger more promising players were introduced, but in early May, despite Green's optimism, Lancashire's situation looked as bleak as the weather.

*****

WE rock up at the town's one and only coffee bar, squeeze in a sixpence to spin the jukebox, tilt our chilled Coke bottles, and tap out the beat with our fingers on the edge of the table top. The Stones and 'Satisfaction' first, just to get things grooving, then a touch of Otis Redding or maybe Wilson Pickett. Mrs B bustles about, clattering cups and saucers and filling up the expresso coffee machine. Fran, slim, dark, and married, so leave off, is also behind the counter.

She points. "What's that in your pocket?"

"Just a book, nothing."

"Let's have a look, what's it called?"

"It's by a bloke called Kerouac."

"Oh...so what's it called?"

"On The Road."

Squeals of laughter.

"So that's where you lot get it from. On the road, eh? Hear that, Mrs B? They're all going on the road. Up the alley, more like it, knowing them."

Embarrassed. But Kerouac comes in useful. I barely understand his 'stream of consciousness' but it sounds good, especially if you read it aloud fast after a few drinks, and the title is terrific. On The Road. It says it all. Breaking free. Bob Dylan, at the outset of his career, said: "I suppose what I was looking for was what I read about in On The Road - looking for the great city, looking for the speed, the sound of it, looking for what Allan Ginsberg had called 'the hydrogen juke box'."

Such a book attracts attention - if you pull it out slowly enough and hold it high enough for the girl in the corner, who works at Boots The Chemists and is worth cultivating for various reasons, to see that you are reading something revolutionary, something with a message, something with a sniff of a wider world. Bouffant hair, thick make-up and downturned mouth, but she can get a 10 per cent discount on certain items. Worth a try.

"Buy you a Coke?"

"Nah..."

And, as you're turning away slightly miffed...

"...but you can get me a Fanta. Only if you want that is."

In the pub, K's eyes are screwed up tightly and he gently scratches the side of his nose with a long, nicotined finger.

"You're doing that bint from Boots, aren't you?"

"What's it to you?"

"Boots have pills."

"Not interested."

"Ok - but get some cough medicine off her. And codeine tablets."

It has come to our attention that a good sniff of legal cough mixture is equivalent to a quick drag of weed (not that I would know because, not being a budding MP, I never smoke the stuff), and that you can get blocked on codeine, mixed with strong cider. So we are told. Such concoctions go side by side in the pursuit of happiness with several strange brews, including cinnamon sprinkled onto piping hot tea. We try them, pretend that they blow our collective mind, if only for a few seconds, and go back to Coke, Fanta, coffee, and, at the weekend, some bizarre alcoholic blends like brown ale mixed with Cherry B, which produces a pink froth and disgusted glares from the gnarled vets of the vault.

We sally forth in search of real cider, having tasted it during a foray to Dorset and find it at a pub named The Fireman's in Manchester's Ancoats district. Mob-handed and camouflaged in our combat jackets we are a formidable force, storming into the pub ready for a big night. We see, in this order: a sawdust covered floor, an old Joanna, two cider barrels labelled 'Sweet' and 'Rough', a 'Wanted for Murder' notice pinned on the far wall and a shotgun resting nice and easy on a counter underneath the bar. This is the 'best' room. Through the serving hatch we can see part of the Tap, full of 'navvies' who, like us, are in uniform - in their case, duffle jackets and string vests. We don't stay long. Neither does The Fireman's, which disappears soon in one of Manchester's massive re-development programmes. A sad loss.

*****

TEMPERATURES plummeted to freezing point in some parts of Britain early that May, making it uncomfortable for the cricketers, and keeping fans away. The first touring side of the summer, New Zealand, weren't powerful or well known enough to boost interest.

Captained by John Reid, it was their first visit to England in seven years. To make it financially viable and to get valuable experience, they had first gone to India and Pakistan, playing seven Tests, but the conditions on the subcontinent were far different from those they were to encounter in England. At the end of the tour Reid claimed the English pitches had deteriorated alarmingly when compared with those he had experienced on previous trips in 1949 and 1958.

Their first game, at the New Road home of the champions Worcestershire, ended in a creditable draw, but a few days later, with the wind still blowing in from Siberia, Lancashire destroyed them at Old Trafford after the entire first day had been wiped out. Green suffered a rare duck after Reid had put Lancashire in, but Pullar's 82 and a half century from Bob Entwistle carried them to 225, far too many for the tourists, who plunged to 114-8. Reid tried to declare at that point, only for Statham to sportingly warn him that in a two day match they could be asked to follow on if 100 or more behind. It made little difference as, with one player absent hurt, they lost their ninth and last wicket only one run later and had to bat again anyway. In their second innings they capsized to 8-6, with Statham and Higgs causing havoc on a badly deteriorating wicket, and were in danger of recording the lowest ever total in a first-class match until Vic Pollard and Dick Motz hit out defiantly. Lacking batsmen and spinners, the Kiwis were also beaten by Yorkshire and Warwickshire, as well as going down 3-0 in the Test series.

Lancashire also had serious problems in the early stages of the season, the easy win over the Kiwis presaging a dismal series of results in May. At Grace Road they came up against former England star Tony Lock, back from Western Australia to play in league cricket but making the first of eight midweek appearances for Leicestershire. The man who had played second fiddle in the Laker Test at Old Trafford nine years earlier quickly made an impact, taking wickets and superb catches. Also in the Leicestershire side were ex Lancastrians Brian Booth, who had left Old Trafford in 1963, and Peter Marner. Booth went on to hit over 1400 runs in 1965, while Marner's all-round talents made a big difference to the Midlands' side. How Lancashire missed both of them. How they also missed Barber, Collins, Grieves, Clayton and another long-serving player, Alan Wharton, who, in 1960, had also gone to Leicestershire.

"It was terrible," admitted Green. "All good players, all lost to the county in the space of a few years. So much talent and experience. Of the team I started with in 1959 there was hardly anyone left."

Barber, sacked as captain in 1961, put it down to lack of leadership, saying: "I should have been offered a friendly hand, a listening ear, given quiet advice. I didn't get any…we had a good team and, if they had been allowed to stick together and allowed to play good cricket, I believe we could have been winning the championship for several years. Players were allowed or forced to leave…and Yorkshire went on to win championships that could have been ours."

Collins, only 28 and a more than useful all-rounder, was astonished by the choice of Joe Blackledge as Barber's replacement. "Joe was a hell of a nice man but his appointment was ridiculous. I did my best to help him without interfering but decided I wouldn't put up with any more of it."

Sad but incisive indictments about the way the club was being run in the early 1960s and, of course, things went even more rapidly downhill with the 1964 crisis. The only way was up, perhaps why Green wasn't too despondent about those early performances in 1965.

At Leicester, Bond's second innings century was remarkable as only three of his team-mates reached double figures, but defeat was inevitable after a lead of 171 had been conceded. In the next game, Statham, bowling magnificently on a decent Old Trafford pitch, claimed the remarkable figures of 33.1-10-69-8 but Lancashire still slumped to an eight wicket defeat against Gloucestershire, whose match-winners were Arthur Milton and off-spinner John Mortimer, who had taken over as captain that season.

Green recalled: "George (Statham) kept going and going, but we couldn't get Milton out until it was too late. He was there for four hours or so and near the end just kept taking well-placed singles to keep the bowling. When I left Lancashire at the end of 1967, one of the main reasons I joined Gloucestershire was the thought of batting with him. I also got on well with Mortimer. He always socialised with the rest of us after the game but didn't drink much, usually a ginger ale with lime, and when the beer really got flowing among the rest of us and the talk got a bit daft, he would make his exit. 'I'm not staying to listen to this cock,' he'd say, but always in a good-natured way."

Mortimer was a good enough off-spinner to play for England, and a batsman who regularly topped 1000 runs. He once took four Lancashire wickets in five balls at Cheltenham and would have played in more Tests but for the talent of his Gloucestershire team-mate David Allen. A man of few words, he could still easily raise a laugh. Asked about the best type of bowler for the Bristol wicket, he responded: "A fast medium, round arm dwarf."

Lancashire were turfed out of the Gillette Cup at Edgbaston, with Barber reminding former team-mates of his class, and then crashed to Worcestershire by 251 runs at New Road, where they were undone by Jack Flavell's 7-40. That was no disgrace. The 36 year old Flavell was nigh on unplayable that season, starting with 8-74 against New Zealand and finishing with 142 wickets at an average of less than 15. Free of injury, he played in every Championship game for the first time in his 17 years career and took a 'five fer' 11 times. Bob Carter, playing in place of the injured Len Coldwell, applied the coup de grace for Worcestershire, grabbing 6-7 in 25 balls, and climaxed the match with a hat-trick, Ken Howard, Goodwin and Tommy Greenhough.

"Carter had an action like a threshing machine," said Green. "Goodwin wasn't too happy. Normally he batted at 11, but the captain put him in at 10 this time, and he told Statham later: 'It's disgraceful that you sent me out there in the middle of a hat-trick!' Middle of a hat-trick...you had to laugh."

*****

I never saw Lancashire play that season. Usually I worked six days a week, five and a half officially for the newspaper and Saturday afternoons earning a few extra shillings by reporting local matches for the MEN. Lancashire didn't play on Sundays.

The town side in the Manchester Association was our premier team, both in league status and downright snobbery, although the ladies who made the teas were nice (they always are, aren't they?), sometimes smuggling me a sandwich or scone. "You're Joyce's lad, aren't you? What's that Chinese writing in your book? Oh, shorthand. I thought only secretaries did that. Here..I'm not supposed to, but have one of these."

A mile or so away was the other club, run by an ebullient pub landlord. Their annual presentation dinner was a red-letter day in the sporting calendar. Under the surface of a heaving bowl of hot-pot you might find chunks of black pudding, and even maybe an oyster. Beer was poured foaming from tall enamel jugs. They once reached the Lord's final of the National Village Cup only to be stricken by the loss of one of their fast bowlers who, while celebrating their semi win, fell off a table and broke his arm. Mutts was an accident prone character who had spent weeks in hospital as an 11 years-old after being knocked off his bike by a car. The Mayor of Manchester, on a flesh-pressing visit to the hospital, spotted him and thought it a good wheeze to invite him for a VIP escorted tour of Ringway Airport (now Manchester International). "When you're better - and bring a friend, if you like." Luckily, I was his best mate. A few weeks later we were high up in the control tower, staring out at the night sky, listening as a controller guided in a Dakota, and I wondering how often Dad had taken off from here on his Parachute Regiment training sorties, the aircraft curving over nearby Tatton Park, then the light flashing and the command 'Go'.

"Had to make sure you missed the mere," he told me. Then the night-time trips into France, although probably from a smaller airfield than Ringway. He never talked about them. Except one, and only then when he was well into his 70s, and then only scant detail, but just enough to understand why he had tried to put it behind him, and possibly to understand a little of why he was as he was.

I *wanted* to watch Lancashire. Not to see Green, nor Pullar. Simply to marvel at my hero Statham. Brought up to believe in justice and fair play, although those motifs faded somewhat each Saturday night and Sunday afternoon when Dad returned from the pub with a sway on and threatening mayhem, I looked up to this cricketer as the embodiment of every quality necessary to become a great sportsman. Modest, honourable, uncomplaining, hard working and always the team man, Statham also happened to be a wonderful bowler and, that season, his 15th with the club, he was to underline just how good he was.

Events took a turn for the better for Lancashire at the end of May when they recorded their first win, Statham and Higgs taking 15 Sussex wickets between them at Liverpool's Aigburth ground. The only resistance came from Richard Langridge, whose uncle, John, was Statham's toughest opponent in the early 1950s.

He admitted: "John Langridge was one of the most difficult to get out. If I bowled outside off stump he wouldn't offer a shot. He wore big, heavy pads and huge thigh pads and always knew exactly where his off stump was and that he would be safe with the lbw law as it then stood. Present day bowlers (this was Statham talking in 1995) have a tendency to take a line perhaps a foot outside off stump, but if I had bowled like that, they wouldn't have put a bat on it. They would have kicked it away all day. They only had to get the pads outside the off stump and you were snookered. I needed a much tighter line to make them play at it."

Cricket aficionados will probably know of Statham's motto: "If they miss, I hit." Of his 1816 Lancashire wickets, 1059 were bowled or lbw. Wasim Akram, Lancashire's Pakistani star of the 1990s, had a slightly better percentage of bowled and lbw victims during his Old Trafford career, but he did not have the sustained accuracy of Statham, who was honest enough to insist that he was never sure how the ball would behave once it pitched and regarded his best ever delivery as the one which bemused West Indies' Jeff Stollmeyer in Guyana. "It pitched fractionally outside leg stump, he went to glance and it just nicked the off bail. Beautiful."

'Beautiful'. It must have been a helluva delivery for Statham to describe it thus. He never boasted. His wife Audrey said: "The only time I can ever remember him talking about one of his achievements was when he put up some fitted wardrobes. He lay back on the bed looking at them and said: 'That's not a bad job'."

Statham once showed me his cricket scrapbook. Dog-eared, with loosened pages, not particularly cared for. The family scrapbook, with photos of children and grandchildren, shone like a new pin.

*****

AIGBURTH, where Lancashire had beaten Sussex, was a favoured ground of Don Bradman and Cyril Washbrook, among others. Photos, just before and after the war, show it as a picturesque spot, bordered by trees, and, even now, from a high perch on the pavilion balcony, you can see right across the Mersey, although towering blocks of flats have spoiled part of the view. Yes, lovely place. On my first visit there I was arrested by Merseyside police, an inspector and a stocky, bearded constable who reminded me of someone.

It's a convoluted tale…let's just say it involved a mislaid Press pass, a know it all young journalist and a bloody-minded gateman. In the ensuing row, the gateman called in the law and they gave it to the journo good and proper. "We're not having any of your Manchester tricks around here, wack," said the bearded one. And it was then that I had to stifle a giggle - he was a dead ringer for the actor Brian Blessed, who had made his name in the Liverpool cops soap, Z Cars. I mentioned it to him. He wasn't best pleased. Eventually the inspector took my arm and, at a fairly brisk pace, marched me through the ground, into the pavilion, up the stairs and onto the balcony where, thankfully, he was able to ascertain my credentials with a club official.

"We won't take it further, but watch your step whenever you come to Liverpool," he warned. And I have.

*****

DAVE and I are in the cab of a large, slow moving van heading home after a weekend jaunt in London. The driver, who has picked us up on the M1 near Watford, doesn't say much. He looks tired.

"Been at it today for 12 hours solid," he admits. "Can hardly keep my eyes open." Dave and I pray that he will stay at least half awake until he drops us off. He has a beard, and longish hair, and has been delivering second-hand furniture up and down the length of the country. A nice, gentle sort of bloke from North Lancashire. "Don't worry, lads, we'll make it."

Sure, we will. It is when the van suddenly veers from the nearside to the outside lane, just after reaching the M6, that we know we won't. Luckily, traffic at that time, around 7pm on a Friday, is extremely light. Hard to believe, now, I know. We are sitting on the front bench seat, Dave next to the driver, and quick-wittedly, he grabs the wheel, pulls it over and our friend wakes with a snort, quickly regaining control. Anything over 40mph we would have been goners, but 40mph, occasionally down to 30mph when he drifts off, appears to be its top speed.

"Need some fresh air," he says. The windows are already wide open. "Hey, got an idea. We'll take the back doors off, and get a real breeze coming through - that'll keep me awake." We brake onto the hard shoulder, unscrew the doors and put them in the back of the van. "And one of these will help," he adds producing, like a conjuror, a white pill in the palm of his hand.

"Ah yes," we agree.

"Sorry, haven't got any more."

He spends the rest of the journey staring wide-eyed straight ahead, knuckles clenched on the wheel, smiling. We smile too. And laugh and sing. And, now and then, get him to deliberately swerve from side to side of the carriageway. It grows gloomy and I mention lights.

"Don't work. Didn't expect to be this late." We laugh some more. He delivers us to our service station, buys us egg and chips and disappears into the twilight, a dark, anonymous van with no rear doors, no lights, and a crazy guy at the wheel. Travelling up the M6. I hope he made it. I hope he had grandchildren and told them the story.

*****

THE season was a month old. Lancashire's cricket committee were arguing. Some members wanted more say in team selection by picking a squad of 12-13 players, from which the captain would choose the final X1. The chairman Dick Bowman resisted, emphasising that the committee were there simply to advise. Defeated on a vote, he asked for his disagreement to be put on the record. And when the name of former player Geoff Edrich was mentioned as a possible assistant coach, Bowman intervened saying there was little point in considering him as certain members of the general committee would not welcome him back to Old Trafford.

Edrich, like his ex Lancashire team-mate Alan Wharton, had been considered a rebel by showing his indignation at the authoritarian treatment of players. During one away game in Washbrook's captaincy, the team enjoyed themselves at a Saturday night dance, until Dick Pollard, the senior pro, began to line them up at midnight demanding that they return to the hotel. Edrich, pointing out that there was no cricket on the Sunday, refused to obey. "I was a prisoner of war for three and a half years and no-one's going to tell me how to spend my Saturday night!"

Washbrook, the strict disciplinarian, found it hard to come to terms with this sort of behaviour. Possibly he never forgave Edrich. John Kay, then cricket correspondent of the MEN, explained: "He tried desperately hard to see the point of view of the new generation, but instead of becoming a father figure he assumed, undoubtedly without being aware of it, the role of all-demanding schoolmaster."

Edrich might have made a good Lancashire captain, but by 1965 was coaching at Cheltenham College. Wharton was involved in league cricket. In the 1990s, at one Old Trafford get-together of old team-mates organised by Lancashire's Players Association, everyone in the room stood to applaud Edrich's entrance. All except Washbrook, who stayed firmly in his seat.

Washy's influence on Lancashire cannot be under-estimated. As player, the first professional captain, the first manager, committee man and president he served the club from 1934 until 1990 and left his imprint everywhere. His fiercely unbending attitude, his determination to instil and maintain 'order' - he commanded me during one interview to call him Mr Washbrook or he would not answer any questions - possibly accounted for some of the unrest which blighted the club, highlighted by the player sackings and members' rebellion of 1964.

The way society was changing was also to blame. Why should a player wear a blazer at lunch, as 'Porky' Marner had been ordered? For heaven's sake, there were long-haired guys out there wearing USA combat jackets. Weirdos, sure, but at least they were doing what they wanted to do.

*****

FOR many good reasons, Cyril Washbrook remains a revered figure at Old Trafford and I know I felt in awe of him, but in his roles as captain and as manager perhaps he could have taken a leaf out of England soccer manager Alf Ramsey's book. Ramsey was also a hard man. But he got 100 per cent from his side. After a long, tough domestic season Ramsey took England on a June tour of South America - Mexico, Uruguay, Brazil.

"We had been playing for 10 months non-stop and had just had three difficult games in searing heat. We were exhausted," said Bobby Charlton. "But we had played well, particularly in the last match against Brazil in Rio. There was a presentation dinner after the match and I sat next to Alf. He asked me how I felt and I said: 'Okay, Alf. A bit tired and I can't wait to get home and see the family.' Alf looked at me sternly and retorted: 'I'm disappointed with you Bobby. If I'd known that was your attitude I wouldn't have picked you for the tour in the first place.'"

Charlton, though gob-smacked at that reply, totally respected Ramsey's professionalism and his management methods. He was in charge, no-one was in doubt of that, but he stood up for his players and created a positive team ethic.

Washbrook and Ramsey died within a couple of days of each other in April 1999. Ramsey was given a decent send-off. Sadly, no-one at Old Trafford was invited to attend Washbrook's funeral. His solicitor son had rowed with Lancashire over an allocation of match tickets and the club were not immediately informed the great man had died. The service, attended mainly by family members, was over before many people knew of it.

*****

WE had seen The Stones live, at Manchester's Palace Theatre. Mick The Lip cavorted across the stage, we shouted and stamped in the cheapest seats, up in the gods. They sang It's All Over Now and V responded by trying to dive over the little safety rail into the pit 30 feet below. I hadn't seen her swallow anything, but she must have done. Luckily Mogsy grabbed her coat hem, held on grimly, and coaxed her back into the seat.

After the show we waited outside the Stage Door on the corner of Whitworth Street. They came out, running towards the black limo parked at the kerb. But we stood our ground. Charlie, Bill and maybe Mick - I'm not sure - signed the proffered programme which I lost at some point over the years.

I didn't know then that Mick was a cricket fan. Next time I bumped into him was 30 years later at Lord's. Amazingly, he didn't remember me! Though, to be fair, while he had worn well enough, I wouldn't have been instantly recognisable, my back-combed locks having diminished to a couple of wisps just above the ears. And when I say 'bumped', I mean bumped, as he came out of the pavilion and I was rushing in, late for a Media Conference. "Sorry" - only realising a moment later who it was.

Anyway, it was the Stones now for us. Not The Beatles. The Stones, with The Who starting to whip up a storm, along with a few British rhythm and blues groups who were beginning to make an impact on the club scene, and, for a short while longer, Dylan - soon to turn 'traitor' in the eyes of the folkies and go electric. And, of course, anyone from across the Atlantic who could growl or squeal the blues and finger repetitive riffs on an electric-acoustic guitar. And Che. And George Best. And, for me, a tall, slim, loose-limbed character in cricket whites or a sports jacket and flannels, who captivated all those who saw him play, and those who played with and against him, and who, 32 years after the summer of 1965, rescued me when I was at a low ebb in the chaotic streets of Calcutta. I needn't go into that story, except to say it involved British Airways losing my bags (yawn) and meeting Prime Minister John Major in borrowed trousers an inch too short. So what? I ended up drinking pints with my hero during Happy Hour in the Oberoi Hotel. Never to be forgotten for what he really was - a great bloke.

THREE

MOGSY and I are walking up the middle of the M6. And why not? After all, it's a warm Spring day and it's the quickest route home. The afternoon is heating up nicely, the tarmac shimmers and sweat eases down our necks, seeping into the collars of our US Army combat jackets.

For a while we don't talk. I kick out at a rusting oil can, leaving a black smear on the instep of my Hush Puppy. Mogsy spits. There are four, hastily stitched bullet holes in my left sleeve. Genuine Korean. Bullets flicking across his arm, sparing him, because I've checked and there are no signs of them anywhere else, not in the chest pockets, nor in the back. Just these four small holes, a couple of inches above the wrist, closely packed together like friends.

Mogsy and I are friends, but not close. Not even now, as we tramp north, with only ourselves for company. Not with the sun arcing and beating down on us and the motorway calling us out for a fight. I demand a halt and we slump onto used up oil drums, staring down at our feet, mine shoved into soft brown suede, his into shiny black leather, supported by two inches high Cuban heels. I think he's suffering more than me, but he's stoic, doesn't complain much, never talks about the mother who upped and left. His nose shines and, out of sympathy, I wipe mine with that scarred sleeve.

"Nice day for a stroll," he laughs. The road stretches ahead. A gang of crows worry at something dead on the hard shoulder, a rabbit or a rat. A buzzard mews over distant fields. In the future, this unfinished stretch of the M6 will link up with the M1 and there will be Spaghetti Junction, Eddie Stobart trucks and lots of other good things that the British motorway network promises, but right now it's quiet, a Bank Holiday, and no-one else around - not even the road-builders because a Bank Holiday is recognised by all as a day off, and so the labourers, housed all week in caravans on the motorway edge, will be in the nearest pub giving it some welly. And all I can hear on the M6 just a few miles north of Birmingham, on Whit Monday 1965 is the buzzard, Mogsy spitting and, in my head, Bob Dylan croaking: "I'm walking down the long lonely road, babe."

For most of my life, London has been a distant star. Not anymore. The M6, though incomplete, offers a fast track to the 'real action'. We hitch rides. Plenty of drivers are willing to stop. It's all so new, this motorway business. Few restrictions. Little danger. A couple of strange looking kids with their thumbs out. Give 'em a lift, what's the harm? And if we sniff danger, well there's two of us, both brought up to look after ourselves.

Sometimes we just mosey into the motorway service station on the outskirts of town, slipping past the police HQ, and wait by a wagon for its driver to re-appear. Or maybe we'll hang around the café which bridges the six lanes, keeping an eye out for a likely benefactor. "Excuse me, any chance of a lift, me and my mate have got to get to London, his mum's been in an accident down there." You might have to try it on a couple of times, but it's easy really. People don't like to say no nowadays.

Today, though, returning north on this work in progress stretch, there's no chance of a lift until we reach Gailey and the latest, completed section of the M6. Where we are sitting on the oil cans - and I'm slowly realising that mine is covered in soft tar - the motorway is empty, the roadsides littered with rubble and the debris of construction, bits of twisted metal, slices of rubber, cans, cigarette ends, bottles, the occasional piece of machinery, a mechanical digger, a roller, silent and menacing, a crust from a half eaten sandwich.

Mogsy came to our school late. His family was new to the area, taking a house on the Manchester Corporation overspill estate built close to the site of the old refuse tip. Their home is neat, clean and characterless, and I much prefer it to mine, because I am embarrassed by mine with its scruffy furniture, its disorder, and its outside toilet where you have to ensure the door is fully closed unless you want to be viewed in all your splendour by the railwaymen in the signal station on the other side of the line running past our back garden.

Initially we treated him as an outsider, but he established himself with his sporting ability - always the chief criteria in electing anyone into our tribe. He had a dry wit and liked to annoy you by sitting behind you on the school bus, constantly tapping your head. When I responded by trying to strangle him, we were kicked off the bus, still four miles from home. It was our first walk together.

"Remember that?" he asks, lifting his head to look directly at me. "You threatened to kill me." The sun catches a tiny, reddened spot on his face. "Did you know you've got a massive wart on the side of your nose?" His finger shoots up to trace it. "Should do something about that," I prod, thinking again about that pat, tap, pat, on the top of my head. "Nothing there, your lamps are on the blink. Let's move."

We are both narked about our wasted weekend. The idea was to hitch to London, but instead of using the M6, to travel the old road, the A50. Bad decision. Bank Holiday, little haulage traffic on the move, and after three short rides, leaving us stranded outside Lichfield, we end up in a pub and sleeping it off in a hay field, waking to feel the mice scrambling over our feet. We call it off and head back home, again having to do a lot more foot-slogging than envisaged. Back safely in the arms of the Rose and Crown, we knock back pints of bitter and lime.

"Where've you two been?" asks Smudger.

"London."

"Good was it?"

"Ace."

*****

ON a damp Tuesday afternoon in early June, Geoff Pullar - Noddy to his pals - climbed behind the wheel of his red six cylinder Triumph, parked behind the wooden pavilion at the Aigburth ground where Lancashire had just won their first game of the season, waited while a couple of team-mates clambered in and made themselves comfortable, heard the engine roar into life at the first turn of the key, and turned into River Lane and then right, heading south. They faced a 200 mile trek, knowing that next morning they would be playing again against Middlesex at Lord's.

Pullar's ridiculous nickname had been easily won when, early in his career, he was caught napping in a hotel lounge chair on the Sunday rest day, while Noddy, the kiddies' cartoon favourite, was being shown on the TV in the corner. But there was nothing noddyish about Pullar. A tall, left-handed opener, he had 28 Tests under his belt, scoring almost 2000 runs with four centuries and an average of 43.86. His first tour, to the West Indies, established him as a high quality batsman. The fiery fast bowlers, Wes Hall and Charlie Griffith, were in full cry, but Pullar and Colin Cowdrey - wearing a rubber padded vest - linked up successfully, their partnership averaging almost 60.

"Only Hall, of their fast bowlers, didn't throw it occasionally," said Pullar, who also claimed a memorable wicket, that of Frank Worrell, when Peter May gave him the last over of the series. Worrell was dropped twice by David Allen and Ted Dexter before Fred Trueman pulled off a stunning one-handed catch at long-off, saying later: "There was nowt to worry about Noddy. I'm not one of those bloody Southerners."

Dexter was one of Pullar's biggest fans. He watched him preparing to take on Hall and Griffith and said later: "There was no pacing up and down, no half-hearted attempt to make a joke of what was a very unpleasant job, just a fag and a pull at his cap before stepping out to meet the blast. I never played forward the whole of that tour to those whirlwind bowlers. Noddy never stopped! Even when Wes Hall went around the wicket to direct the bouncers more purposefully at his head, that right foot kept probing down the wicket defying anyone to make him change his style for the sake of the odd extra 20 mph or more."

Courageous against red-hot pace, Pullar was technically superb against spin. Added Dexter: "He played Benaud and Simpson all day on a turner at

Sydney in 1962 and never looked in trouble. He refused to be flustered, even when I asked him to lend me a fiver after the trip to get me home."

In 1960 at The Oval, Pullar took South Africa apart with a Test best of 175, sharing in a stand with Cowdrey of 290, but he failed badly against the left arm expertise of Alan Davidson in two Ashes series. By 1965, his England days were over and after a run of indifferent championship form, questions were being asked about him at Lancashire. His request for a benefit in 1965 had been turned down flat, on the basis that they were only awarded to players who had served the club for 10 years after winning their county cap, which meant he had two more years to run. Instead, the committee had nominated the scorer Mac Taylor as the beneficiary. Few whinged about that, Mac being a hugely popular and respected figure, but there's little doubt that Noddy's career was approaching a crossroads. However, the drive to London that evening was pleasant enough, radio on, the highways fairly quiet, and a good win over Sussex to celebrate with a couple of pints at the team's hotel.

"We had used trains now and then in earlier years, but cars gave us more flexibility and no-one minded driving," said Green. "Trains were okay but I can remember coming off the field sometimes and Mac Taylor, who did a lot of the organising, telling us that we had half an hour to shower, get changed and get to London Road station (Piccadilly) in Manchester to catch a train south. You can imagine how, say, Tommy Greenhough or Brian Statham felt about that after bowling 30 overs.

"I remember a couple of train journeys. We were stopped at Crewe once and it was a bit cramped in our compartment. Tommy stuck his head out of the window, saying he needed fresh air, it was like a cattle truck, and Porky Marner said: 'Get your head back in here, Tommy, otherwise people will see your mug and think it *is* a cattle truck.'

"Another time we had to get from Manchester to Hove via Euston and Victoria and we didn't get there until 1.45am. Outside the station we looked around for a taxi but there weren't any around. We were wondering what to do when a car pulled up and offered us a lift. Some of us got in and the driver, who we'd never seen before in our lives, shouted to the rest of us: 'I'll be back.'

"We didn't expect him, but he came back and eventually ferried us all to the hotel. The astonishing thing about it was that he was completely pissed. I got in at 3am and we were playing that morning! But we couldn't stop laughing about it. By the mid sixties it was the era of the car, quite a few of the lads had one and didn't mind using it. I had an Austin Somerset. The lads called it The Leaper because it had a carburettor problem and went in surges. We got a mileage allowance, I think sixpence (2 1/2p) a mile, petrol was about five bob a gallon and you could have a bit of fun, cruising down the M1 with the radio on. I liked a bit of rock 'n' roll, Elvis."

The motorways were a bonus for Green and his mates. Cyril Washbrook certainly would not have looked sympathetically at any complaints over travelling arrangements. He recalled: "Travel was much more tiring in my day, before the motorways. I must have had more cups of tea on Crewe railway station between midnight and 1am than anywhere else in the world. They talk about the pressures of the modern game. We travelled from Bradford to Weston Super Mare once, arrived at 8am, and were waking up players to go in to bat."

Motoring was fast becoming the only option for cricketers who didn't want to rush for, or, alternatively, to hang around for a train. So Pullar put his foot down and they reached London in good heart. Next day, another championship fixture, but still plenty of time for a drink and some decent kip.

"When you've won a game, you don't feel tired," said Green. "And anyway we didn't start playing until 11.30am and we didn't have to get to the ground until about 10. No physical jerks or anything like that, just a good net, and we were ready. Nowadays, they're doing all sorts of exhausting looking exercises and things by 9.30am. At that time I was only just out of bed, having my first fag."

*****

UNDER the controversial Beeching Plan, train services were being cut, many district lines ripped up.

Richard Beeching, a friend of the Transport Minister Ernest Marples, had an industrial background and was brought in to re-organise the nationalised British Rail system. The facts were unarguable. The railways were haemorrhaging money. Everyone, freight carriers and passengers, was shifting to the roads. Un-used rolling stock rusted away in sidings. Change had to come. But he became Public Enemy Number 1 for the trade unions, those country folk who still relied on the branch line, and, of course, every kid who had spent the day on some platform, or railway embankment, jotting down the names and numbers of the steam monsters which trundled by, while referring to the appropriate Ian Allan handbook - in our case, the London, Midland and Scottish Region - to research them, their Class, designer, sheds. We would amble home with grimy faces, lungs full of soot, and hungry, but jubilant at bagging a 'Clan' or a 'Coronation'.

His supporters claimed that Beeching saved the railways, but all we knew was that he killed train-spotting. It would have happened anyway, but we blamed him. Steam was replaced by diesel and our beloved locomotives disappeared in a puff of smoke.

By 1965 the future was at the end of a long strip of tarmac. While there were lots of gaps in BR's new 24 hour timetable, the motorway system was expanding rapidly, with extensions and improvements to the M1, M6, M2 and M4. These long-range thoroughfares were lightly used in their early years and, one Saturday morning, I was able to hitch-hike from Cheshire to London with three lifts, reaching Trafalgar Square in only three and a half hours.

A mile from our town centre, Top Rank had built a service area in 1963 for £340,000, creating 200 jobs and promising waitresses in 'especially attractive outfits designed by a couturier'. Top Rank claimed they wanted to provide the perfect stop-off for all drivers, from the family man to the long distance haulier (or the 'Logistics Solutions' as they now term themselves).

"Their own special club atmosphere will be encouraged," said a company spokesman. Drivers, he added, could relax, have a meal, read a magazine, make a phone call, etc, although he had to admit one drawback - there was no alcohol on sale. We loved the service station. As long as you evaded detection when creeping down the prohibited approach road, you could get into the café at any time of the night, when everywhere else in our district was closed. It was also the ideal launch-site for a free and quick trip to The Smoke.

The first of my three lifts that fine Saturday took me into Staffordshire where, at Gailey, the M6 ran out of tarmac. On a nearby roundabout I joined two girls who were also thumbing it to the capital. Good move, that. The trick was to hang back, let the girls make the contact - which they did almost immediately - and, as the door opened, rush up to dive in with them. A sort of pimping, I suppose. Anyway, the motorist was always too embarrassed to kick you out.

Sticking together we grabbed the third lift on the other side of Birmingham, taking us down the M1, and when he dropped us off in Barnet, we completed the journey by rail. One of the girls, named, I think, Helen, was spaced out. "Taken all sorts," grimaced her friend. We half carried her into Trafalgar Square and dumped her on a bench. "Do you want to go for a coffee," I asked the other one. "No, I'll have to stay with her. Look after her." I saw Helen a little later, laughing, with a bunch of Mods, trolling through Oxford Street and her friend, looking miserable, trailing behind.

In Wardour Street, Soho, a youth collapsed that weekend and was rushed to hospital, where a stomach pump extracted an almost lethal cocktail of amphetamines. It was, for the times, an unusual incident, and made the newspapers.

While the motorways injected some excitement and a little glamour into our lives, I couldn't fully comprehend why Britain was pulling apart the world's first and best railway system. As our garden had backed onto the Manchester-Chester line, I must declare an interest in the road versus rail debate, because from early days I had rushed to the fence to wave to the drivers, firemen and guards as they rattled past, just a few yards away. It wasn't just train-spotting. Being so close, feeling the house shake a little when one of the heavy freights went past, you felt part of it. Saw the sweat on the fireman's face as he shovelled coal into the boiler, the sparks flying into the air, sometimes setting off small fires on the embankment which divided our garden from the tracks.

Sometimes, when a train passed the backs of our houses, the fireman would shout and throw something out of the cab. A few minutes later, one or two of the neighbours could be seen walking slowly along the side of the track, eyes peeled for lumps of coal. Old Mrs H, scrawny and beady-eyed, was usually there, scooping up the fireman's gifts with mittened hands, pushing them into a bag or hessian sack. But this type of open cast mining was soon to end.

You could write good songs about trains. They had done so since the 19th century and in 1907, a 12 year-old North Carolina girl called Elizabeth Cotten wrote one of the best of all, 'Freight Train', spawning a whole genre. To write a train song all you needed were a few simple chords, a flag, a whistle, a kettle (steam for atmosphere) and just a touch of whimsy. Oh, Lizzy Cotten…'Freight train, freight train going so fast'... And, hurry up or you'll miss it, because here comes Johnny Duncan and the Blue Grass Boys with 'Last Train to San Fernando' - and, whoa, look out, Lonnie Donegan is getting up steam on the 'Rock Island Line'.

Yes, I know there are catchy ditties about roads and cars. But they're not quite the same even when Mick Jagger or Bruce Springsteen is roaring them out. Not for me, anyway. You can shout all you like about 'Route 66' and 'Thunder Road', but there's not a lot to say about the exhaust fumes, except 'Ugh', whereas the steam, smoke and soot of a locomotive just reek of romance.

Britain's countryside was ravaged during the Victorian railway building boom. Elizabeth Gaskell in 'Cranford' and Charles Dickens in 'Dombey and Son', among others, wrote of how the approach of the fire-breathing machines divided communities. But the benefits of a rail network quickly came to be appreciated and the locomotives to be loved. Soon writers were exploiting this new passion, stations and trains were loaded, not merely with passengers and freight, but with excitement and drama. W H Smith saw the opportunity, opening up station bookstalls where they sold cheap thrillers called yellow backs. Even our small town station had a W H Smith until the early 1960s, when the M6 arrived and changed our life.

Motorways have also been appreciated, but never loved. The M6, which, in the back of someone's car or in the cab of a lorry, we cruised down almost unhindered and at a steady 60-70 mph in 1965, has turned into a log-jam of frustrated, angry, sick-to-death of these roadworks drivers. The service station is like the centre of so many towns, indifferent, nondescript. Sadly, the remains of the railway system are just as charmless. Poet John Betjeman fought successfully to save the cathedral edifice of St Pancras station, but, in the general dismantling of the tracks, the voices of railway afficionados fell on ballast. In his BBC Home Service 'Back To The Railway Carriage', Betjeman said: "Roads bury themselves in the landscape. The railways carve out a landscape of their own."

He spoke tenderly of the artists who painted railway scenes, viaducts, embankments and cuttings and, of course, the locomotives. But he knew then only of steam trains, the tank engine puffing its way slowly along the branch line, the dashing express whistling its way to London. Individuals, identified from a distance by their smokestacks and windshields, and then as they chuntered, growled or whooshed past, by their numbers and names. Guided by men in filthy blue dungarees at the front and guarded at the rear by one in a uniform, waving a green flag. Vehicles with character, and with a human touch. I can't see those qualities in modern rail travel, and the fact that I can get from Manchester Piccadilly to Euston an hour quicker than before does absolutely nothing for me.

*****

In June 1965 President Lyndon Johnson authorised the first major American offensive in Vietnam, a 'search and destroy' mission north of Saigon. It was at this stage that the USA's theory of 'protecting' South Vietnam, to meet the perceived threat of the Red Horde sweeping down from China, turned into war. The public didn't get to hear about it for another month.

When President Johnson did feel ready to inform his nation, he said: "I do not find it easy to send the flower of our youth, our finest young men, into battle. I have spoken today of the divisions and the forces and the battalions and the units, but I know them all, every one. I have seen them in a thousand streets, of a hundred towns, in every state, working and laughing and building and filled with hope and life. I think I know, too, how their mothers weep and how their families sorrow."

Like every war, there was the initial belief, hope, illusion, that it would all be over quickly. No problem, according to one of the candidates for the governorship of California, a certain Ronald Reagan. "It's silly talking about how many years we will have to spend in the jungles of Vietnam when we could pave the whole country and put parking stripes on it and still be home for Christmas."

Harold Wilson's government said little about the USA's escalation. There is evidence that they privately supported it all the way. On the front pages, there were snippets about Da Nang and other places I'd never heard of before. I didn't know what to think. Much of my left-wing drum-beating was superficial, it was cool to dig Che and Castro and Dylan singing 'With

God On Our Side' etc., but I came off a council estate, deeply steeped in its working-class conservatism. Dad had served bravely in the Parachute Regiment and the SAS, all his mates had been in the forces. "The Americans are ok, they'll stop the Commies," they'd say.

Naturally, given our rebellious nature, we formed an unofficial branch of the Communist party. Meeting occasionally, in the pub. No names, no pack drill. It was a real gas to weigh up the fate of millions of people over a few pints.

I know I look back at some aspects of those days with rose-tinted specs, but only with disdain at my comfort zone politics. Opportunities to get involved, to help, to protest, were eschewed in favour of a hedonistic lifestyle. Earnings were spiralling, prices of major items like cars were falling and consumerism was on the march. No wonder a former member of the Young Communist League admitted: "It was the beginning of the end for us." They claimed a national membership of over 6000 in 1965, actually it was under 5000, and falling. But they raised £1000 in medical aid for Vietnam, while I gave sod all. How could I afford to, saving as I was for a scooter and needing the rest for clothes and our weekend orgies? Dad had it spot on. "You're all talk, you and your lot."

*****

DAVID Green and his team-mates probably had little inclination to debate Vietnam. If, on a rainy day at the ground, there was the time, there was always something else to think about. A game of cards, where they would take a drink that evening, doing the Telegraph crossword. Please don't think for a second that I'm accusing them of superficiality. I take the rap for that. No, the point is that a county cricketer's life is, by definition, all about the game and its minutiae. During the season, there is little time to glance at the wider world.

"Cricketers eat and breathe the game. It's all consuming," said Green. "We were either playing it, waiting to play it, or travelling to it. Never travelling away from it, because one match led automatically onto the next. The road always headed towards a cricket ground. So you talked about it. All the time. There wasn't a lot of room for anything else, no matter how sharp you were on world affairs or literature or whatever. And there was team spirit to consider. Arguing with a team-mate over politics or religion was hardly the right preparation for a difficult game.

"If we were rained off, we found something to occupy ourselves. There was always a cards school, ours was usually Jack Bond, Roy Collins, Porky Marner and Tommy Greenhough with a few watching over their shoulders, having a bit of a laugh. You could read the paper, do the crossword. I hadn't a clue as to how to do the Telegraph one, until Peter Lever showed me. I was surprised he was so adept at it. Can't believe we nicknamed him Plank."

Off the pitch, some players certainly can surprise you. One wet August morning in 1994 I spotted Lancashire's Peter Martin, a tall seam bowler with a Boris Johnson flop of hair, sitting in front of the Lord's pavilion, reading a thick volume.

"What's that Digger?"

"Mein Kampf."

I chuckled disbelievingly. But it was. 'Digger', though, was a bit different. During the 1996 World Cup on the sub-continent, he left his England teammates insulated in their five star hotel on the edge of town to walk alone into the old city of Peshawar, in Pakistan's North West Frontier province, a haven now and then for the Taliban. His height and mop of straw coloured hair, along with the large Canon camera wrapped around his wrist, made him an easy and valuable target, but he emerged unscathed. "Enjoyed it, got some brilliant pictures."

He became an artist, using a shed at the bottom of his garden as a studio, and one of his most colourful pictures, showing the Old Trafford ground with some of the personalities who have graced it, was bought by Lancashire and was hung in the pavilion.

*****

OF the 31 days of May, Green was involved in 25 days of active cricket. Or would have been if it hadn't monsooned so much. One day of the game against New Zealand was washed out and a lot more time was lost in the fixtures of that month. In nine first-class matches and one Gillette Cup tie he had scored consistently, but Lancashire's only centurions were Jack Bond and Mike Beddow. In fact, Lancashire's entire line-up had twice failed to reach 100 - 96 against Somerset and 55 (Worcestershire). No-one had scored a century against them, nor were they to all season.

It was already a bowlers' summer. Jack Flavell, the Derbyshire pair Harold Rhodes and Brian Jackson, Statham, Trueman, and Tom Cartwright of Warwickshire, led a host of seamers who enjoyed themselves, along with one or two top-class spinners like Ray Illingworth and Fred Titmus. Twenty bowlers claimed 100 or more dismissals, yet one of them, Kent's Alan Dixon, finished 77th in the national first-class averages with these jaw-dropping statistics - 1190.1 overs, 375 maidens, 2978 runs, 121 wickets, average 22.61.

This did not mean that a bowler like Statham simply had to turn up to grab a bagful. Many pitches were poor for batting, some of the smaller grounds had only one sightscreen, and the tail usually caved in quickly with few recriminations, providing rich pickings for the bowlers. But you still had to bowl well, as Green emphasised: "There were lots of good batsmen about and they didn't give their wickets cheaply. And while there were lots of bowlers taking six, seven and eight wickets, it was no good if it were 6-80, or 7-100. Expectations were greater than that. 7-40 ...fine, a slap on the back and a 'well done mate' for that, because it gave you a chance of winning."

THE bowlers' top 10 of 1965 went like this:

	Ovs	Ms	Runs	Wkts	Ave
H J Rhodes (Derbyshire)	646.5	187	1314	119	11.04
A B Jackson (Derbyshire	807.5	262	1491	120	12.42
J B Statham (Lancashire)	771	205	1716	137	12.52
T W Cartwright (Warwicks)	735.1	305	1505	108	13.93
F S Trueman (Yorkshire)	754.4	180	1811	127	14.25
J A Flavell (Worcestershire)	910	217	2100	142	14.78
J D F Larter (Northants)	589.2	169	1333	87	15.32
D J Shepherd (Glamorgan)	1062.2	460	1765	112	15.75
L J Jones (Glamorgan)	654.3	203	1336	84	15.90
D Shackleton (Hampshire)	1246	529	2316	144	16.08

Alan Dixon, said the Kent cricket correspondent, was much under-rated and proved himself again as one of England's best all-rounders. He mixed off-spin with medium pace and bowled for lengthy periods under varying conditions. Several years earlier he had given the game up to become a sales rep - and then one sunny day, a strange chemical reaction persuaded him to give it another go.

"It came around to the spring," he recalled in the Wisden magazine, "and I stopped the car by a cricket field where they were mowing the grass. And the smell of the new mown grass meant so much. I got out of my car and rang Les Ames, the secretary of Kent. 'Leslie,' I said, 'it looks as if I've made a mistake.'"

Apparently, what saved Dixon to Kent cricket was a breakdown of fats and phopholipods in grass when it is cut. This leads to further reactions and that smell which we all love so much. "It taps into the memory and into our sub-conscious emotions," said a scientific report.

As Green pointed out, bowlers were expected to get lots of cheap wickets. Everything seemed in their favour, but the national selectors were finding it harder and harder to develop replacements for the likes of Trueman and Statham, who were coming to the end of their Test careers.

"All our young prospects have this awful chest-on action," lamented the former Test fast bowler Bill Bowes, adding: "It is generally agreed that the present emphasis, to the great detriment of the game, is the preponderance of swing bowling."

This followed criticism by the highly influential commentator Jim Swanton of England's fast bowling problems on the previous winter's tour of South Africa. Tom Cartwright, he pointed out, was, predictably, steady in the one Test he played in, but 'unhostile'. Swanton went on: "He is, essentially, an 'English bowler', as are most of those who lead the field in the county season." In other words, a bowler who would prosper from medium paced seaming, slightly short of a length, to defensive fields, and on under-prepared wickets. The problem came when they were promoted to Test cricket.

There was potential. John Snow at Sussex, for one, but Bowes was pessimistic. "England's selectors, I imagine, gaze on a bleaker prospect of finding bowlers for next winter's tour of Australia than at any time in the history of the game."

Lancashire's June game with Middlesex was a dour affair for the most part, although only 15 minutes remained when the home side clinched a seven wicket win. John Sullivan's second innings 50 was easily Lancashire's best contribution, and despite another eye-catching display from Statham (25-6-38-6), Middlesex were left chasing 162 in 150 minutes. Peter Parfitt led them home, adding an unbeaten 67 to his earlier 76. But Parfitt escaped when dropped on two, underlining one of Lancashire's biggest problems.

Explained Green: "All through the summer we missed catches. Dozens of 'em. We didn't have a slip cordon worth talking about. The best slippers, particularly Ken Grieves, had been shown the door. It cost us dearly. We might have won a couple more matches, and I'm sure Statham's figures would have been even more impressive."

Statham would have agreed. But he remained phlegmatic. "I never let that sort of thing get me down because I knew there would be more opportunities." Peter May, when England's captain, said of him: "He is the most even tempered cricketer I have ever met. His composure hardly alters on the pitch." Just a slightly puzzled grimace having suffered another appalling piece of luck was a characteristic of Statham's career. He dismissed 2260 batsmen, but the everlasting image of him is the moment after the ball has grazed the off stump, or when first slip has failed to hang on. The batsman wondering how on earth he has survived, Statham, hands on hips, and that momentary, frowning silence before turning back for his next effort.

He looked askance at the wicket-taking celebrations of modern cricket. "Hugging and kissing and doing war dances was not in vogue in my day - and I'm very pleased it wasn't," he said. "It leaves me cold. A lot of players from my era feel the same. When I dismissed a batsman, all you heard was a couple of handclaps. Usually none of the other players said anything to you, never mind rush up and throw their arms around you. I would perhaps take my sweater and put it around my shoulders while waiting for the next one to come in, maybe have a couple of words with the umpire, but that was it."

That was Statham talking in 1992. Old-fashioned? Of course. And he was just undemonstrative. For once, though, I could not have agreed with him less. Cricket needs constant injections of that magical ingredient named buzz. Not enough of it around in the mid 1960s, and the admittedly unedifying sight of Green or Pullar racing up to plant a kiss on Statham's forehead after taking a wicket would have really got people talking - trouble is he took so many wickets they soon would have got sick of it.

Statham didn't get much out of Yorkshire in the first Roses match of the season, but there was plenty of encouragement for Lancashire in the performances of three younger players. Gerry Knox, a Tyneside schoolmaster who had scored a mass of runs for Northumberland, hit his maiden century with 15 fours, and there was stout resistance from Sullivan and Mike Beddow against the pace attack of Trueman, Nicholson, and Richard Hutton, and the spin of Ray Illingworth and Don Wilson. Higgs and Greenhough also showed plenty of defiance in a last wicket stand of 40 and that, with some late rain, ensured a draw. Ken Howard, an uncapped off-spinner, also had a match to remember, twice bowling Geoff Boycott. Sadly, of this particular group of youngsters, only 'Sully' was to feature prominently in the Lancashire revival which carried them to glory in the one-day game between 1969 and 1973.

David Green maintains that cricket was on the verge of a breakthrough in the mid 1960s. "There were signs that people were waking up to new possibilities," he said. "In some ways county cricket refused to change. But the Gillette Cup had been brought in, the John Player League was only a few years away and The Cavaliers touring sides had helped to generate spectator interest. We felt something was in the air."

Soccer's nearest equivalent of The Cavaliers were various All Stars sides, comprising ex-players, showbiz personalities and media types, who had a bit of fun and raised cash or charity with low-key games at local grounds.

An All Stars bunch, captained by Malcolm Allison, came to our patch one Sunday morning to take on the town's Chamber of Trade XI. I recognised their ginger haired defender immediately. Tony Kay was not long out of jail, having served 10 weeks of a four months sentence for his part in a 1962 match-fixing ring, involving Sheffield Wednesday team-mates Peter Swan and David 'Bronco' Layne and a string of lesser known players. Kay and Swan were England internationals and, before the scandal was broken by the Sunday People, had moved from Wednesday to Everton for a British record transfer fee of £60,000.

Kay's downfall was sealed by the use of taped conversations which had only recently been introduced into British courts. He had been a 1966 World Cup possible, one of the biggest names in the game, but now was disgraced, an ex con, and barred for life by the FA from playing in any football under their jurisdiction. Which meant anywhere, with anyone. And here he was breaking the ban, right under the nose of the local scoop, who just happened to be playing up front for the Chamber of Trade.

After the game I grabbed the team sheets to find him listed under a false name. I went into the away dressing-room, explained I worked for the paper, and asked Allison for his full line-up to use as a caption for the team photograph. And, hee hee, to clinch the story that would earn me some real bread from the national newspapers. Big Mal stood up, wrapped a strong arm around my shoulders - rather too tightly, I thought - and said: "Listen, son. I know what you're after. But is anyone here causing any harm? We're just in it for fun. Doing our bit for charity. You wouldn't want to spoil that, would you?" Squeeze.

Well, yes, Mal, I would. But I didn't say that. After all, I was a mere 17-year old novice and felt under some pressure, particularly around the throat. As a fellow footballer, albeit at many levels below Kay's, I also had a bit of sympathy for him. I couldn't imagine what it would be like never to play again. And I put off writing the story until I eventually abandoned it. Later, though, I wished I had written it. Kay got involved in further scurrilous activities. He even boasted about meeting the gangsters Reggie and Ronnie Kray, who had been arrested early in 1965 and wanted Kay to take them through the new procedures of tape-recorded evidence.

Years later, Big Mal unwittingly gave me ample compensation for that incident. By then I was reporting on Manchester City matches and loved going to their Maine Road ground. It had a lovely atmosphere, and, with Mal around - cigar in one hand, glass of bubbly in the other - there was always plenty to write about.

*****

One Saturday night early this wet summer, we make our 'eight pints of lager and a Ruby Murray' debut, ducking out of the soft drizzle and into the garishly lit New Embassy. My friend Ken goes for a 'Madras'. I chicken out, opting for the 'England Meals' section on the menu and pointing to Ham Omlet (*sic*), Chips, Peas. The English chippy is taking a hit from the Indian curry house. Some go with the flow, offering curry with the chips, but the sauce is a strange concoction, brown and lumpy with sultanas, offered in white polystyrene containers. And scoffing a bag of chips in the rain, spiced up or not, is fast losing its attraction as the perfect climax to a Saturday night out.

Chucked out of the pub at 11.10pm, the night is young, you still have a quid or two in your pocket, and, if not clubbing it, you are up for some decent grub, another pint and somewhere comfortable to sit. Only society's hardest workers can provide all that so late at night. The Bangladeshis and Pakistanis and some Indians - Punjabis - of every city cash in. Only they are prepared to wait until the glassy-eyed hordes roll out of the pub, only they are prepared to cook and serve until the early hours, only they are prepared to stomach the drunken, ignorant insults.

In 1960 there were only 300 'Indians' in Britain, although curry powder had been used by British cooks since late Victorian times and the term 'currye' was used in Richard II's royal cookbook. By 1970, there were 1200 and at the turn of the century there were 8000 with a £2billion turnover. These determined entrepreneurs changed British culture, but their impact on English cricket was, for many years, negligible. Why? With their roots embedded in the sub-continental hotbed of cricket, you would have expected them to quickly push their way into local clubs and leagues and then into the county game. But it was 2002, for example, before Lancashire's first home-bred player of Asian descent, Sajid Mahmood, made his debut for the county.

I've heard various reasons, none satisfactory, but I fear the problem was double edged. English cricket at grass-roots level was not open enough, and many immigrants and first generation Brits lacked the confidence, and/or the desire, to make the first move. They could be clannish, too. Some formed their own clubs and leagues. A shame, because, on the evidence of what you see on any street in India and Pakistan, a lot of natural talent never had the chance to blossom in England.

*****

OLD Trafford attendances were in freefall. Lancashire's new-look side were losing, the weather was dreadful, and there was little chance of sitting back, warm and contented, as your favourite batsman chalked up a century. You couldn't usually nod off because it was too chilly and damp - and, if somehow you did, you would wake up to find that wickets had clattered. Edna, the kindly lady who printed Old Trafford's updated scorecards at lunch and tea on a clattering old press, often had her work cut out to keep up with the progress of the game. Indeed, scorecard sales tumbled, and there were other substantial falls in revenue from car parking, catering and broadcasting. The lack of a Manchester Test was the main reason, but the team's early Gillette Cup exit and their struggles in the championship also took their toll, resulting in a loss for the year of over £7000. Put into context with the overall turnover of £81,000, it was a worrying deficit. Gates were also affected, apparently, by too many fans sliding off the plate. The club's Year Book reported: "As a result of *many* deaths, the County's disappointing performances during the last few years, and with no Test Match, the membership fell slightly." Well, it would, wouldn't it? At the end of the summer, Lancashire mounted a recruitment drive. "The importance and urgency of members continuing to introduce new members cannot be over emphasised."

Other counties were feeling the pinch as well. Desmond Eagar, secretary of Hampshire, wrote an impassioned letter, pleading for supporters to become members: "...the modern game is competing with so much more. Most families have a car - some have two - almost every home has a television set. It is the age of full employment, the age of the Beatles, - the age of speed and excitement. Thank heaven for cricket where one can at least relax." Although Eagar was forced to admit that the game was short of personalities and character, he persevered: "There is still much to applaud and let's face it, Shackleton bowling to Cowdrey, who makes 100 in three and a half hours, is certainly not without interest."

Hampshire's concern was that it cost £35,000 to run the club - about the same price as an over the hill footballer - and, with a membership fee of three guineas, they needed another 2000 members to balance the books. Eagar was confident his appeal would work, but William W. Caldecott of Farnham, in a letter of reply to The Cricketer magazine, caught the mood of many fans: "I feel the Counties could do a lot more in the way of public relations to gather support. The other day, whilst awaiting for three hours during the rain, we were given no indications as to when the umpires would inspect the wicket. In other cases, if the batting order is changed or a player retires from the field we are given no facts. I know this causes considerable resentment."

Forty years later, the same complaint could still be made at some matches. Many times during that four decades we, in the Press Box, knew the game was 'off' well before the 'speccies', who had to wait, wet, chilled, fed up, for another 20 minutes or so for the decision to be made official and for it to be relayed over the PA. Improvements have been made. Public relations is treated far more seriously, as are other aspects of 'customer care', but, in general, county cricket still lags behind other sports.

Lancashire had various membership categories. Full members over 21 years of age (£5 5s); full members over 18 (£2 2s); and Country Members. No matter what age these paid £2 2s as long as they 'permanently reside 50 miles in a straight line from Manchester Town Hall and who do not have business interests in the Manchester area; *distance is not calculated on road or rail mileage.*' Why 50 miles from the Town Hall and not Old Trafford? I've wondered about that....

Members were members, and ladies were subscribers, which was something quite different. Women were not allowed into the Pavilion, a fortress of male chauvinism until it crumbled on a vote at the 1998 AGM.

"What next?" demanded one indignant male after that historic meeting. "A creche? Are we going to have kids running around all over the place? Mothers suckling their babies at the end of an over?"

There would have been very few subscribers, and not a lot of members, for the visit of Hampshire on June 9. Those who stayed away missed one of the best games of the season. Forty wickets, just 489 runs, and all over early on the last day. What they also missed was the no-ball of the season. Hampshire's paceman Butch White, stumbling in his run-up, threw the ball playfully at Green - and was promptly called for throwing by umpire Syd Buller at square leg! That caused a laugh, but a little later in the season Buller was to be the central figure of a major no-balling row.

Wisden described the Old Trafford pitch for the Hampshire fixture as 'treacherous'. Hampshire, however, first batted doggedly against Statham and Higgs, so doggedly that it took them 96 overs to eke out a total of 174. The second day provided much more entertainment. Shackleton sent back Knox for 10, hardly a surprise, and the rest of the innings was dominated by sensational displays from Green and Bob Cottam. Driving powerfully, Green hammered a superb 61, well worth a century in better conditions. Pullar weighed in with 37, taking the score to 102-1, but Cottam, Hampshire's first change seamer, devastated Lancashire by dismissing the last nine batsmen for 25 in 67 deliveries. Not to be totally outdone, Higgs (6-33) and Statham (4-41) blasted Hampshire out for 77 in 32 extraordinary overs, leaving Lancashire to chase 116 for victory. At the end of a second day, which had seen 252 runs and 27 wickets, they were 99-8, but could add only three more singles on the final morning.

A meagre 13 runs, maybe one of the many dropped catches that Green referred to earlier - but it didn't only bring about Lancashire's sixth defeat, it signalled a new dawn for Old Trafford. Next day Middlesex were the visitors, and Lancashire decided on dramatic changes. Pullar and Greenhough were dropped, Statham ruled out with a groin strain and in came the diminutive batsman Harry Pilling, paceman Peter Lever and left arm spinner and batsman David Lloyd. This was the side: Green, Knox, Beddow, Bond, Sullivan, Pilling, Lloyd, Lever, Higgs, Howard, Goodwin. Eight were uncapped. Five were to go on and play in the team called the 'Kings of One Day Cricket'. Lloyd, particularly, will never forget that game.

"I made nought in my first innings for Lancashire. For good measure, I made another nought in the second innings. As I was also implicated in a run out, dropped an important catch and we lost by nine wickets, it was not exactly the debut of my dreams," he wrote in his autobiography (subtitled 'Anything But Murder').

'Bumble', as he became known, was 18, still to earn his second XI cap, and had gone to the ground without any kit, not thinking for a second he would be picked. His biggest supporter, his dad, finished work at Accrington General Hospital just in time to get to the ground and see his son walk out at 140-5 only to be bowled by Fred Titmus for a duck. Next, the teenager was caught behind by John Murray off Titmus's spin partner Don Bick to complete his 'pair'. But nothing could dilute parental pride. In the notebook where he maintained his son's cricketing progress, Lloyd snr wrote of a 'very proud Mum and Dad' with 'tears and lumps in the throat.'

Lloyd was grateful to the discarded Pullar. "He gave me plenty of advice before I went in to bat as he would do on the numerous occasions in the weeks and months to come. In hindsight, I was obviously being groomed to succeed him and I'm sure he was far more aware of this than I was, but he offered to help genuinely and in the right spirit. Against Titmus, he told me always to get well forward but always to play with the bat in front of the pad …I followed the code faithfully and it succeeded inasmuch I didn't give my wicket away lightly. I was in so long and pushed forward so relentlessly that I needed a salt tablet for a bout of cramp."

Not surprisingly, considering the lack of experience in the side, Middlesex won comfortably, but this was the start of something big. Pilling, Sullivan, Lever, and Lloyd became key players in the side which won the John Player Sunday League twice and the Gillette Cup three times under Bond's captaincy.

*****

DAVID LLOYD is well known, and well liked, as a cricket commentator. Early in his TV career he was asked to do a voice-over for an obscure Channel Four programme on fruit growing. They didn't want him to appear on screen, but thought that his earthy Lancashire accent would come over well. "Didn't know anything about flippin' fruit," he said. "But all I had to do was read a script so it was easy."

A week or so afterwards, he answered a knock on the front door of his house in Bramhall to find a sweetly smiling lady asking: "I wondered if you could look at my plums - I've heard you're a bit of an expert."

Bumble was always good for a laugh. The first time I ever walked into the Lancashire dressing-room, he screamed and threw a snake at me. Ok, only a rubber one, but just for a moment as it wrapped itself around my neck…And he wasn't exactly an ignoramus on fruit. On his debut as a first-class umpire, Cambridge University v Essex, paceman John Lever secretly swapped the ball for a juicy orange, which was duly despatched to all parts, literally, by the uni opener.

Everyone has a soft spot - and a daft story - for Bumble, a genuine, caring character imbued with a rarely matched enthusiasm for the game. Not the best choice as Lancashire captain when he took over from Jack Bond in 1973, but a good player from 1965 to 1983, an innovative and motivational coach, and an entertaining broadcaster.

*****

ONE notable absentee from the Middlesex XI in both encounters with Lancashire was the up and coming Clive Radley, who played in half the championship games and was rated as having 'a good fighting spirit'. Later in his career he played well against Lancashire at Aigburth where left-arm spinner Ian Folley bowled immaculately for a lengthy Saturday afternoon spell. A Sunday newspaper report, heavily biased in Lancashire's favour, hailed Folley as an England candidate, claiming that he had troubled the Middlesex star. Before play on the Monday morning, Radley buttonholed the reporter concerned on the balcony outside the dressing-rooms and gave *me* a finger wagging re-appraisal of his duel with Folley.

"He bowled well, certainly, but he genuinely beat me only once - with one that turned square," he said. His Middlesex colleague Phil Edmonds, who knew a bit about left-arm spin, made his opinion plain by hanging a washing line in front of the Press table and slowly tying on his laundry, jock straps and all, obliterating their view. Protests were met with a withering: "What do you want to see the pitch for? It's obvious you don't bother to watch!"

Folley died in 1993 at the age of 30 suffering a heart attack while being operated on for a head injury, sustained while captaining Whitehaven in a North Lancashire League match. He was a likeable, popular man and it was hard to take in. I received the news on my mobile as I entered Worcestershire's New Road ground on a bright, sunny morning. Neil Fairbrother was just going onto the pitch for some fielding practice.

"Harvey, I've got some terrible news - Ian Folley has died in hospital."

Fairbrother was visibly shaken: "No. Foll? It can't be. Are you certain?"

"Yes," giving him what detail I had.

Fairbrother called to the dressing room: "Athers, Athers. ….Jesus, not Foll."

If I had been over the top in championing a new left-arm spinner for England, then historically I wasn't alone. The Daily Express in 1965 said this: "The left-arm spinner English cricket is seeking will appear in the championship in the middle of June…his name is David Lloyd, he is 18 years old and he will be playing for Lancashire." Well, he did make his debut, as the Express forecast, and he did make it to the top, but not because of his bowling. Barely out of Sunday School, he still played soccer for Accrington's Cambridge Street Methodists when he joined Lancashire. In the winter Bumble worked in the Old Trafford ticket office where there were a couple of battered typewriters, or maybe he'd help out the maintenance staff.

"The Lancashire of the 1960s was a cottage industry compared to modern times. It was run on a Victorian shoestring," he said. Yet Geoffrey Howard, the secretary who quit at the end of 1964, recalled in Stephen Chalke's book, 'At The Heart of English Cricket': "They knew how to be generous at Old Trafford. At Christmas we'd get boxes of chocolates, bottles of wine from Tommy Burrows, even a crate of whisky from one of the vice-presidents, Stanley Holt."

And in 1965 they were talking of giving players two year contracts at a much improved salary of £1000 a year. However, when it came to a request from one of the players, Ken Snellgrove, to help with his 14shillings a day petrol costs from Bootle to Old Trafford, Lancashire were not quite so forthcoming. There was a danger, they thought, that it would create a precedent.

As to the rows and controversies which engulfed the club, Lloyd admitted: "Most of the problems passed over my head, to be honest. They didn't mean much to a teenager whose only interest was in playing the game, rather than its internal politics. There was an atmosphere about the place which surprised me, but, for all I knew, it was natural for there to be an Upstairs Downstairs divide. For all I knew the 'Dogs Home', as the below stairs dressing room was called, was the fate of the juniors at every club. I probably thought such conflict was commonplace in county cricket, though I did know that for a big, well-supported club like Lancashire, the record of our first XI in the early 1960s was neither commonplace nor acceptable."

Lancashire's solution was to turn to the younger brigade. Lloyd, Pilling, Sullivan and Lever all advanced confidently, but there were still obstacles to overcome on the club's road to redemption.

*****

IF, as some would have it, our rural wild bunch was careering along the road to perdition, then we were determined to do so in style. We bought for a fiver a ready to be scrapped icon of the motoring industry, a Ford V8, probably manufactured in the late 1940s but the same model which was used by mobsters and FBI agents alike in America's Prohibition battles of the 1930s.

Favourite car of America's once Public Enemy Number One, John Dillinger, and also of Clyde Barrow of Bonnie and Clyde fame. They had the audacity to write to Henry Ford praising it, Dillinger saying: "It's the first choice for getaways."

Ours was black, with deep runner boards and brown leather seats, but a roaring exhaust and a steaming radiator dissuaded us from using it in bank robberies. Proudly, though, we drove it slowly through town, aiming pointed fingers at innocent pedestrians while taking care to avoid our own crime-fighters, the two local bobbies, Lionel and Doddy. Not the brightest lights in the HM Constabulary firmament, but even they would have quickly discovered the wanton breach of a number of motoring laws, eg:

No insurance;
No tax disc;
No full driving licence;
Unroadworthy vehicle - faulty brakes, lights, tyres, horn, exhaust, radiator, etc;
No log book;
Dangerous driving having regard to an excess number of passengers (eleven).

While not having the charisma of a steam loco, The Pilot, as it was named, was a thing of beauty. We cleaned it, plugged some of the holes in the radiator with mustard powder and egg white and cruised to a nearby town to watch the Swinging Blue Jeans. What we hadn't reckoned on was a petrol leak. At the top of a hill it coughed to a halt, but there was still a last ride left in it. Having hauled it around, we climbed back in, one or two riding the runner boards. Ken released the handbrake and the Pilot, silent and dark as a ghost ship, coasted back down the slope, picking up speed into the starless night until the road straightened and it spluttered to a resting place on a grassy verge where, in another act of sheer irresponsibility, we left it for someone else to bury.

FOUR

IT was tough up North. Like the Rochdale Cowboy Mike Harding joked: "We was so poor that me mam gave us a knife and fork with our soup to make it go further." In Wigan snotty-nosed kids went down to the chippy on a Friday night to ask for a bowl of 'pea wet', the juice of the mushy peas, a tasty and cheap accompaniment to a tanner's worth of chips, if you couldn't afford the peas themselves. Obviously, the pea wet could not be immediately slurped over the chips, because it would soak through the newspaper so you took your bowl, had it filled with the luminous green nectar and carried it carefully back home. The things we eat...

In 'The Road To Wigan Pier', depicting Northern life when it was really tough, George Orwell investigated the weekly food bill of a typical out of work miner's family of the early 1930s and found that almost as much was spent on jam, tea and sugar as on meat and potatoes. No wonder, thought Orwell, that they were all under-sized with bad teeth. An article in the New Statesman had the answer, showing that such a family could live much more healthily, and cheaper, by sticking to the following shopping list:

3 loaves;
1/2lb margarine;
1/2lb dripping;
1lb cheese;
1lb onions;
1lb carrots;
1lb broken biscuits;
2lbs dates;
tin evaporated milk;
10 oranges;
Total cost - 3s 11 1/2d a week per person.

That was perhaps taking it a bit far. One school of dieticians reckoned the minimum amount to keep someone alive was 5s 9d a week, while another put it far more generously at 5s 9 1/2d. But, as Orwell said: "...the less money you have, the less inclined you feel to spend it on wholesome food."

Living, if that's the right word, in a terraced heap, with crumbling walls and an outside lavvy, you don't exactly yearn for Ryvitas and orange juice. No, it's a plate of greasy chips, or a lick of cream, or a blob of jam on your bread, followed by a fag. Just a little of what you fancy - after all, what else is there? Sod the oranges.

Strangely, Orwell made no mention of pea wet. Folk ignored the New Statesman recommendations, kept on smoking, and spreading jam on their crust. And, of course, they also continued to cough and splutter and to die young. Apart from the poor nutrition, it also rained a lot in the North, which made it doubly hard for those whose toilet was 30 yards up the alley. Chamber pots came in useful, but were hardly hygienic if left until brimful under the kitchen table.

*****

According to George Orwell, the working class philosophy of 'grin and bear it' exposed rows of rotting teeth. Blame the Victorians for that. Sugar flooded into Britain during the 19th century and quickly embedded itself as a staple of our diet. A 'little of what you fancy' usually entailed something sweet, an extra spoonful in a mug of char, a cake, a slab of chocolate and so what if a couple of molars started to give you grief. Dad, however, was one of the few who didn't have a sweet tooth. He preferred offal. Put a boiled calf's head in front of him and he was as happy as a pig in muck. A pig with all its innards, that is.

His favourite dish was tripe (the stomach lining of a cow). Mum presented it in various ways, raw without accompaniment, raw dressed in vinegar, boiled in milk, boiled in milk with onions. Each time he spotted my look of disgust and remonstrated: "What's up with your face? Nothing wrong with this. I lived on a farm and we had to eat anything that was put on the plate, and if we didn't it would be there again for breakfast."

Dad was born in 1914. His mother, Gladys, was a Victorian of the old school. She didn't need the Suffragettes' help. In her household, she already had the vote - the only one. Born in an army camp, wife of a soldier, restrained by corsets and the discipline of military life, not to be disobeyed. "There's a bit of sheep for you boyo. Don't dare ask which bit. Now get it down you."

Dad pulled his nose up at anything exotic, yet covered his food with white pepper. When I told him I'd discovered curry, he snorted: "Muck." Strange, really, considering he had Indian blood. But, apparently, he didn't know about that. A secret was that, and my tight-lipped Grandma was good at keeping secrets.

*****

I was born and lived for the first 15 years in a pre-war council semi - built about the same time that Orwell was conducting his rather snobbish examination of working-class mores - certainly a cut above the hovels of Wigan and other industrialised towns, which so depressed him, but not exactly anything to boast about. Even now, I would dearly love to meet the architect who designed a house where you had to go outside to get to the inside lavvy. Very strange, and embarrassing. I rarely invited friends around.

By 1965 we had 'flitted' to a more modern estate with inviting open squares, neat little cul-de-sacs and green playing spaces. And our new home had two toilets, one upstairs in the bathroom, one in the adjoining brick outhouse. The neighbours were a little more up-market too, though not as neighbourly. One was the manager of the local cinema, another ran a taxi firm. At last we were respectable. Dad had to calm his temper - "you don't want next door to hear you carrying on, do you?" jibed mum. Given the chance, she would have stayed at the old house where she could chat for hours over the yard wall with 'Mrs W' - never 'Margaret', always 'Mrs W', despite years of convivial gossip. One day, returning from school, I found her sitting thoughtfully in the front room, staring into the empty grate. "We've been offered another house," she said carefully. "What should we do?" She knew the answer, of course. I think she was scared. She had lived in that place most of her life, her father had died there, in the back bedroom overlooking the railway line and the fields and woods beyond. I had been born there, in the front bedroom overlooking the street.

Living conditions in the mid 1960s had improved beyond most people's dreams. Terraced rows still guarded the factories, and some people still had to go out of the back door for a crap, but there were cars parked outside many houses, a Mini here, a Ford Cortina there, and the roofs were littered with TV aerials beaming in the latest antics of Coronation Street's rampaging Elsie Tanner, British TV's first anti heroine There were fridges, electric cookers and Dansette record players, which held several 33 rpm Long Players at a go and provided the first genuine excuse for teenagers to spend long periods in their bedrooms.

"We're not having that noise down here - take it upstairs."

"Don't you like Howlin' Wolf then, Dad?"

"Bugger off."

"Thanks, Dad."

As well as social improvements, there was a new regional pride. Our big cities were still dirty and unromantic, but Liverpool had provided The Beatles and all the spin-offs of the Mersey Sound, and Manchester was emerging from its industrial shadows with a peculiar mix of cultural innovation. Mods danced the night away to American soul music in The Twisted Wheel and other clubs but, twice a week, settled down with the rest of the family to watch Elsie's latest rows and romances in a soap opera which portrayed the North to the rest of the nation as backward and ignorant, indeed as lacking any culture at all. But it captivated Britain, and we, up North, revelled in its popularity.

Granada TV, the region's first independent station, also generated a brighter, sassier feel about the place. Its garish red sign lit up Manchester's night sky. Its actors, presenters, directors and VIP guests could be seen buzzing around the studios' foyer, or up and down Quay Street, or noisily drinking in the Old Vic or The Grapes. There was a vibe of creativity about the place. And there was also United, one of the world's top clubs. Sometimes, if you were lucky, you would spot soccer's first heart-throb George Best darting into one of watering holes, or his hairdresser's.

But it stayed forever wet. Bob Dylan warned that 'A Hard Rain Is Goin' a Fall', but Northerners already knew that. Hard and bloody heavy. If it were any consolation, the rest of the country suffered just as much in 1965. Who'd be a cricketer that season - especially a batsman? To appreciate that runs were at a premium, forget Lancashire's problems for a moment, and take a look at Yorkshire. Geoff Boycott, whose international status was growing rapidly, headed their batting charts with an average of 34.88 - and like Green he failed to score a first-class century, although he did hit one to help them win the Gillette Cup final when, with the cares and woes of the Championship season over, he delighted a 25,000 Lord's crowd by hitting three sixes and 15 fours in his 146.

Ten days earlier he had been dropped for the third Test against South Africa as a slap on the wrist for slow scoring! You could imagine him muttering …"I'll bloody show 'em." However, captain Brian Close, who went to the crease in the Lord's final with Yorkshire a meagre 20-1 after 12 overs, took some of the credit for Boycott's startling transformation, claiming that he stirred him into action by threatening to 'wrap my bat around his bloody neck.' Boycott denied that, but the fact remains that it was only after Close joined him and had words in the middle of the pitch that he took the attack to the bowlers. Close explained: "He had never played like that before. I forced him to do it by relieving him of responsibility. If he got out he had an excuse - he could say: 'It's the captain's fault.'"

No other Yorkie that summer averaged 30. John Hampshire came in second to Boycs with 27.52 and the experienced Doug Padgett had a paltry 20.68. Considering those figures, Yorkshire did well to finish fourth in the championship. However, that was nowhere near good enough for supporters who had gorged on four championship triumphs between 1959 and 1963. Their nadir came in mid May at Middlesbrough when, on a lively pitch, Hampshire routed them in the second innings for 23, the lowest total in their history. There were four byes and a four off a no-ball. Yorkshire's first effort would have been a total disaster as well, if not for Fred Trueman's hurricane 55 off 22 balls, including 26 in an over off Derek Shackleton, after Boycott had spent 36 minutes for a duck. No-one reached double figures in the second knock, Butch White tucking in to the tune of 6-10.

Commentator Gordon Ross lamented Yorkshire's negative approach. Why, he asked, didn't some follow Trueman's example and have a go, rather than prodding around and getting out without achieving anything? And, on a wider scale, should not English batsmen learn to be more adaptable to conditions? One-day cricket, in its infancy, still had lessons to impart.

Yorkshire's 23 was the lowest championship total by any side since Glamorgan's 22 against Lancashire at Liverpool in 1924. Trueman's 115 wickets at 11.36 each gave Yorkshire respectability at the end of the season, but he ran into hot water with the Headingley committee over a Press article, and he lost his England place after disappointing displays against New Zealand at Birmingham and Lord's. Typically, he hit back by reverting to his longer run-up and taking 74 wickets at 10 each in 25 innings, including the 2000th of his career.

His spat with the Yorkshire hierarchy stemmed from breaking the rule that a player needed consent from his club before publishing any article. Fiery Fred was 'severely reprimanded and warned that any future breaches of his contract will result in instant dismissal', provoking a heavy-handed cartoon in The Sun where one long-haired schoolboy told his pal: "Fred Trueman's case proves that a first-class cricketer doesn't need education - if you can write, you are not allowed to."

Yorkshire were not the only county to suffer major batting collapses. There were nine other county totals below 60:

> Hampshire 31 (v Worcestershire at Bournemouth)
> Leicestershire 33 (v Glamorgan at Ebbw Vale)
> Leicestershire 36 (v Derbyshire at Loughborough)
> Leicestershire 40 (v Glamorgan at Leicester)
> Worcestershire 42 (v Somerset at Bath)
> Derbyshire 52 (v Surrey at Chesterfield)
> Leicestershire 52 (v Worcestershire at Worcester)
> Derbyshire 56 (v Kent at Derby)
> Leicestershire 59 (v Lancashire at Manchester)

In addition, Ireland were dismissed for 25 by Scotland and Cambridge University for 37 by Essex. A glance at that list of flops suggests that Leicestershire were easy meat, but they finished in 14th, an improvement of two places from the previous season, and only two points behind Lancashire.

However, it was Yorkshire's failure which spurred the Wisden Editor to attack county pitches. "Is it any wonder," he railed, "batting has become so unattractive? Surely it is time that groundsmen returned to the old method of using marl, cow manure, and the heaviest possible roller. The way back to better first-class cricket is to remember that the state of the pitch governs the play. Fine weather is essential and, when the sun shines, batsmen should be able to know that the ball will behave reasonably as it comes off a fast, true surface....

"The worst pitches," he continued, "were considered to be Bath, Old Trafford, Bradford, Chesterfield, Edgbaston, Headingley (county matches), Hove, Loughborough, Middlesbrough, Northampton, Romford, Sheffield, Southampton, Trent Bridge and Worcester."

Which didn't leave a lot. Some groundsmen might have retorted that yes, of course fine weather *was* essential - and they hadn't had any! But, generally, there was disquiet about pitches, and in September the Lancashire cricket committee agreed that the Head Groundsman, the redoubtable Bert Flack, should be told 'very firmly' that they wanted hard, fast wickets. And, they asked, was the roller heavy enough, and was it used enough?

The furore over pitches was a central theme that summer. But no-one could do anything about bad weather. At the Cambridge University ground, tables, chairs and parasols had been planted outside the beer tent to give it a Continental look, producing a rueful comment from one critic: "One fears that the parasols will be more frequently employed as umbrellas."

May had been a shocker, with 72 mm of rain in Manchester and a maximum average temperature of 15.3 deg C. June and August were warmer and a little drier but July was a wash-out. The season was concentrated into these four months. Now it starts in mid April, sometimes in desperate conditions. While writing this, newspaper images and reports of the first county championship matches of the current season portrayed nearly empty grounds, with the few faithful fans frozen to the bone, and some critics pleading for a re-think on the fixtures programme. But a later start doesn't guarantee better weather, at least in the North. One May morning only a few years ago, Lancashire's ground staff had to chip off two tons of ice which had gathered on the polythene covers overnight and on June 1 1975 a blizzard, which left two inches of snow on the ground, wiped out a day's play between Lancashire and Derbyshire at Buxton.

The season also closes later nowadays, in late September, when, perversely, Lancashire have suffered from too much sun, as a result of their unusual east-west laid pitch, now re-positioned in the re-development of Old Trafford. Late afternoon rays shining on the executive box roof of Old Trafford's Stretford End occasionally reflected into the batsman's eyes, causing this message to be sent out - Sun Stopped Play. In Manchester, of all places. However, rain usually was the chief enemy for Lancashire, and not in April, but in late summer, wrecking a couple of recent title bids, to the despair of the club chairman Jack Simmons, who, in the middle of a debate over the future of the Old Trafford ground, joked, a little forlornly: "If we ever do move maybe we should relocate to the south coast."

Cedric Rhoades led the Lancashire members' rebellion which produced a new committee for 1965. Rhoades later became one one of the club's most influential chairmen but his 18 years reign ended in bitter controversy.

Jack Dyson, who helped Manchester City win the FA Cup in 1956, was also a talented Lancashire cricketer, but he was one of four players sacked in the pre 1965 purge.

Peter Marner in the blazer that caused a row when he was ordered to wear it at lunch. Marner was kicked out along with three other players and joined Leicestershire.

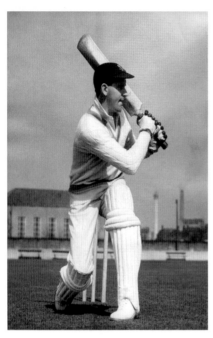

Ken Grieves, who was relieved of the Lancashire captaincy at the end of a dismal 1964 season during which manager Cyril Washbrook complained of poor behaviour. Grieves went into league cricket.

Brian Statham is congratulated by Lancashire captain Nigel Howard on making his county debut. Fifteen years later in 1965 Statham himself became the club's captain but only after the committee had controversially considered other less worthy candidates. Statham emerged as an inspirational leader.

Legendary West Indies spinner Sonny Ramadhin in a less familiar pose. Ramadhin played for Lancashire in 1964 and 1965 when old racist attitudes had faded. Thirty years earlier, admitted one Red Rose star of that era, the thought of a black player taking the place of a white player, was 'anathema' to the dressing-room.

One of Lancashire's greatest - Cyril Washbrook. A strict disciplinarian, he condemned some of the team's behaviour during his managerial stint and, at the end of 1964, four players were sacked leading to a members' rebellion.

Always fond of a leg glance, George Best, brilliant footballer and ladies' man, steps out at Old Trafford to grace a charity cricket match. With him is Manchester United coach Jack Crompton who took the Lancashire squad through some agonising fitness routines.

Geoff Pullar had to play on some diabolical pitches - but this was ridiculous! 'Noddy' as he was known enjoys a back garden knock-about with family members. He scored three of Lancashire's eight centuries in 1965.

Brian Statham put everything into it when he was on the field. Off it, he knew how to relax and at the end of play there was nothing like a good pint. A few drinks after a hard day was quite acceptable and, if you had one too many, you simply went to bed 'retired hurt'.

Groundsmen were under fire in 1965 over the poor quality of their pitches. But no doubt the 'flak' bounced off Old Trafford's redoubtable and aptly named Bert Flack, pictured here. The committee resolved to firmly instruct him to prepare faster surfaces, but his reply was never recorded.

Old Trafford pulled in massive crowds just after the war -
here fans try to get a view of the pitch from the Warwick
Road station adjacent to the ground. But by the mid
1960s cricket attendances had nose-dived and critics
were calling for change.

Not a 1965 picture - but one which shows the old wooden
Press Box on top of the Ladies' Stand in the background.
Built in 1947 as a 'temporary structure' it lasted for 40 years
and provided the author and more famous correspondents
such as John Arlott with many happy memories.

Star of the future. A young Frank Hayes who, in 1965, was beginning to make an impression in the Lancashire 2nd X1. Hayes, then 18, had the chance to join the Old Trafford staff but elected to delay his cricket career to complete a degree course at Sheffield University.

Jack Bond, to emerge as one of the club's finest captains, failed to command a regular place in the mid 1960s and more than once seriously considered leaving the club. Thankfully he stayed to lead Lancashire to glory as the first Kings of One Day Cricket.

Peter Lever was the crossword solving genius of the Old Trafford dressing-room. Patient, determined, he emerged as a high-class Test pace bowler after waiting for many years to come out of the shadow of Brian Statham.

What the summer of '65 meant to a pseudo teenage rebel....Manchester's Twisted Wheel club was a hub of youth culture; the Richmond Festival poster shows a great line-up headed by The Who; the eye-catching Ford V8 Pilot - a throwback to the days of Bonnie and Clyde; Mods congregating outside Horners motorbike shop on Ayres Road in Old Trafford and Manchester's Central Station, where the summer ended for the author, before it was closed.

Yorkshire's fall from grace at Middlesbrough coincided with a Neville Cardus article in 'Playfair Cricket Monthly' which trumpeted:

'YORKSHIRE The Greatest of all Counties'

"The greatest of all county cricket teams over years and years has been Yorkshire, not only in point of technical achievement but for original, uninhibited character. From Tom Emmett to Freddie Trueman, Yorkshire's cricketers have expressed the broad nature of their county. With them the game has been a pride and the possession of a jealous, self-contained region."

My favourite Yorkies of the 1950s and 1960s included Trueman, Willie Watson, Jimmy Binks, Doug Padgett, Len Hutton and Doncaster's Diana Rigg, who with Audrey Hepburn, Doris Day and Jane Fonda was voted as one of the hottest actresses of 1965.

One Sunday afternoon in the late 1970s, while doing a shift for a national paper, the news editor threw a PR handout in front of me. Research, claimed the leaflet, proved that Yorkshire people changed their underwear less often than those of any other county.

"Get onto that" was the command. "Get some Yorkshire legends out of the contacts book and ask them about their mucky habits."

I rang Diana, a dark-haired beauty who, in 1965, had shimmied into a skin-tight, black catsuit for her new role in The Avengers. "Erm, it's the Daily Mail Manchester here, Diana. Erm, I know this sounds daft, but can I ask you how often you change your knickers?" I can't remember the answer, but I know she giggled and I'm sure came over as very hygienic, as well as extremely good-humoured.

I rang Sir Len Hutton at his home in Surrey. His wife answered. I explained my predicament. She laughed: "Oh, I can answer that for him. After all I do his laundry. I'd say twice a week in the winter, a bit more in summer."

I didn't ring Geoff Boycott.

*****

LOOK up a few 1965 mid-season scoreboards and the scarcity of runs quickly sinks in. Worcestershire's game on a 'travesty of a pitch' at Bath was all over just after 3pm on the second day. Somerset won by an innings and five runs, despite making only 190. The champs also hit trouble at Hove, where they struggled to 30-3 off the first 30 overs.

On June 17 three batsmen were struck on the head when Hampshire took on Glamorgan at Southampton, where a wet pitch steamed under a hot sun. There was a wet patch on the Southampton wicket during another game, against Kent, only that one wasn't attributed to rain."On the Monday night an intruder watered the pitch at one end," it was tactfully reported.

Not every side was rolled over. At Bristol Gloucestershire batted defiantly, exasperating Glamorgan to the extent that they put on everyone to bowl. Keeper David Evans recorded figures of 3-0-8-0. Yorkshire resorted to similar tactics against the West Country side, this time at Lydney where wicketkeeper Jimmy Binks bowled in his pads with Trueman taking over behind the stumps. Some fans laughed, others grimaced.

And there were fun and games in a one-dayer at Lord's, Middlesex meeting Surrey in a Past and Present XIs encounter which yielded 569 runs, Denis Compton hitting 48 and Jim Laker 52 not out. Compton also appeared in a one-dayer for MCC at Worcester where, at the age of 47, he reminded fans of his 'former majesty when he went down the pitch to deal with the turning ball'.

Usually, though, bowlers had the upper hand. There were 11 hat-tricks, including three for Worcestershire (Bob Carter, Len Coldwell, and Norman Gifford) and two from Tony Buss of Sussex. Three bowlers, Bob Cottam, Jim Presdee and Don Shepherd, had nine wickets in an innings. Only one Englishman, John Edrich, got a double century.

One of the grounds which escaped Wisden's censure was Tunbridge Wells, which Lancashire visited in mid June, but runs were hard to come by there, too. Green (37), Mike Beddow (59) and Harry Pilling (42 not out) provided a 40 runs first innings cushion against a table-topping Kent side lacking Colin Cowdrey, but the match turned on brilliant bowling from Alan Dixon and Alan Brown, who reduced Lancashire to 24-4. Brown and Green were pals, but that didn't stop the Kent paceman from banging in a bouncer which smacked the opener in the chest before bowling him for a duck.

"We had been out together the night before; we got on really well," said Green. "But he saw nothing wrong in giving me one, neither did I. Cricket was a lot different than now, but it was always very competitive."

Statham declared, leaving Kent to score 151 in 95 minutes, and although Mike Denness promptly cracked him for two sixes in his first two overs, they had to settle for a draw, leaving Lancashire two points for first innings lead - one of nine ways of championship scoring.

From Tunbridge to another spa town, Buxton, to face two bowlers who were already causing havoc and who were to claim first and second places in the national charts with an aggregate of 239 dismissals. Harold Rhodes and Brian Jackson were such a formidable force, aided and abetted by the superb wicketkeeping of Bob Taylor, that, despite moderate batting resources, Derbyshire harboured title hopes.

And, as expected, the deadly duo were quickly among the batsmen, bowling Lancashire out for 88, only for Statham (6-16) and Higgs to underline the imbalance in the Derbyshire line-up, demolishing them for 61 in 36 overs - no-one else had to bowl. Statham, though, suffered some acute embarrassment. Green explained: "He was always disconcerted on those very rare occasions the ball swung for him. One was in the Buxton match. Boggy run-ups caused him to cut down his approach from his customary 13 running strides to eight or nine. Bowling rather tentatively at something below fast medium, he started the ball on his normal strict off stump line only to find that the banana-like movement away from the bat resulted in several near wides, an unheard of thing for him.

"At the end of his second over he was ashen-faced and said despairingly: 'I don't know what's going on.' However, the ball picked up a light coating of mud, movement through the air diminished, then eased, to his huge relief."

Rain spoiled it with Lancashire 150 ahead, a wicket left and every chance of a 10 points outright victory. Instead, they had to settle for another two points. If that dented Derbyshire's ambitions, then what happened in their next game, against the South Africans, put them completely off their stride and provoked one of the biggest rows in cricket's history.

During the second innings of the Chesterfield game against the tourists, Rhodes was called for throwing by Syd Buller, the world's leading umpire, who had recently been honoured with the MBE for services to the game. Rhodes had been no-balled for throwing before, in 1960 and 1961, each time by Paul Gibb, putting a permanent question mark over his action, and, after appearing twice previously for England, he had not played Test cricket since. However, in mid 1965 he was rated the fastest bowler in England, headed the averages table, and had Derbyshire fans clamouring for him to be re-instated in the Test side. Which left the selectors in a pretty pickle.

The incident at the picturesque Queen's Park ground came as a debate over the action of West Indian star Charlie Griffith's action continued to rage, particularly after claims by several Aussies, including former captain Richie Benaud, during the winter series in the Caribbean. Benaud had also claimed that there were seven chuckers in county cricket. Some thought that rich, considering that the notorious thrower Ian Meckiff had played under Benaud's captaincy, and accusation and counter accusation left a trail of sparks throughout the world-wide game.

A county bowler suspected of throwing had to be reported to Lord's, who would then ask his club to take remedial action, but it lay within an umpire's discretion to call him immediately. Usually this was the job of the square leg umpire, although an Australian umpire once did it from the bowler's end in a match between North Melbourne and Kilda, pointing out there was nothing in the laws to prevent it. In any event, Law 26 informed that that discretion came into play if the umpire was 'not entirely satisfied of the absolute fairness of a delivery'. Rhodes had sent down 15.3 overs on the first day of the game without any apparent disapproval from the other umpire. But, next day, Buller observed Rhodes from square-leg, crossed over to cover point to watch one delivery, and then returned to his normal position from where he signalled no-ball and put county cricket on the front pages, along with Princess Beatrix of Holland and a story about price-fixing.

The Daily Mirror blasted:

'Rhodes, Test Colossus, country trundler, or outlaw... DECIDE NOW ENGLAND!'

Reporter Brian Chapman wrote: "..the fastest bowler in England had his cricket career cut short yesterday as ruthlessly as though he had ridden the tumbrils to Execution Dock."

A Daily Sketch report led on a middle-aged man, brandishing a walking stick, who rushed at Buller only to be restrained by police, although a witness thought that the man was using the stick merely to walk, and what was brandished was simply a rolled up newspaper. In any event, all hell was let loose and Buller needed a police escort to avoid angry fans when he walked off the ground.

Left out of the next two games, Rhodes was recalled by Derbyshire and continued to ravage batting line-ups for the rest of the summer. MCC sub-committees pored over film of his action, but it wasn't until 1968 that it was declared legitimate and by then his chance of an England return had long gone. Public opinion, outside Derbyshire, was divided over the issue. Rhodes' immediate reaction was: "This business stinks. There is a thrower witch-hunt. I feel I have been made a victim and example."

Rather like Statham, Rhodes had loosely jointed limbs. The Derbyshire paceman also had extremely long fingers, leaving a distance of about 10 inches between the ball held in his hand and his wrist. If the Lancashire star was Mr Bendy, so flexible that he once won a limbo dancing contest, then Rhodes was Mr Whippy with a hyper-extended arm action which caused almost constant suspicion. But why hadn't other umpires called him? Buller, himself, had not raised any questions in recent seasons.

Was there a high-level conspiracy to keep him out of the England side? Certainly, with the Griffith storm unabated, England would have been crazy to pick a suspect bowler, yet how could they omit the country's most potent fast bowler? The conspiracy theory was compounded by the revelation that MCC had written to Derbyshire earlier, hinting that they should drop Rhodes.

But Buller was a highly principled character. A Yorkshireman who rolled up his sleeves before leaving the pavilion to do his day's work, giving the impression that he wasn't to be messed with, although one story had it that the real reason was his allergy to washing powder particles left in his shirtsleeves - his skin itched if he kept them buttoned down - he believed Rhodes to be a chucker and called it, knowing it would wreck his England chances, and knowing that he had to work with his victim's father. For when South Africa faced England in the first Test at Lord's the umpires were J S Buller and A E Rhodes.

Ten years after the Harold Rhodes throwing row, it was snowballs, rather than no-balls, which concerned Lancashire and Derbyshire. Their Buxton game began on a red-hot Saturday with Clive Lloyd in majestic form, scattering sixes into the surrounding tennis courts and bowling green, but an overnight blizzard, leaving two inches of snow on the ground, wiped out play on Monday June 1, despite it dawning bright and sunny.

David Hughes and Jack Simmons were rooming together in the team's Buxton hotel. A waiter, with a 'He's from Barcelona' accent, brought them morning tea, opened the curtains and said: "It snow." From their horizontal position, all Hughes and Simmons could see through the top half of the window was pure blue sky and Yosser, not one to suffer fools gladly, suggested that he should vacate the room - pronto. "It snow, it snow," the waiter protested. Later Clive Lloyd was pictured enjoying his first ever snowball fight in front of the pavilion. Next day, with the sun blazing once more, the pitch was steaming and spiteful, and as the ball zipped past his head, Derbyshire's Ashley Harvey Walker calmly took out his dentures, wrapped them in a hankie and handed them to the square leg umpire Dickie Bird for safe keeping.

But, of more concern to me was the dressing room rebellion that I walked straight into during that strange three days. Wanting to know about a variety of injuries and illnesses afflicting both sides, I walked into the Lancashire dressing-room and found three of them huddled together, Peter Lever, Frank Hayes and Barry Wood, who broke off from the murmured discussion and asked me courteously to leave, as they had something to talk about.

Obviously! I suspected that it was something to do with a new pay deal - I had heard one or two complaints - and checked with the chairman, Cedric Rhoades. He assured me that there was no problem, negotiations were continuing and all would be well. The following Saturday Lever, Hayes and

Wood, having been involved in the World Cup which was being played in England, reported to Old Trafford but were omitted from the side to play Derbyshire at Old Trafford. Lancashire initially took the field with 10 men, and the 11th Bob Ratcliffe appeared some minutes later, looking flushed and a mite agitated. Something was 'up'. A check with the secretary 'Jimmy' James secured the information that all three were injured, a claim met with disbelief in the Press Box. Chairman Rhoades was attending the World Cup Final at Lord's, but eventually the truth emerged.

STRIKE! roared the headline in that afternoon's Manchester Evening News Pink edition. Written by Brian Bearshaw, then cricket correspondent of the MEN, the story told of how Lever, Hayes and Wood were the first cricketers to withdraw their services over a pay dispute (although there were other issues at stake). Had they succeeded in persuading the rest of the side to take action, it would have been even more serious, but David Lloyd, the captain, was reluctant and when he asked Harry Pilling, who was having treatment for a minor injury, whether he would be playing or not, Pilling replied: "Am I picked? If I'm picked I'll play." Jack Simmons went along with that and other players were hurriedly drafted in to fill the gaps.

Bearshaw was covering the World Cup Final at Lord's that Saturday, but explained later: "I had a good idea of what had been going on and when I heard that all three were missing from the side, I knew what had happened. I got it confirmed in time to write the story for the Pink." His scoop wrecked Lancashire's attempt to play the row down. The Pink was being distributed all over the ground and the rest of the Press fed voraciously on it. Agreement was later reached over the players' pay and conditions but Lever, Hayes and Wood, all England players, were disciplined by the committee. Lever and Hayes were suspended for two matches, Wood for six. Ratcliffe gave it all a humorous twist, admitting: "I was shopping in Woolworth's in Accrington when I was told that Lancashire needed me and to get to Old Trafford quick."

*****

ONE of the greatest ballads in Western popular music was born on June 14 1965. Its title? 'Scrambled Eggs'. At least that's what Paul McCartney called it while working on the song which was to become 'Yesterday'.

'Macca' and the rest of the Beatles were recording their 'Help' album at the Abbey Road studio, London, with George Martin acting as producer. He had started writing this haunting melody in early 1964 at the George V hotel, Paris, but now it was being laid down on tape for the first time. He was the only Beatle to take part in it, the other musicians being a string quartet, Tony Gilbert, Sidney Sax, Francisco Gabarro and Kenneth Essex.

George Martin, the producer, said (Official Story of the Abbey Road Years): "Paul said he wanted a one word title and was considering 'Yesterday', except he thought it was perhaps too corny. I persuaded him that it was all right."

It was on this day that McCartney revealed the full extent of his musical genius, agreeing to backing from a classical string quartet and working with Martin on cello and violin parts of the score. Martin added: "There is one particular bit which is very much his ..where the cello groans onto the 'seventh' the second time around. He also liked the idea of holding the very high note on the first violin in the last section. To be honest, I thought that was a bit boring...."

McCartney then sang and accompanied it on acoustic guitar. 'Yesterday' was a trend-setter and The Beatles continued to use strings and orchestras on their records.

*****

COUNTY cricket was struggling, but Test cricket had found new impetus. During the 1964-65 winter, West Indies, captained by Gary Sobers, had beaten Bob Simpson's Australia in a captivating series, featuring great bowling by Wes Hall and Lance Gibbs, some wonderful batting from both teams and a fair bit of controversy involving Charlie Griffith, who had broken records in league cricket in Lancashire in 1964. Also during the winter, England had tussled successfully with South Africa and, now, after sending New Zealand packing, were ready for the return.

The South Africans had landed, making their way to Chesterfield for the first of 17 first-class matches, including three Tests, and aiming to avenge their 1-0 series defeat by England during the winter. They were an all white squad. Anti apartheid demonstrators were planning to greet them with demos at various grounds.

If I'd had the courage of my convictions, I would have been one of those demonstrators. I have always hated racism. More to the point, I have never understood it. There seems no logic to it, and in those hearts where hate and intolerance burn, it is as deeply entrenched as any religion. But in 1965, I welcomed the South Africans as readily as any member of the cricketing community. After all, the players themselves were not to blame. They, as Wisden later put it, were 'gay young men' simply intent on producing attractive cricket in a season which badly needed a lift. However, South Africa's political leaders looked on it in a more cynical light.

Four months earlier Prime Minister John Vorster had issued the Group Areas Act, which prohibited any mixed sporting activities, performances or audiences except by permit, thereby segregating white, blacks and coloureds, and this tour was a way of maintaining official and open links with The Commonwealth while vigorously pursuing white supremacy policies.

Basil D'Oliveira, a coloured cricketer from Cape Town, had been forced to come to England in 1960 to further his career and, encouraged and helped by broadcaster John Arlott and cricket writer John Kay, had been playing for Kay's club Middleton in the Central Lancashire League, using the residential qualification rule to become an 'England' player. In 1965 he was in his first full season as a county player with the title-holders Worcestershire and, as the South Africans began their tour, he carved out a masterful century against Gloucestershire at New Road with a six and 16 fours. His class was undoubted, good enough to earn him a place in any South African squad, only he wasn't white.

Over in the States, Martin Luther King, the black rights activist, had been arrested for his part in a demonstration in Selma, Alabama, and black people were segregated, brutally beaten and murdered simply because they were black. Even now, it makes me feel sick because it's not over. You don't eradicate a faith with legislation, nor by electing a new President, and while all the racial equality laws and the ban on golliwogs have helped to bring about a better, less discriminatory society, racism in the UK still simmers and breeds under the surface. If you don't see it, you can sense it - and, sometimes, hear it.

"...he heard some fans calling him a nigger, so he went to see the manager and told him what had happened, and he said: 'Well, you *are* a nigger, what are you complaining about?"

This, in 2008, on the touchline of a junior soccer match where everyone involved was white. The speaker was the father of one of the players. His mates chuckled. Which doesn't automatically mean that they enjoyed the tale, or had any empathy with its sentiment. Maybe they were just too embarrassed, or too weak, to protest - I should know. The story concerned an international soccer star, who had suffered racist abuse many times in his career, but the identities of those involved is not important. It had the ring of truth as I knew of several racist football managers during my stint as a soccer reporter. So why didn't I put the phone down on the one who sometimes referred to 'those black bastards'? Why didn't I demonstrate against the South African tour? How many racist remarks and 'jokes' - from relatives, friends, acquaintances - have I let go unchallenged?

Philosopher Peter Singer asked: "Who can say with confidence that all his or her attitudes and practices are beyond criticism? If we wish to avoid being numbered amongst the oppressors, we must be prepared to re-think even our most fundamental attitudes."

The truth, and it's a hard truth, is that you have to be a special character to cast off lip service and, instead, to stand tall and shout for justice and equality, to risk losing your mates, your job, perhaps your whole comfortable lifestyle. And I'm not a special character. Actually, in 1965 at the age of 17, I was, in the eyes of my father: 1 - a tearaway; 2 - a big headed trendy. I'm not sure which I preferred.

The D'Oliveira Affair is well documented. Eventually it led to 25 years of sporting isolation for South Africa. They didn't tour England again until 1994, when Archbishop Desmond Tutu was barred from entering the Lord's pavilion, not, thankfully, because he was black, but because he wasn't wearing a tie. The man on the door was polite but firm - no, a dog collar wasn't acceptable.

Led by the dark-haired, bespectacled Peter Van der Merwe, the 1965 South Africans slumped to a seven wicket defeat in their opener against Derbyshire. Rhodes took 4-34 in the first innings but, even when he was withdrawn from the attack after Buller had no-balled him, Derbyshire's bowling was too potent for a team badly lacking match practice. A series of draws followed, but soon the batting of Graeme Pollock, the bowling of his brother Peter, and the snappy fielding of Colin Bland, were winning admirers throughout the shires en route to the first Test. They managed to skirt the anti apartheid protests and, back in Pretoria, Vorster and his cohorts smiled their thin smiles as they planned further ways of putting the blacks down.

*****

John Arlott, the much loved broadcaster who helped to bring Basil D'Oliveira into English cricket and the poet Dylan Thomas to the forefront of the literary world, was always the most welcome of visitors to the Old Trafford Press Box, although I'm not sure how much he looked forward to having to climb three steep flights of metal stairs to reach it. Perched high on the top of the old Ladies Stand, the Box was a long, rickety wooden shed, built as a 'temporary' structure in 1947. It leaked badly and swayed and creaked in the wind. One other minor disadvantage was its position immediately above a kitchen, which meant that a number of cricket correspondents were in constant danger from any over ambitious chef experimenting with flambé dishes. The only means of escape was by leaping 40 feet onto the concrete below. It didn't get to that, but there was a fire in the kitchen, luckily on a non-match day, resulting in the staircase being closed, and when Arlott appeared for an Old Trafford Test he found to his horror that he had to climb a set of builders' ladders to get onto the flat roof and, from there, gain entry into the Box.

His mind probably went back to when, just after the war, he went to Old Trafford and found the handrail and some of the steps to the old commentary box (inside the scoreboard) had been blown away, along with other parts of the ground, by Hitler's bombers. In front of him was the illustrious Olympian

CB Fry, then in his 70s. Arlott said: "To see him swing his way up, monocle firmly fixed, was to know genuine admiration for the tradition of athleticism and the Royal Navy." Perhaps not as agile as CB, the heavily built Arlott puffed and gasped his way up the rungs. I followed immediately behind, feeling sorry and anxious for him - until, when he stopped for a breather, I suddenly realised that if he fell he would take me with him. Then I felt anxious for me.

In earlier years I had waited for him to finish his match report for The Guardian at the end of a day's play. His handwriting was small, in tightly linked paragraphs, and sometimes difficult to read at first sight. He handed it to me with a gruff: "Make sure you get all the punctuation in." My task was to phone it over to one of the copy room typists. The Guardian had the best in the business, super fast, but they constantly had to wait for me as I pored over Arlott's sentences, desperately searching for any reclusive commas. Afterwards he would dig out a couple of pound notes, shove them into my hand and say: "Well done lad." (I was over 30). I enjoyed the little compliment more than the cash.

Arlott had promoted the cause of Dylan Thomas on his regular BBC radio programme in the early 1950s and I often wanted to ask him about the Welsh writer, particularly about his short stories such as 'Old Garbo', which romantically recalled Thomas' time as a reporter in South Wales. But, sometimes, at the end of a working day, Arlott looked weary. Copy dictation completed, I returned to his seat to find him dozing, head lowered, cushioned by his forearms. Shortly after the ladder climbing episode, Lancashire built a new Press Box, the Neville Cardus Suite and, appropriately, Arlott came along to officially open it. I reminded him of the ladders and he admitted: "I thought I wasn't going to make it to the top." But I never did get to ask him about Dylan Thomas.

*****

BRITAIN'S cultural revolution was spreading across the world. With MBEs about to be dangled around their necks - a brilliant tactical move by Prime Minister Harold Wilson - The Beatles were now ambassadors as much as rock musicians. Designers and painters such as Mary Quant and David Hockney were at the cutting edge of fashion and art. Carnaby Street and Kings Road, Chelsea were the places to be seen, with vividly dressed trendsetters diving in and out of the boutiques. Dandys in peacock plumage. Inspired by groups like The Who and The Kinks, they spent their wages on striped blazers and tight pink trousers, and topped these ornate costumes with exaggerated back-combed hairstyles. And where the Chelsea Tractor became de rigeur in the 21st century, the original Mini, designed by Alex Issigonis and so cheap they called it the charlady's car, zipped in and around the high streets of London.

The Who had made their TV debut early that year, just after the state funeral for Sir Winston Churchill. Churchill's exit nailed the Second World War. It was all over now. No more looking back for us. Even my father's 'then and now' rants began to fade, although the sight of a young woman with her skirt 'halfway up her backside' would quickly fire him up again. He gave the fleshless Twiggy some fearful stick.

Prime Minister Wilson, however, cast an approving eye over the unclad thighs of Ms Mod. Fifteen years earlier, as a minister in Atlee's immediate post-war government, Harold had done his bit to stabilise the collapsing economy by bizarrely warning housewives against the folly of wasting cash and material on the new fuller, calf-length fashion inspired by Christian Dior. With a wink at every male wage-earner in the country, he sniped: "You ladies will know that longer skirts mean fewer skirts."

The Who's entrance signalled a new dynamic. We took to them instantly, liked the aggression which was in their music before we saw Pete Townshend and Keith Moon trashing guitars and drums on stage. The Stones, though, were something else. They didn't appear likely to follow the Beatles' footsteps to Buck House, not after three of them had been fined for urinating in public. In a private prosecution, brought by the manager of an East London service station, West Ham magistrates heard that Jagger, Brian Jones and a 'shaggy haired monster' (Bill Wyman) got out of a chauffeur-driven Daimler asking to use the toilet. When the manager refused, they lined up and peed against the wall of the forecourt. The Sunday Express headline captured the mood of the Press with the headline 'Long Haired Monsters' and, for a while, the Stones were portrayed - and persecuted - as the leading lights in Britain's moral disintegration. Facing another court on a series of minor traffic offences, Jagger heard his solicitor deliver a long, heart-felt plea that the length of the star's hair should not count against him.

"The Duke of Marlborough had hair longer than my client and he won several famous battles. His hair was powdered, I think because of fleas. My client has no fleas."

Definitely anti Establishment, this lot. Yet society, released from its post-war burdens and awash with consumerism, was learning to live and let live. Sort of. Amid the Establishment warnings of a cultural Armageddon, there was talk of tolerance, freedom, civil rights, and reform. Only two years later, when Jagger and Richards were jailed by a high-handed judge for possessing four amphetamine tablets they had brought back from Italy, there was public outrage, led by William Rees-Mogg in The Times.

He wrote: "If we are going to make any case a symbol of conflict between the traditional values of Britain and the new hedonism then we must be

sure that the said traditional values include those of tolerance and equity."
The article was headlined: Who Breaks a Butterfly on a Wheel? Richards'
sentence was quashed on appeal and Jagger's downgraded to a conditional
discharge.

*****

AMPHETAMINES and other chemicals were of no concern to our cricketing
heroes. Alcohol, though, was another thing.

"Nowadays I keep hearing this phase 'binge drinking'," said Green. "It
didn't apply in our day. We just drank until we'd had enough! Or we couldn't
stand. What was my limit? Didn't have one. The point was that we didn't let
it affect our cricket. You'd get up, scoff your breakfast and get to the ground.
Then you'd fetch your breakfast up and feel fine. Playing as much as we did
kept you fit."

Before they left Buxton, where their game with Derbyshire finished on
June 22, they probably had a few in the pavilion. No problem - drink-driving
laws were lax, as Green fondly recalled:

"We were in Swansea for a game once and George (Statham) and I
were invited one night to a golf club down on the Gower. We had numerous
pints, and, ok, maybe one or two gins, and got lost on the way back to the
hotel. George was driving and I told him to stop and ask a passer-by for
directions. He managed the first bit okay, - winding down the window. But
he just couldn't form the words properly. I don't know what the bloke on the
pavement must have thought.

"George's head was hanging outside the window, and he was obviously
trying to say something, but it was just a blurb. I'd had enough, leaned across
and asked where the hotel was. He was still looking at George, but he pointed
across the road and said: 'It's there, right behind you.' We got in and I went
to have a nightcap in the bar with Noddy (Pullar). George went straight to his
room, retired hurt."

But a cloud hovered over the driver who liked one for the road. The
dreaded breathalyser was on its way, although it took a few years for the B
test to truly bite. Right up to the 1980s it was considered prestigious to go for
an evening or weekend drive, have a drink and maybe some bar food, and as
a result the traditional country inn prospered. Now it barely exists.

*****

As for Lancashire they could look forward to a rare break from action. Out
of the Gillette Cup, they had a week off before the next championship fixture
and fitted in a 1st XI v 2nd XI game, played under cup rules. The1st XI won

comfortably. Only one of the 2nd's top five batsmen got into double figures, an 18 year old named F Hayes joining the list of promising youngsters who, in a few years, would haul Lancashire cricket to the heights.

On his day, unleashing his speciality cover drive, Frank Hayes was worth paying money to see. A big favourite at Old Trafford, he seemed to have a great Test future when he made a second innings century on his England debut against West Indies. If, as it proved, he wasn't consistent enough, he was certainly brave enough to stand up to the most scary fast bowling. Andy Roberts smacked one into his head during one county game on a green and difficult Old Trafford wicket, forcing Hayes to hospital.

Three hours later he was back at the ground, the left side of his face grotesquely swollen. "Broken cheekbone," he told me. "In three places." He smiled ruefully.

"You'll be out for a few weeks, then," I said, scribbling into a notebook.

"Maybe - but I'll be going back into bat later."

"You're joking, Frank, you can't go out there with an injury like that," - forgetting that, when his mind was set, you had to be wary about trying to change it. His rejoinder was brief and to the point. Exit one chastened hack. As it happened, he didn't resume batting, he just hated the thought of surrendering.

"Colin," said the switchboard lady one morning late in 1984 when I answered the sports desk extension, "Frank Hayes is in reception to see you." A surprise - he didn't court the Press. One sunny Wednesday morning, for instance, when captaining the side he refused to give us the line-up, even though play was about to start. But down in the MEN reception area he looked vulnerable. "I'm giving up," he said without preamble. "I've got to accept the medical advice." He'd suffered a lot of injuries. I said I was sorry. What more can you say?

*****

AFTER their week's break from the Championship, Lancashire returned to action at the end of June to produce their best performance so far, hammering Nottinghamshire by 108 runs at Old Trafford. Geoff Pullar, with a century including 12 fours, spearheaded a strong batting performance in which John Sullivan (67), Harry Pilling (51 not out) and Green (40) also prospered on an easy-paced pitch, and then Statham took over. Five wickets in the first innings was followed by an inspirational display in the second after Notts, facing a victory target of 218, had launched their chase just before lunch on the last day. The Lancashire captain dismissed their top five with only 67 on the board, and he finished with 6-36 as Notts slumped to 109 all out.

Notts, it must be said, were a poor side. In Mike Smedley they reckoned they had unearthed a much-needed prospect, and there was experience in the form of Brian Bolus and Norman Hill at the top of the order, but their overall batting performances were abysmal and, at the end of the season, after taking the wooden spoon for the fifth time since the war, their bowling was weakened when top wicket-taker Andrew Corran emigrated to Australia and Bomber Wells retired after featuring in only 12 games. Despite the quality of the opposition, this was a hard-earned morale-booster for Lancashire. Only 15 minutes remained when Tommy Greenhough wrapped it up with an lbw verdict. The leg-spinner had bowled exceptionally well, claiming 15-11-12-2, while off-spinner Ken Howard had 2-20 from 17 overs, but, again, Statham was the outstanding player on the field with a match haul of 11-88 and the Notts side joined in the applause as he led his team back to the pavilion.

That evening Lancashire climbed wearily into their cars for the 200 mile trip to Swansea. Their game with Glamorgan started the following morning. "It was a good win," said Green. "No-one would have been complaining about the journey. We would have been a happy band of travellers."

FIVE

"YES. No - sorry." With Colin Bland around, the batsman's indecision became utterly decisive. Few had seen fielding of such prowess. Yorkshire were the first to suffer when they met the South Africans at Sheffield at the start of July, just as news filtered through of the death of Wally Hammond in Durban at the age of 62. The England all-rounder, rated by many as the greatest ever, had excelled in the field, particularly as a slip catcher. Bland was an adrenaline fuelled patrolman in the covers. Swift, strong, accurate, he turned an apparently comfortable single into a prayer for survival. Batsmen could never feel safe in his presence. Bland eroded confidence in the opposition and inspired his team-mates with a series of dazzling run-outs. Ironically, he was run out himself at Sheffield, but Yorkshire suffered five such dismissals - Bland being responsible for three - and Boycott was a victim in each innings. England had been warned.

Bland stood out, it is sometimes argued, because fielding standards were generally moderate in comparison with later years. Frank Tyson, England's Ashes winning fast bowler who became a highly respected coach, agreed that there was greater athleticism in the modern game, but added: "When I hear stories about modern fieldsmen being better, I wonder whether they would be able like Neil Harvey or Bland to repeatedly hit the one stump that they could see." England fielders certainly lacked that ability, particularly at one-day international level, when I watched them regularly over a 15 year period.

Bland practised the skill through his schoolboy days on the family tobacco farm near Bulawayo. One source claimed that he saved his side at least 20 runs per innings. Another raised the bar to 30 runs. And in the Oxford Dictionary of World Cricketers his fielding was 'worth 50 runs'. That's cricketing gold. Much of Lancashire's one-day success between 1969 and 1973 stemmed from a new emphasis on fielding, with captain Jack Bond insisting that every player got his whites dirty - but even Bond was more than happy with a 'saving' of 20 runs from the whole side, never mind one individual. One of my abiding memories from those days was the sight of Clive Lloyd accelerating through the covers, swooping on the ball, and flinging it hard over the stumps into the gloves of Farokh Engineer.

Unable to get to the Test Matches, I saw only glimpses of Bland that summer, on TV, and when the South Africans visited Old Trafford late in the season, he didn't play. But if he was as quick as Lloyd, and if he could regularly knock over one stump, then he must have been a fearful sight for any batsman.

After the first Test, The Times correspondent said: "It would be worth watching the South Africans simply to see Bland in the covers, or at mid-wicket, or wherever he might happen to be."

In the 1990s another South Africa star, Jonty Rhodes, set the example with his cover point acrobatics, and, in most polls of today, he would be a candidate for top spot in a list of all-time fielding greats. Bland would be up there, of course. Other than Hammond, I wonder how many England contenders? Bond's side revolutionised the strategy of one-day county cricket, but at the highest level, England have failed to consistently shine in the field - certainly in comparison with the Southern Hemisphere teams. Why? When Bob Simpson was invited to coach Lancashire in 2001, he was appalled at the fielding of one younger player, saying in astonished tones: "He has never learned to throw the ball properly!" The Aussie, in his day one of the best 'slippers' in the business, added: "I never thought when I came here that I would have to go back to teaching someone the basics."

Despite reservations over Simpson's judgement in some matters, I felt he was justified in making this point. Professional sportsmen, no matter who, where or when, should ensure they are proficient in the basics. I can't for the life of me understand the constant debate over left-footed, right-footed footballers. "He's missed a great chance - a pity it was on his weaker foot"... how many times have you heard something like that? For example - Trevor Brooking, in his TV commentary days: "He's chanced his arm with his left foot." Jimmy Hill reckoned that: "David Beckham has two feet which a lot of players don't have nowadays." Joking aside, footballers shouldn't have a weaker foot. It should be regarded as unprofessional. All they have to do to rectify the problem, and, as a result, make themselves much better players, is to practise.

Former England captain Paul Ince once talked to me of his time with Inter Milan and compared Italian and English attitudes towards self-improvement:

"The football culture was so different to England, and if we are ever going to win a major tournament again, we have got to change the whole concept of how we develop our players. It's such a massive thing I'm talking about, I'm not sure whether it will ever happen.

"It's not just Italy, I'm talking about Spain, France... you name it. Countries in Central and South America. In England you have a training session and at 12.30pm everyone is away. At Inter we hung around for a couple of hours afterwards, practising our skills. Maybe the climate has something to do with it. Italy, bit of sun, ball at your feet, you feel comfortable, you just want to keep working with it.

"For instance, how many times do you hear talk in England of finding decent left-footed players. In other countries you will find teams with any number of genuine two-footed players, at all age levels. Because it is in their culture, they work on their technique from a very young age. Even teams like Macedonia, for example. They don't have the experience that we have but their technique is excellent.

"If you want passion, effort, commitment, etc, you won't find anything better than in English football. We've got lots of talent as well. But you see the difference at international level. Because of the success of the Premiership, our expectations are high when we go into a major tournament, but England haven't won the World Cup since 1966, and we haven't won the European Championships. Look at Italy's record.

"I remember Eric Cantona coming to Old Trafford and everyone being dazzled by his skill. But not many knew how hard he worked at it. He would put in the extra hour. He helped me with my left foot, as well as people like Lee Sharpe and Giggsy."

Hell, I was only ever a two bit local league striker, but, from the age of 11, I could shoot, cross and manouvre a ball with either foot having learned a lesson from a certain Bobby Charlton, who advised all young wannabes (in an article) to wear a boot on the weaker foot, a slipper on the other and to keep hammering a full-sized ball against a wall. Eventually, he claimed, you will automatically use the booted foot. Problem with that method now is that all boots are as light as slippers. But it worked for me, though Mum wasn't too happy with the state of my right-footed slipper after an hour's work-out on a muddy back garden.

"Why, for heaven's sake, are you playing football in your slippers?!"

"Bobby Charlton told me to, Mum."

"You're heading for a slap if you come out with that sort of rubbish."

And, anyway, I remained as slow as a carthorse, which is why I decided sports writing was the best way of getting into Old Trafford free. Some, though, reckoned that even as a journo I continued to put both feet in it - especially when snooping around for exclusives, or 'scoops' as they were once known in the newspaper trade. When, for example, I got a tip-off that the aforementioned Cantona was about to complete his move from Leeds to United, I nipped down to Old Trafford, and was lucky enough to spot the Boss in the reception area. No newspaper or local radio rivals around - get in there, my son.

"Morning, Alex. Heard Cantona is going to sign on the dotted line this morning. Okay if I hang around and have a quick chat with him?" Now, this is in the days of yore, when Fergie fumes often enough, but, also, can be most charming, even with the Press - honest. And, yippee, I've caught him on a good day. "Sure, he's due in at 10. Just wait here, I'm going up to see the chairman."

Just as he is going through the door, I spot a suspicious looking character sidling through the front of ground car park, keeping close to the stadium wall. He is in disguise, baseball cap pulled tight over the eyes, scruffy track suit top, but it's Cantona, I'm sure. One of the most influential players in United's history has arrived unheralded and almost incognito. Not even Fergie instantly recognises him.

"Alex - there's Eric now."

"Where? Are you sure? Jesus, so it is."

"Can I just grab him for five minutes, our deadline is coming up. Just five minutes, Alex. OK?"

"Go on then, but I warn you now his English isn't much good."

"Don't worry, I'll do it in French."

Course I will. After all, 25 years previously I scraped a GCE 'O' level pass in the lingo. Fergie drags Cantona into the reception area, introduces us, sits him down and wags his finger at me: "Five minutes...can you really speak French?" He leaves us to it.

"Bienvenue, Eric. Je m'appelle Colin Evans du Manchester Evening News. Erm... pensez-vous que er, um...pouvez-vous, er, help Manchester United...."

"Comment?"

What I'm attempting to ask is whether he thinks he can help United win the title. All I need is to make him understand the question, say 'oui' - and I've got my angle for the back page lead story. 'Cantona predicts title glory' (allowing, of course, for a little tabloid author's licence). Only I can't remember the verbs for to help and to win, nor the best word for title, which makes conversation a little tricky. I opt for a pidgin Franglais, with a heavy Northern accent.

"Eric ... Manchester United, beaucoup de tasses, n'est ce pas?" - a clumsy effort to ask him how many trophies (cups) he might win with the Reds, but, later, I learn that he probably interpreted it as to how many cups of tea he will have at Old Trafford.

"Beaucoup de tasses?" he asks, pushing up the peak of his cap to reveal questioning eyebrows and making a drinking motion with his right hand. Flustered, I miss the Gallic irony and take it that he wants a drink, so turn to the lady behind the reception desk and ask her if it's possible for Eric to have a brew.

"Coffee or tea?" she says.

"Er café ou thé," I relay to Eric.

"Non, merci."

"De l'eau?"

"Non, merci."

"I thought, j'ai pense, er vous er thirsty," mimicking his drinking motion to underline the point.

"Comment?"

By now we are both totally perplexed. I try again.

"Vous helpez United win title, er, tres successful, oui?"

"Comment?" But now there is a petit smile playing at the corners of his bouche.

Desperately, I cast back to my French lessons in the third form at grammar school and, momentarily, recall our voluptuous, red-headed teacher Miss W, sitting on her desk at the front of the classroom and revealing far too much leg for my own good, especially when I accidentally drop a pencil to get a better look. Oh hell! .. It was maths, she taught. Come on Evans. Pull yourself together.

One last go…

"Er, j'ecrivais Cantona et United champion, oui?"

"Bien sur. What you like."

Cantona spoke to me only once after that, a week or so later, when he asked me: "Parlez vous Anglais?"

And I was up to my knees again when I once questioned John Crawley about his testicles. It was during his Lancashire captaincy. Nipping out of the Old Trafford Press Box for a late afternoon stroll around the ground, I heard a gasp from the crowd, peered through a gap in the stands, having to shield my eyes from the sun, and glimpsed, through a crowd of players, a fair haired batsman writhing on the ground clutching his wedding jewels. Obviously the skipper wouldn't be having much fun tonight. And, I thought, I'd better handle him with kid gloves, if you know what I mean, at his post match Press conference less than an hour away.

My casual stroll had a purpose. Morning, before the start of play, and late afternoon were the best times to bump into a few acquaintances and pick up the latest gossip. This time I was delayed longer than usual, and, instead of returning to the Press Box, decided at the close of play to go straight to the dressing room for the customary interview with the captain, a change of plan which meant that none of my journalistic colleagues got the chance to tell me that it was Graham Lloyd, not Crawley, who had collapsed in agony.

Crawley emerged from the showers, clad only in a towel, motioned me into the captain's room and sat down heavily, obviously tired after batting. As he leaned back the towel slipped a little, so I got the kid gloves out and said: "Well, mate, how's your bollocks?"

"Er - fine, thanks," said Crawley, throwing me a strange look and tightening the towel around his waist.

Returning to the issue of fielding…finding someone who didn't have a decent 'arm' was, I have to say, a rare occurrence at the cricketing Old Trafford where, particularly since Bond's regime, fielding techniques always received due importance. From a Lancastrian viewpoint, I always enjoyed Clive Lloyd, before knee trouble slowed him down, and Frank

Hayes, who used his speed as a 400 metres champion to good effect. Then there was the ever alert Neil Fairbrother, Freddie Flintoff, shovel like hands and powerful throw. Statham was good too, a reliable catcher with a good arm. But none would give the side anything like a 50 run start. In 1965, the fans flocked to see the South Africans, salivating at the prospect of entertaining batting and bowling, but praying that they would see Bland in run-out mode.

Hammond was perhaps the world's greatest all-rounder, and his fielding, by all accounts, could influence matches just as much as Bland's. George Duckworth, the Lancashire and England wicketkeeper, claimed: "Hammond justly earned the title of the game's greatest slip fielder and there was no more electrifying sight than to see him on an English sticky wicket, standing only a yard away from the wicketkeeper and catching everything."

Hammond was only 62 when he died in South Africa in reduced circumstances following business failures, and the world of cricket paid tribute. Neville Cardus wrote: "Wally indeed was cricket in excelsis." One of his most remarkable performances came at Old Trafford when he plundered a double century, taking five boundaries and a single through the covers in one over off Lancashire's famed Aussie fast bowler Ted McDonald. Duckworth recalled the single off the last ball would have also sped to the rope, but the fielder, having already recovered five boundaries, was obviously tired, maybe a bit fed up, and hadn't bothered to return to his proper position in time for the sixth delivery, allowing him to make an interception.

Not only does that story illustrate the majesty of Hammond's batting, it also highlights how easily poor fielding was tolerated - or, at least, what we would now consider to be poor fielding. Even 30 years later, in the mid 1960s, a similar aberration in the field might have raised a caustic comment, but, just as likely, a joke. No wonder fielders of the calibre of Hammond and Bland were so conspicuous.

Hammond was a natural athlete who even took to surfing during a trip to Honolulu, but there were many who were not. David Green said: "It was generally accepted that each side had some reasonable fielders, some good ones, and a couple of cart horses. But attempts were occasionally made to render us more agile. Lancashire brought in Jack Crompton, who was training Manchester United and had been their keeper for many years, to loosen us up a bit. Some of us, particularly the burlier ones like Ken Higgs, Peter Marner and me, had extreme difficulty in performing the contortions which Jack requested. We weren't built like the soccer players. We hobbled about for days after he had finished with us.

"Fielding practice was basically longer and middle distance work being done by the coach, or senior pro, hitting the ball at us. Close work was provided by the old wooden slip cradle. But, for all the primitive preparations, we were well armed to play the game *as it was then,* and not too many broke down, despite the rigours of a season with 30 or more three day matches."

Green's reasoning is backed up by the fact that only a handful of Lancashire team changes were caused by injury in 1965. Statham suffered a couple of niggles, Pullar was absent once through illness, but generally the selectors had a full squad to choose from. As Green said, they were 'fit for purpose'. Which brings to mind the case of Ian Austin, who had to work hard throughout his career to convince certain people at Old Trafford that his physique was perfectly adapted for the job.

Green was once described as 'heavily built, tending towards rotundity', but that was a description, not a criticism. He was a top-class batsman, in that season was the model of consistency both in scoring and in availability, and his body shape was not important. Austin, though shorter, had a similar appearance, and for several years through the 1990s was one of Lancashire's most reliable players. Best known for his feats and many honours in one-day cricket, he also excelled in the first-class county game, and, in a spell of three years in the mid 1990s, was an ever present member of the Lancashire championship squad. To clarify this, while he did not play in all those games he was always available for selection, never sidelined by injury.

Many other Lancashire stars of that era, although outwardly fitter and faster in the field, missed games through injury, and Austin was justifiably proud that his thicker and rounder trunk took the strain of so much cricket better than some team-mates. What is more valuable, he used to ask, a fat bloke who is ready to play, or a skinny sod who is out with another hamstring strain?

"Judge me on my figures, not my figure," he said.

Green had sympathy for him. "Players hurl themselves at or over boundary boards in attempting to save runs - something we would have considered imprudent. If I had tried it, I would have a good chance of breaking my neck. I am filled with admiration of the modern outfielder. I sometimes wonder though whether the concentration on physical conditioning has led to some neglect on technique. Athletic excellence puts a gloss on basic cricketing skills, but it is no substitute for them."

Of course, modern coaches would say that it is perfectly possible, indeed imperative, to combine the two. Certainly Austin lost the argument and his Red Rose career ended, prematurely in my view, in 2001.

Earlier in 1965, Bland had played for Rhodesia against Worcestershire during the county champions' world tour. The sides met in a three day game in Bulawayo, which Bland missed, and a superb four day clash in Salisbury - now Harare - which provided the stage for a rarity, a coloured South African cricketer mixing it at first-class level with a South African Test star on their home soil. Basil D'Oliveira failed to make a great impact in the game, scoring 14 and 13 and not doing much with the ball, and Bland got the better of it with a hard-hitting 62 in Rhodesia's 156 run victory.

That Worcestershire tour, however, was a huge success. Yorkshire had visited America, but this was the most extensive tour ever undertaken by a county side. They took just 12 players and two members, with Joe Lister the manager and Don Kenyon the captain. Covering 34,000 miles they played in Kenya, Rhodesia, India, Singapore, Malaysia, Thailand, Hong Kong and Honolulu. The climax was to be a one-dayer against the South Californian Cricket Association in, of all places, Hollywood, and, of all things, it poured down! Away from early February, they returned two months later - just in time to start preparations for the defence of their title.

The Cavaliers had also boosted English cricket abroad with a winter trip to West Indies. A strong squad of 15, including nine Test players, drew three of their four first-class matches and lost to a Jamaican XI, whose outstanding performances came from Gary Sobers, 129, and Wes Hall, 4-48.

Two months later Hall gave one of his finest performances, bowling fast and straight on an erratic pitch to earn a match haul of 9-105 in West Indies' maiden home victory over the Aussies. West Indies went on to take the series 2-1, deepening Australia's chagrin over the action of Hall's pace colleague Charlie Griffith. Although never reaching the heights with bat and ball, Sobers was always influential, and at the end of a memorable five match series, West Indies celebrated their first series success over Australia and, with it, the status of unofficial world champions.

While Bland was wowing English fans, he would have received news that back in Rhodesia the white nationalists, having walked the latest election with 50 out of the 65 seats in the 10th Legislative Assembly - election rigging is nothing new in that country - were deep in debate about the country's future. Britain's de-colonisation policy came under the awkwardly worded banner of No Independence Before Majority African Rule (NIBMAR), but Ian Smith, the Prime Minister, and his cronies didn't fancy that one bit. Rhodesia was heading for their Unilateral Declaration of Independence (UDI) and, like South Africa, towards economic and cultural upheaval.

D'Oliveira, who should have been playing for South Africa on merit, was quickly getting to grips with Championship cricket. No doubt he would have loved to have taken on the South Africans that summer, but Worcestershire were not one of the 13 counties they played. While the tourists were shivering in a cold easterly in Sheffield, D'Olly was hitting 99 against Warwickshire, foiled of a century when bowled by Jack Bannister. In the next game against Glamorgan, he became the first Worcestershire batsman to pass 1000 runs.

*****

Although it took three more years to boil over, the injustice of the D'Oliveira affair simmered throughout the summer and brought home what was happening in South Africa. D'Olly didn't aspire to political eminence. He just wanted to play first-class cricket.

Mohammed Ali, formerly Cassius Clay, was another sporting hero at the forefront of the human rights battle. However, whereas D'Oliveira was content to let his cricket do the talking, the Louisville Lip punched his weight in and out of the ring. Backed by the Nation Of Islam (aka the Black Muslims, motto 'A White Man's Heaven Is A Black Man's Hell'), Ali vowed to refuse to fight in Vietnam if drafted. And he stuck to his vow, saying: "War is against the teachings of the Holy Quran." He later put that in a more idiosyncratic way... "I ain't got no quarrel with them Viet Cong - they never called me nigger."

To win the world heavyweight title and then to retain it, Ali beat Sonny Liston twice, the second time provoking allegations of a fix. Liston, linked with mobsters, fell as if poleaxed by an apparently innocuous right-handed chop, which seemed to graze the side of his head. It won fame as The Phantom Punch. Ali, I thought - and still do - was, as he so outrageously proclaimed, The Greatest. He fought not just with flashing hands and dancing feet, but with intelligence, bravery and sometimes blood curdling ferocity.

Liston disgusted and equally intrigued me. One of 25 children to a hard drinking cotton worker, he followed a similar route to a number of other American boxers, runaway, petty criminal, hard man, 'leg breaker' for the gangsters, schooled in the art of boxing while in jail and so forth. He was taken up by a certain Frankie Carbo, known as the Czar of Boxing, and not even a brute of a man like Liston, whose fists measured 19 inches in girth, argued with Frankie, a fully paid up member of Murder Inc. The cops had nabbed him a few times, only for him to beat the rap when vital witnesses suddenly refused to give evidence or died in strange circumstances, like Kid Twist, who 'fell' out of a bedroom window in the Half Moon Hotel on Coney Island.

Eventually Frankie was accused of conspiracy and extortion, and just to make sure he was banged up this time, none other than Robert Kennedy masterminded the prosecution case. By then, though, Sonny was in the grip of other shadowy figures. His moody demeanour, his associates and his lack of social graces made him an unpopular world champion, so it was a welcome relief for boxing fans when Ali - or Clay as he still was - wrested the title from him in their first fight. And, for American blacks, they now had a sporting and political champion, just as capable as Martin Luther King of shaking up the white establishment.

The 1965 return bout with Liston, staged in Central Maine Youth Centre in front of a mere 2434 fans, ended in disarray with the first round Phantom Punch. As Liston lay on the deck, Ali stood over him shouting at him to get up, and refusing to go to a neutral corner so that the ref Jersey Joe Walcott could begin the count. After a while Liston did stagger to his feet, only for Walcott to be told that he had been on the floor for 20 seconds. Ruled a KO, it sparked off controversy and rumours of Mob involvement, although, in one interview, Liston allegedly told a reporter that he was under threat of death from The Nation Of Islam. Whatever the truth, that victory cemented Ali as a new black hero. Liston made a comeback, indeed he kept fighting until around 50 years of age. Then, like so many others involved with the Mob, he died, in 'strange circumstances', possibly through a heroin overdose, administered by whom remains a mystery. Buried in Paradise Memorial Gardens, Las Vegas, his simple headstone bears an even simpler epitaph: 'A Man'.

*****

MAKE Swansea a Test Match venue was the demand from one fan. "It has a ground as big as any in England and at least the seam bowling monotony would be relieved," enthused Mr David Roberts of Winchester in The Cricketer, referring to the help that spinners traditionally got from the pitch.

But Wales had to wait another 41 years before it won Test Match status. One late afternoon in March 2006, I was in the office of Lancashire's Commercial Director Geoff Durbin when the club's Chief Executive, Jim Cumbes, walked in, sat down heavily, and said: "We've lost the Ashes Test."

Cumbes was ashen-faced. Durbin, wearing a look of blank astonishment, asked him to repeat it. "It's gone to Cardiff," exclaimed Cumbes, who had received the news in a call from David Collier of the England and Wales Cricket Board. Lancashire and other clubs had been massively out-bid by Cardiff in the auction for the 2009 Ashes series. It was a shock to anyone involved with Lancashire cricket. "A kick in the teeth," said the Chief at the following day's hurriedly called Media Conference. Less than 12 months earlier, Old Trafford had been crammed full for five days, locking out 20,000 fans on the last, as Ashes Fever gripped the nation. Now the club had to ponder their entire Test Match future.

Some critics of Old Trafford, dismayed by what they perceived as a lack of investment in the ground, stuck the knife in. Lancashire deserved to lose the Test, Old Trafford was run down, lacking modern facilities, stewarded by people who knew nothing about cricket and so on. Okay, but did the North-West deserve to lose the Test? Some of the criticism was spiteful, opportunist and directed at the club to avenge past grievances. The cricket fans of the region, who had packed Old Trafford in 2005 little caring about the state of the stadium because the game itself was the sole attraction, were pushed to one side.

But there was no doubt that Old Trafford had slipped its sell-by date. Where did it go wrong? Back in 1965, the new committee man and chairman to be Cedric Rhoades was already thinking big. Soon he was talking big. But the doing came only here and there, now and again. Development was piecemeal, uncoordinated.

When John Arlott opened the new Press Box in 1987, a draught whistled through the gaps between the window frames and the wall. Years passed before they were sealed properly. The double-decker Washbrook-Statham stand was a white elephant, although the top tier made a useful platform for launching fireworks during floodlit matches, and while the Executive Box Stand pulled in much-needed cash, it was hardly an architectural gem. Noses sniffed at the re-developed pavilion with its all glass frontage, as seen from the main entrance, contrasting so inelegantly with the beautiful Victorian edifice as viewed from within the ground. And so on. Nothing ever gelled.

Finance was the major problem. Lancashire were a big club, but not as rich as many believed. In fact, they plunged deeply in debt, up to £3m at one point. Their ground was difficult and expensive to maintain, they lost money through stewarding and other costs as soon as they opened the gates for a Championship match. Then Health and Safety laws kicked in. Stands had to be demolished, the pavilion re-roofed - and that alone cost almost £1million. Yet when initiatives were taken, such as using the stadium for summer rock concerts, members denounced the club for putting commercial affairs before the cricket. So did I, come to think of it! Something had to change and so was born the plan, first in 2003 to move to a new site, later to completely re-develop the existing ground.

I got a call in October 2003 promising to give me a 'massive' story, perhaps the biggest in the club's history, but I passed the caller on to a colleague without even asking what it was all about. Why? Well, the previous evening my wife and I had dined on mediocre fish, chips and peas accompanied by Guinness for me, cider for her, while being bored to death by a German social worker whose ambition was to visit every one of Britain's off-islands and had, sadly, just happened to have picked the one where we were spending our wedding night. It had been a very low-key wedding day, but a good one, until, misguidedly, we invited Gunter, bespectacled, intense, and looking oh so lonely on the other side of the pub, to join us for dinner, whereupon he proceeded to list his experiences studying the tides on the Outer Hebrides, the Inner Hebrides, the Shetlands, Lundy Island, Caldy Island, Isle of Wight, Isle of Man, Anglesey and the Isles of Scilly - you name it, he had seen its waters.

"Nice meeting you Gunter, got to go now," inwardly cursing him for destroying any hope of a wildly passionate night, although the cold peas also had something to do with that. "Ok, maybe see you over at Hell Bay tomorrow. Mein Gott, I could sit all day there watching the waves."

We didn't tell him we had said "I do" to each other only five hours before. I prayed that the only waves we'd share with him were ones of goodbye.

Anyway, when the mobile rang next morning, as I lounged on the patio of our honeymoon cottage, basking in the radiance of our newly wedded bliss - after decades of living over the brush - I felt it imprudent to get involved in anything like work, and so I handed the story of how Lancashire might ditch Old Trafford for a new ground to a colleague. Although, if Gunter had been around, I would have accepted the job with alacrity and left the missus to keep him company for a few hours.

In Sept 2008 after five years of talking, planning and designing, Lancashire unveiled a model of the new Old Trafford. Oh dear! Apparently they wanted something with a Northern flavour and what immediately came to my mind was the container depot at Trafford Park, but I'm sure that, like the M6, it will come to be appreciated, if never loved.

Funny thing though. In 2006, during preparations for the 50th anniversary of the Laker Test, I walked onto the Test wicket with Alan Oakman, one of the main players, with five catches off Laker's bowling in Old Trafford's most famous match. The sun danced on the square, and, looking back at the pavilion, and then around the rest of the place, I thought: "Hey, it doesn't look *that* bad, in fact not bad at all." And Oakman, a charming man, agreed. Maybe sentiment played a part, but a number of former players, who came to Old Trafford that day for a special dinner, were of similar opinion. No way should an Ashes Test have been taken away from Manchester.

Losing it to Glamorgan was salt in the wound - if it hadn't been for Lancashire, the Welsh club would not have been admitted to the ranks of the first-class counties in 1921. Glamorgan needed eight votes from the existing counties and, facing strong opposition led by Lord Harris of Kent, were struggling to get the necessary support until Lancashire stepped in. Tony Lewis once revealed: "There is an unwritten law in Glamorgan which forbids a deaf ear to be turned on any request from Old Trafford." That law had obviously been written off by 2006!

Lewis, praised for his stroke-play - as highlighted in a glittering century against the South Africans - but urged to find more consistency, was 'something of an enigma' when Lancashire visited Swansea in early July 1965. Green couldn't remember, but maybe it was the match where he and Statham had trouble finding the way back to the team hotel.

I had a fondness for Swansea. My Auntie Lou lived there, in the crescents of council houses which make up the Mayhill area, and, when I was 12 or so, we had stayed with her for a couple of summer weeks, taking the bus through Sketty down to the bay, and, at night, tramping down to the docks with my cousin to fish for bass with a simple line and bait dropped over the quayside. We lay on our bellies, peering over the concrete edge, tightening with excitement at a glimmer of silver in the darkened water, waiting. We never caught a thing.

Dad was born a few miles away, over the mountain in Ammanford. He hadn't lived in Wales for years, having served in the Army during the War, but it could be said that he had never left there either. "God's Own Country". According to the Gospel of Thomas Avery Evans, the air was cleaner, the food tastier, especially the leeks, and you worked hard - down at the pit face in his case - and played hard.

Built like a bull, with bigger hands than Flintoff, he was digging into the coal seam with pick, shovel and explosives within two years of leaving school, earning wage bonuses from the senior miners he partnered, seeing his 'mam' right with his weekly contribution towards the household expenses, and having a good time with what was left. He was a man's man, nothing better than Saturday night in the pub after the rugby, a bellyful of beer, and a good old sing-song with the lads. And he was a fighter with a devastating burst of temper. Noticing his older sister had a black eye, he sought out her bullying husband, ignoring her pleas to forget it because he was older and even bigger than Tom, and hammered him to the ground. When he watched Ali's fights on the box, his fists clenched, his shoulders hunched up and he began to throw short left and right hooks.

In his short story 'Old Garbo', Dylan Thomas talks of a Saturday night out in Swansea town while working on the local newspaper. In one busy hotel bar he sees a group of young men chatting up a pretty barmaid, asking 'to see her garters'.

"Other young men," he goes on, "sleek-haired, pale, and stocky with high cheekbones and deep eyes, bright ties, double-breasted waistcoats and wide trousers, pocked from the pits, their broad hands scarred and damaged, all exultantly half drunk, stood singing around the piano…"

A good description of Dad I thought when I first read it many years ago. And then I realised that he and Thomas were the same age. And that, sometimes, perhaps at Easter or Christmas, Dad and his pals from the pit would get the bus over the hills into Swansea for a big Saturday night out. But he and the poet never made contact. If Dad had spotted Thomas, a lonely, unattractive figure, he would have called him over to join the party. And, unlike Gunter the island-hopping German, Thomas would have made an excuse and declined.

Lancashire lost at Swansea. So did I. Just before that game I had one of my two weeks of holiday and got a lift down to South Wales to spend a few days with relatives. They looked askance at my clothes and my hair. It rained and I stayed indoors most of the time, irritating my cousin's wife, who kept having to shove me out of the way of the vacuum cleaner. I made my excuses. Stretched my sleeping bag on the floor, placed spare clothes, toothbrush and the other bare necessities of teenage life into the hood, rolled it up, tied it with a leather belt, slung it over my back and started for home. Glenda, drying her hands on her pinny, asked kindly: "How will you get home? You haven't much money."

"Hitch it," I replied. "That's the only way to get around." I walked a few miles. The rain got heavier, trucks splashed me. I dived into a pub, advertising cheap rooms, sorted one out, shot back downstairs for a few rum and blacks and, in the morning, hopped on a train to Manchester.

On Swansea's slow turner, Lancashire's spinners Tommy Greenhough and Ken Howard picked up 11 wickets, Tony Lewis among them, but Glamorgan were far too strong. Having led the table in late June, they stayed in the top three for the rest of the season. Howard's 4-79 in the second innings was his best of the summer, but Lancashire, set a target of 246 in 320 minutes, had little chance and were bowled out in under two hours for 135.

By the time I got home, Lancashire were back at Old Trafford with David Green in good nick against Leicestershire, heading for his first century only to be run out for 78. "I was playing well, knew that a hundred was well within my grasp, but I got a 'yes, no, sorry' from Mick Beddow. I went past 80 a couple of times that season but I think that innings was the best chance I had. It was just one of those things. I didn't feel sorry for myself. After all, there was still half the season to go, plenty more chances. Or so I thought."

He never made it. Before that, the highest total of runs in a season without a century was 1709 by C B Harris (1935). Cyril Washbrook scored 1665 in 1939 with a highest of 91. Three others, James Langridge (1937), T C Dodds (1947) and J D Robertson (1955) went past 2000 with just one century.

Lancashire dominated the first half of that match, skittling Leicestershire for 59. Jack Birkenshaw top scored with 17 and Higgs, striving harder than ever in the absence of the injured Statham, produced career best figures of 16.4-5-19-7. Green and Pullar's opening partnership of 113 steered Lancashire towards a lead of 142, only for Leicestershire to fight back with 341-9 dec, leaving a target of 200 in 135 minutes. Green, as acting captain, went for it with a belligerent 37, but this time Pullar was run out, a collapse set in and Lancashire had to settle for a draw. Peter Lever, filling the gap left by Statham, teamed up efficiently with Higgs, taking eight wickets in the match and showing his usefulness as a number seven batsman with 35 not out in the second innings. Birkenshaw made 68 in the Leicestershire revival before edging Higgs behind.

A decade later Higgs and Birkenshaw were Leicestershire team-mates at Grace Road, sharing in a stubborn last wicket stand to deny Lancashire victory. A thunderstorm washed out any lingering Red Rose hopes and half an hour later, I went into the dressing-room, a little tentatively knowing how they would be feeling, to get a quote from captain David Lloyd.

"What can I say?" groaned Bumble. "You can tell him to piss off," shouted someone from the back with utter sincerity. Facing a Gillette Cup tie the next day, Bumble ignored me for a few minutes and tried to rally the troops. "Right lads, 9.30 at the ground tomorrow." Moans all round, particularly from Jack Simmons. "You're not expecting me to be there at that time, are you? ...I've got to get all the way from Great Harwood."

"Flaming heck," Bumble retorted. "We're playing at Old Trafford, Jack, not flippin' Lord's."

Jack Bond, restored to the team after being dropped for the previous three matches, scored a few runs in the next match at Trent Bridge, but rain cut deeply into the first two days and washed out the third. A draw and 'no decision' as it was then recorded. Green, though, had just enough time to chalk up his 1000 with a free flowing 66, putting on 93 at a run a minute with Pullar. Green's 1000 came in his 35th innings, with an average of around 30. "I was fit, strong and didn't pick up injuries. But I hadn't felt that great at the start of the season, and it surprised me a little that I had got to 1000 so quickly. It's always a mark. And we were having to play on some awkward pitches. I knew now that I had the chance to make a lot of runs by the end. I was playing well."

*****

Jack Bond was nearly lost to Lancashire well before he was offered the captaincy in 1968, giving him the chance to restore the county's fortunes with a new, aggressive brand of one-day cricket.

During the mid 1960s he was repeatedly dropped in mid-season, but then brought back. There seemed no rhyme nor reason to it. A senior player with over 7000 runs, he had already been mentioned as a possible future coach. True, his batting had lacked something since having his wrist broken by the West Indian fast bowler Wes Hall in 1963, but in this transitional phase of the club, his immense experience and hard graft were thought essential by most of the other senior players. The selectors thought differently. They were determined to give younger players a go, and Bond was 33. Lancashire's youth policy, in part forced on them by their own folly of the past few years, generally proved fruitful.

But they were lucky that Bond hung around. At least twice he was on the brink of leaving. And then what? Who would they have turned to for salvation in 1968 after Brian Statham packed in? He had been tempted to leave Lancashire before the start of the 1965 season. He was offered a job as a sportsmaster at a school in Norfolk, thought hard about it, and, as he was due a benefit at Lancashire, eventually said no. Then, in 1967, he was again ready to call it a day, only to be named as 12th man for a match at Cheltenham, mainly because a sportsmen's service was planned for the Sunday and a Lancashire player was to read the lesson. Who better than Bond, a staunch Methodist and a regular church goer. Even so, it was only when the unfit Geoff Pullar had to pull out of the game that Bond actually played, and he took his chance with two good knocks. Divine intervention?

*****

CRICKET was slow and, to some minds, getting slower. The Gillette Cup was gaining in popularity, and there were calls for Sunday play and better pitches. All very encouraging. But in 1965 the fastest century was by Jim Parks and it took him 102 minutes, earning him the National Sporting Club's Café Royal Centenary Trophy and 100 guineas. Parks also hit the quickest hundred in 1959, when he needed only 61 minutes, "...a fact which," noted Wisden, "emphasises the change of tempo in County Cricket in a comparatively few seasons."

David Green was one of the quicker scoring players, and Colin Milburn also liked to rattle or clear the boards, as he did against Gloucestershire at Northampton where, after a rain-delayed start, he blasted 152 not out in 210 minutes, 'smiting' seven sixes and 15 fours - 102 in boundaries. But, generally, scoring was restrained, or impossible.

The cricket writer EM Wellings was one of those who believed the game could be, and should be, speeded up. In his annual report on public schools' cricket he referred to the bad weather, but added: "A vintage year it may not have been, but, turning from much false, dreary and often meaningless county cricket, I found the play of the boys decidedly encouraging." However, Wellings castigated King's Canterbury who, apparently, had boasted about averaging 122 balls - more than 20 overs - an hour. "Do they really think such a tempo good, or even satisfactory?" he asked. With growing indignation he went on: "England averaged only 106 balls an hour during their six Tests. Set against that wretched figure, 122 may seem excellent, but, if I had the job of cricket master, I would not do any boasting until my school side averaged something in the region of 25 overs an hour....Before the war we used to expect 22 overs an hour from all first-class sides, youthful and elderly alike. Young teams, such as the universities, habitually maintained higher averages... England, for instance, averaged 23 overs an hour at Lord's in 1930 during an Australian innings of more than 700 runs."

Wellings felt that more overs would have produced more results - proper results, not those obtained by contrivance - and he could have used a couple of Lancashire matches to underline the point, Lancashire v Leicestershire and Lancashire v Warwickshire both produced draws after virtually three full days in which an average of 93 overs a day was achieved. Even with some weather interruptions this was snail's pace cricket.

Colin Cowdrey had voiced concern about the game's entertainment value, right at the start of the season, noting that in 1964 the national over rate had slipped to 19.38 an hour. "I would like to see the captains unite in an attempt to average 20 an hour."

One fan claimed that cricket had become far too conscious of the clock and that it was media exaggeration which led to criticism of slow scoring and over rates. But Geoff Piper of Bakewell in Derbyshire was one of many who thought something had to be done about the preponderance of seam bowling: "…I am afraid that in the modern age we are committed to becoming increasingly clock conscious. Outside cricket grounds everything is happening faster and faster. If cricket is to survive, the reverse must not occur inside them. If Barrington can be dropped for slow play, many of the 'faster' bowlers in this country might be omitted for the same reason, and the popular Press might more often shift the blame for dull cricketing days from the frustrated batsman to the frustrating bowler."

Something else earned E M Wellings' ire that summer. English Schools had a "good, workmanlike" wicketkeeper in CEP Carter of Radley. He was, however, "among those who looked as though they were avoiding the barber in the hope of qualifying for the award of the MBE. Long hair may be fashionable for those who strum a guitar but is to be deprecated on the cricket field. Hair which screens the eyes is an impediment to efficiency."

Carter was behind the stumps for Radley against an MCC XI when a batsman skied one to mid-off and, the catch taken, walked off only for the square-leg umpire to invoke Law 43 saying: "Not out - the wicketkeeper had his gloves in front of the stumps as the bowler delivered." It is not known whether Carter's error was due to his Beatle-style locks.

OTHER GREAT CRICKETING ESCAPES OF 1965

In Lancashire's game at Taunton, Somerset veteran Bill Alley played a ball from Ken Higgs onto his stumps without dislodging a bail. But that was nothing compared to the luck that Tony Buss of Sussex enjoyed against Yorkshire. First, a delivery from Yorkshire's seamer Tony Nicholson clipped Buss's off stump and raced away for four byes. The off bail moved but somehow jammed in its groove at one end and just refused to fall off. Then, in the second innings, a ball from Chris Balderstone bounced off Buss's foot, and rolled against the stumps. Again the bail stuck. The funniest escape was that of RL Burchall, of Winchester, whose cap was knocked off by a bouncer from Harrow's CA Holt. The cap fell onto the stumps and hung there 'as though from a dressing-room peg'. The story was headlined: An Extraordinary and almost Unbelievable Incident.

Holt, incidentally, was Harrow's hero against Eton at Lord's, where because of a fixtures pile-up they were playing in midweek for the first time. After breaking a stump in the first innings, he won the game with a late spell of 5-1, one lbw and four bowled.

The most amazing escape was made by Monkton Coombe School. The scorecard read, Monkton Coombe 67 all out, Bryanston 68-5, indicating a comfortable five wickets win. Until a Monkton Coombe schoolmaster checked the scorebook and found the total had been added incorrectly and that his lads had scored 68. The game was re-started for Bryanston to score the one run needed to correct matters, only for three batsmen to be run out and two to be caught without addition, making it a tie.

*****

CRICKET wasn't the most pedestrian game around. That was surely snooker, even when you had a giggle by viewing it on your old black and white telly, listening to Whispering Ted Lowe's attempts to describe it in colour. John Pulman, the tall, bespectacled Devonian was the world champion, with the title being decided on a series of tedious challenge matches rather than a KO tournament. In mid 1965 at London's Burroughs Hall he beat Fred Davis 37-36, Rex Williams 25-22 and Fred van Rensberg 39-12.

But snooker changed dramatically in the early 1970s, with the world championships held in the City Exhibition Hall, Deansgate, Manchester, now part of the Museum of Science and Industry. Masterminded by the West-Nally public relations firm, in which the popular broadcaster Peter West was the figurehead, the transformation was based around a new format, live TV coverage, and a young man little known outside the snooker world. Alex Higgins was a few minutes late for the initial Press conference. Probably deliberately. He swept in, wearing a fedora hat, vividly coloured waistcoat and brown and white shoes. We hadn't seen him play a shot. But we knew we had a star to write about.

Despite the hair, which he constantly flicked away from his eyes, Higgins, who had won the world title the previous year, had an engrossing game with the veteran Fred Davis in the quarter-finals until a bizarre interruption. Rain Stopped Play. I know we were only two miles from the cricket ground, but we were *indoors* for heaven's sake. Eddie Booth and I were covering the championships for our freelance agency, the only reporters there every day and all day. Eddie came rushing breathlessly into the Press office to tell me what had happened - rain seeping through a leak in the roof right above the table where Higgins and Davis were playing. What a story. We phoned it around to every national newspaper and arranged an exclusive photo shoot for the Daily Mirror. Next day there it was, a middle page spread, with the picture showing a spot of moisture glistening on the top of a snooker ball in the middle of the table. The headline? 'Raindrops Falling On My Red'.

Ray Reardon won the title, beating 'Steady Eddie' Charlton from Australia in a close but wearying five day final. At least Reardon made the spectators laugh with his jokey approach. I liked him. During one interval I went to the toilets and found him standing over a wash-basin, stripped to his vest, lathered up for a shave. He chatted away as, bending towards the grimy, pock-marked mirror, he wielded the razor. No edge to him at all, no pretence. Just an ex-Welsh miner, like my Dad, who also happened to be pretty nifty with a snooker cue.

No doubt, though, that Higgins was the biggest draw. But, in time, relations between him and the Press became strained. He didn't like reporters, felt we were following him around, looking for dirt. As if! At the following year's championships, in the Kings Hall, Belle Vue, Manchester, he had another quarter-final battle with 'the old man of the baize' Fred Davis and, at a crucial point, the referee Jim Thorpe called a foul against him for a push shot. Davis went on to win a nail-biter and The Hurricane blew, threatening to sue Thorpe, the organisers, everyone involved. Another good Higgins story. Only we knew him a little better now, the mood swings, the sudden changes of direction. He insisted he would take matters to the High Court, so we asked him to put it in black and white and sign it. Which he did. Whereupon we filed the story.

Higgins, who had been drinking, drank some more and returned well after 11pm to say he'd reconsidered and wouldn't be suing anyone after all. We had to pull the story, he said. Too late, we told him, with, I must confess, a tinge of provocation. Thorpe was a friend of mine - I didn't like what Higgins was saying about him. This is how, in his autobiography, he remembered our confrontation: "After that fiasco of a match, I was doing a Press Conference in the players' room, slagging off Jim Thorpe, and, as usual, a reporter started winding me up. I gave him a real mouthful, swearing and shouting in front of everyone - not a smart move…but I have to say that I believe every row or scuffle I had with a tabloid 'journalist' was justified, although not everyone would agree with me on that one."

Actually the reporter who enraged Higgins that night was my mate Stan, sat next to me at the Press desk. Higgins just *thought* it was me who called him a 'great poof'. Which of course he wasn't. While The Hurricane was blasting me with every known obscenity and some others of his own, one of the tournament managers, a hefty bloke named Bill, stalked him from behind, grabbed him around the chest and hauled him away. He was a great player, and, like George Best, a very vulnerable person. But I know, if ever invited, who I would have preferred to have had a drink with.

*****

WEST Indies had upset the world order by knocking over the Aussies, England had beaten South Africa on their 1964-65 winter tour - their first overseas win in five years - and now had comfortably disposed of New Zealand. Despite the weather and the threat of anti-apartheid demos, the return series against the Springboks, as they were then nicknamed, promised to be a cracker. And Van Der Merwe's side were warming up for it nicely.

Officially, this was an 'unofficial' series because South Africa had left the Commonwealth, automatically losing their status from the world's governing body, the Imperial Cricket Conference - in 1965 this was re-named the International Cricket Conference, but South Africa remained outside its boundaries.

No-one but the statisticians bothered too much with all this nonsense. This was England v South Africa, a full-blooded Test series, the first of three crucial series for England, with the Aussies in the winter and the West Indies the following summer, to come. They would need to be at their very best to repel a side considered by some to be the best in the world, notwithstanding the results in the Caribbean.

South Africa's first win of the tour came against the Minor Counties at Jesmond, where Ali Bacher hit a century and Lancashire's Peter Lever made his mark by taking 3-64, including Graeme Pollock and Bland. Bacher was again in top form with another hundred in their next game, against Leicestershire, but although South Africa reached 350, the off-spin of Lancashire born John Savage, who eventually came to play and to coach his native county, threatened to embarrass the tourists. Bowling Graeme Pollock for a duck, Savage earned 6-79 and South Africa declined to 159-8 before a whirlwind stand between Bacher and Jackie Botten, of 181 in 137 minutes, put them in charge. Rain washed out the last day with Leicestershire struggling.

*****

Peter Lever, a first-rate fast bowler and a crossword expert, was a bloke who stuck to his guns. In 1969 he was one of a handful of players who said they would refuse to play against South Africa, underlining opposition to a proposed tour the following summer. But at Lancashire's AGM that year, a call to pull out of the county's fixture against the South Africans was overwhelmingly rejected by members.

Lever was also patient. As understudy to Statham and Higgs, he had to wait five years for his county cap and he was 30 by the time England picked him. "It was the best of all cricket educations," he said. "George was the most undemonstrative man I've known. Nothing ever aroused him to an outward show of excitement. He said to me early on: 'I'll give you what help I can but I'm not much of a talker. Just stand at mid-off and watch…' I watched all right and I reckon old George must have had a little black book with every batsman's name in it together with their strengths and their weaknesses."

*****

In 1965, Lever was happy enough to play against the South Africans, both for the Minor Counties and for Lancashire in the end of season game against the tourists. But, four years later, his opinions had hardened and he was brave enough to make a stand. So did Mike Brearley. Other players considered it right to play against them. One such was D'Oliveira, who thought it 'essential' to keep contacts open.

Lever would have waited a long time before seeing Statham exploit one particular weapon in the fast bowler's armoury. David Green said ruefully: "George didn't like using the bouncer, and he could bowl a very good one. We had to nag away at him before he bowled one. Nothing to do with him not being aggressive enough, he obviously thought it was a wasted delivery, unless in exceptional circumstances."

Batsmen did not wear helmets. They didn't always have a sightscreen to help them. The only protection against a good bouncer, or a ball which reared up off one of the many poor pitches, was quick reflexes. Which John Edrich had, yet he was felled by a ball from Peter Pollock which hit him on the side of the head when the Test series got under way at Lord's. Edrich, bowled for a duck by Pollock in the first innings, had scored only seven in the second when he was forced to retire hurt and, although he recovered to play a few more matches for Surrey, he did not re-appear for England that summer.

The incident once again called into question the use of the bouncer. Fred Trueman had knocked out New Zealand's Bert Sutcliffe in the Edgbaston Test, effectively ending the 41 years-old left-hander's career. Sutcliffe appeared to duck into the ball which hit him on the right temple. With New Zealand in trouble at 71-3, he bravely carried on after an eight minute interruption, but 20 minutes later he felt dizzy and retired hurt. Sutcliffe hit a half-century in the second innings but took no part in the second and third Tests.

Significantly, not one bouncer was seen in the third and final Test against South Africa. Perhaps that had something to do with England recalling Statham for his Test finale. He claimed 5-40 to prove once more that there is nothing quite like bowling at the stumps.

Apart from the blow to Edrich, the first Test with South Africa is usually remembered for Bland's fielding. A total of around 100,000 fans saw a thrilling see-saw game - the 100th Test between the countries - and many of then went away enthusing over the vibrancy of the South African cricket. England, too, deserved praise. Superb catches by Bob Barber, Fred Titmus and David Brown, on his debut, had South Africa in trouble on the first day, but, at the end, the match was delicately balanced with England needing 46 short of victory with only three wickets left.

Ken Barrington was one of the stars at Lord's with a fine innings of 91, including a six and 11 fours, a complete contrast to his century in the first Test against New Zealand when 'adopting the most exaggerated two-eyed stance ever seen' (Wisden), he occupied the crease for seven and a quarter hours. He was stuck on 85 for over an hour while 20 overs were completed, having particular difficulty with John Reid's leg cutters and off breaks, yet when he clinched his century he celebrated by slamming 14 in an over off Pollard's off-spin.

Broadcaster Peter West later wrote: "I said on TV that this was the sort of thing which would kill Test cricket dead and on further reflection I do not wish to amend that view."

Annoyed with Barrington's performance, and under pressure to provide more positive cricket, the selectors, led by chairman Doug Insole, dropped him for the second Test against New Zealand. Insole stated: "We can talk about it until we are blue in the face about the right methods on playing cricket and nothing happens. Only by practical action are we likely to achieve anything. We have agreed that we have to show the younger players, in particular, that we are prepared to leave out and discipline a man whatever his status if he does not play in the proper manner."

Insole, only recently put in charge of selection, was determined to get English cricket back on the right track. He had three daughters, forcing him to extend his musical education, and he could now tell a 'Kink from a Hermit', said a tongue in cheek report of his appointment as chairman.

Obviously the message had got home, and Barrington seemed set for a wonderful Lord's century against South Africa until falling victim to the irrepressible Bland who, sprinting from midwicket, swooped on a push to mid-on and hit the one stump that he could see at the bowler's end. Bland struck again to run out Jim Parks. If not before, England's batsmen knew then that here was a fielder you tempted at your peril.

Controversy stalked Barrington. During the previous winter's tour of South Africa, the third Test at Cape Town, he 'walked' - after staying at the crease for a few seconds - to a shout for a catch behind. As the umpire had not responded to the appeal, Barrington could have continued his innings, but he gave himself out. This contrasted with Eddie Barlow who, earlier in the match, waited for the umpire's verdict when England felt he had nicked one to Peter Parfitt at slip off Titmus. Barlow, on 41, got the benefit of the doubt and went on to make 138, with a noticeable lack of applause from the England players as he reached three figures. Titmus, who had expressed his feelings on the pitch, was told to apologise by his captain Mike Smith, and the story, billed as an international incident, ran and ran, building into a major debate over sportsmanship and 'Englishness'.

Walking, it was believed by many, exemplified the true spirit of the game with, presumably, England taking the lead. Others disagreed. A number of umpires, for instance, claimed that Barrington's action undermined their authority. "He waited for the umpire's decision, then flouted it," said one..."if players are allowed to make their own decisions one way, why not the other? And, in that case, why have umpires?"

Rebuked for walking, dropped after hitting a Test century, then beaten to the punch by Bland - poor Barrington couldn't do right for doing wrong.

On the walking issue, Insole appeared to have some sympathy with Barrington, saying: "I believe that walking is one of the pleasing aspects of cricket and I hate to think it is in disrepute because of the reluctance of all players to put it into practice. I hope that, given time, the habit will spread... it will add to the pleasures of playing the game and also help to maintain the kind of image of cricket which, one would like to feel, is held by the majority of people whether or not they are actively interested in sport."

Thankfully you rarely see anyone walk in today's ultra-professional first-class arena. And it seems to me that, in any class of cricket, if a batsman believes that walking is part of the spirit of the game, and that his duty is to uphold that spirit, he should walk in every instance, no matter what the situation. The acid test, is one wicket left, two runs to win the Ashes or the local league cup. How many batsmen, past and present, would walk then? My bet is not one.

The British have many, many qualities and have given much to the world. More specifically, I'm proud to be English, glad that Dad stayed in Cheshire after the war rather than returning to south Wales. But the notion of 'English' fair play gets right up my nose, and walking plays a small part in the hypocrisy of it all. No doubt, we want to be fair, we often are, but the truth is that if it suits us, we are as ruthless, double-dealing and self-serving as any other nation, especially those which have power and are desperate to retain it. 'It's not cricket', the world's starving, homeless and downtrodden could plead. Oh yes, it is...

By the middle of 1965, Britain and the USA were plotting to use the Indian Ocean outpost of Diego Garcia, part of The Chagos Islands, as an American military base. Problem was the 2000 people who happened to live there. The Americans wanted them out of the way completely, but how to do that without any opposition or fuss?

Britain, who controlled the island but were being offered £14million of American aid as part of the Polaris nuclear deterrent programme, instructed her civil servants to come up with a solution. And, being inventive and caring little for the spirit of the game, they did. Sir Bruce Greatbatch, governor of Seychelles, set the tone in a 1965 Foreign Office memorandum. "These people have little aptitude for anything other than growing coconuts." They were "unsophisticated and untrainable".

Neither use nor ornament then, old sport. Kick the beggars out and hand them a few sheckels to keep quiet. Which is, essentially, what happened, although it had to be done covertly to avoid international condemnation and it was 1971 before the USA were able to start building its base. The process began in 1965. Mauritius held sovereignty over the archipelago, an obstacle easily cleared by persuading the Mauritian Prime Minister, Seewoosagur Ramgoolam, to sell it for a bargain £3million. Ramgoolam had, surprise, surprise, just been awarded a knighthood. With the Chagos and a handful of other islands, Britain founded the British Indian Ocean Territory and the following year they agreed with the USA to use Diego Garcia for their joint defence needs for the next 50 years.

Gradually the island was 'de-populated'. Some islanders were virtually kidnapped, being refused to return home from supply trips to the mainland. It was a remote island without communications and the rest of the world never got to hear the full story until it was too late. Even though eventually it became a cause celebre, the British government constantly fought the islanders in court to avoid paying further compensation.

USA used Diego Garcia for long range bombing missions to Iraq and Afghanistan and rendition flights in the Allies' War Against Terror. Apart from one brief 'courtesy' visit to see how their paradise home had been transformed into a war zone, the islanders were barred from returning until 2116. But cricket and the spirit of 'English fair play' survived. A rough pitch was prepared between the hangars and depots and a British side from Naval Party 1002 hammered a a visiting Australian Air Force crew to win the Ashes of Diego Garcia. Apparently one of the Brits walked for a catch behind the stumps, although, by then, the game was as good as won.

SIX

MOST professional sportsmen turn off when you start spouting history at them. They dislike comparisons with past and present, just want to focus on what is in front of them. Lancashire's cricket coaches and captains down the years sniffed disdainfully at my questions about this and that from yesteryear. Tell you the truth, they sniffed disdainfully about most of my questions, but the game's history was the biggest turn-off.

"What do you want to write about that for? It's got nothing to do with what we're trying to achieve." And don't even mention Lancashire's last Championship triumph!... Of course, to get a mention in the newspaper about their benefit year they would talk about 'Cricket And Its Place In The Agrarian Revolution' until it came out of their ears, and in retirement they would gladly answer anything about the game's characters, the greatest matches of 1864, etc - as long as it was at a sportsman's dinner where a few hundred quid would be stuffed in their back pocket. Only joking. Most players that I dealt with, especially at Old Trafford, were extremely co-operative and patient, as for the others, it's understandable that they wanted to concentrate on the next ball rather than natter about irrelevant (to them) heroics and failures of the past.

But history is vital to the 'Member', the regular supporter of Championship cricket, partly I suppose because he/she has a fair amount of history him/ herself. Early in the 21st century, the average age of a full Lancashire member was in the mid 50s and rising. This vintage crew have long memories of the game and like to remind everyone else of them. So do I, which is, of course, why I'm boring you stiff with this book.

At an Old Trafford Championship game in mid 2008, I sat with a member friend in Old Trafford's C stand, looked around and saw a crowd of tanned pensioners with a sprinkling of grandchildren - the school summer hols had just started. Next to me was a sociable, quietly spoken bloke. Our combined age was 130 and the chat went like this:

"Look, Corky's on, if he can just break this stand...."

"I like Corky. Always gives it everything."

"Maybe. Statham certainly did. I loved watching him."

"Oh yeah. And Washy."

"Yeah. When we were kids we usually sat on the grass behind the rope."

"Winston Place was still in the side when I started coming here."

"I always came to the Roses match. Trueman…"

"And Statham."

Pause to applaud a useful Cork delivery

"I hate all this effing and blinding, don't you."

"No effing need for it."

Another pause to applaud Cork

"Well done, Corky - he deserves that wicket."

"These comedians, that Chubby Brown, awful. Morecambe and Wise weren't like that."

"No. Remember George Formby, only man to win the Grand National and the Isle of Man TT!"

"Ha ha - yeah, that's always a good 'un. Made me laugh, those films."

"Liked him, George Formby. Got some of his records too."

"Some of them were a bit naughty, weren't they? Y'know, bit of double entendre."

"Oh, yes, very risqué...Remember that song, 'My Little Stick of Blackpool Rock'?"

Another round of applause.

"Ooh, that's two wickets in an over for Corky."

"Isn't he after a new contract?"

(He was ...but he didn't get it and joined Hampshire)

And so on. Strange. I enjoyed that day, the first time in 25 years that I had watched Championship cricket as a supporter rather than a reporter. Much of the conversation revolved around the glorious past. But there was also deep and sensible debate about the match in progress. They knew their stuff.

While watching that game I wondered whether I might become A Member. Even the thought made me take a deep breath. I couldn't be old enough, surely! But then I remembered the senior citizen's bus pass in my pocket. So what else did I have in common with my fellow Red Rose vets at the Brian Statham End, most of whom had voting rights at the AGM? Not surprisingly, I found myself sadly lacking, and still do.

For one - I don't know enough about the game;

Two - They show restraint, applauding politely, maintaining decorum. Nowadays, enjoying my freedom from the Press Box, I'm more likely to jump to my feet, punch the air and shout "Oh Lancy, Lancy; Lancy, Lancy, Lancy, Lancashire".

Three: I believe Membership is far too cheap;

Four: I like a pint, but I would campaign for an alcohol stand, instead of a non-alcohol stand - then when someone throws ale over someone else, at least they can't complain they don't like the smell of it;

Five: I can't find the energy to complain about chips not being available in the pavilion after 3pm (see Chapter 9).

There are many other flaws in my Membership credentials, I accept - the above are just a few that come quickly to mind. In fact, throughout my lifetime holiday as a cricket writer, I refused to join the official Lancashire brethren for fear that Membership would prejudice my reporting objectivity.

'Crap, Evans' - comes the call from the back of the room. *'You were prejudiced anyway.'*

Well, OK. Sometimes. It was difficult, for instance, in a bad season to have continually criticised players that you knew fairly well. Especially if you were travelling around with them, as I did with Lancashire. Especially if you liked them as blokes rather than just as players. Now and then I hit out causing a reaction. David Hughes once threatened me with legal action, Neil Fairbrother told me that 'my attitude' was wrong and that I wasn't well liked in the dressing-room of that time (and perhaps other times), Wasim Akram blasted me on a couple of occasions, John Crawley cold-shouldered me after his acrimonious switch to Hampshire, Jack Simmons barred me from entering the Old Trafford offices, one Chief Executive threatened to ban me from the ground - although later we became so friendly that we shared a bedroom in India - and Mike Atherton's mum stopped talking to me (which remains a matter of sincere regret).

But, generally, I leaned towards the club rather than away from it, and, sometimes, not in an effort to be ultra positive or optimistic, but simply to make life a bit easier for myself. My predecessor at the Manchester Evening News, Brian Bearshaw, might have been accused of doing the same, as, in his reports, he even refused to identify the culprit of a dropped catch. But that wasn't about dodging the issue. His reasoning went thus: "Everyone misses 'em. It's not fair to pick one poor sod out." So his report might say: "Tavare was missed at slip off his second ball and stayed another five hours for an unbeaten 31." Or something like that.

Quiet, unassuming, going out of his way to give the benefit of the doubt - that was Bearshaw. But when there was something to stand up for, he stood tall. One morning, during an Australian tour and before the start of play, an Aussie writer brought his young son into the Old Trafford Press Box, just to show him around, only for a senior home-based reporter to order the youngster out.

"This is for working journalists, not for kids," he rasped. (And he did 'rasp'). Technically he was right, but some, including Fred Trueman, then working for the Sunday People, remonstrated with him, trying to persuade that the boy should be allowed to stay for a short while. To no avail. Bearshaw, livid, kept his distance, but, after the row had died down, I saw him approach Mr Nasty and whisper something in his ear.

"What did you say to him?" I asked afterwards.

"Oh, nothing, really. Just told him to crawl back under the stone that he came from."

As well as not particularly desiring unimpeded entry to the Pavilion, or to have my say at the AGM, another average Membership quality I lack is a love of cricket quizzes. These usually crop up at the wrong time, either when a newspaper deadline looms or you feel like a little mid-afternoon snooze. Just at that moment, someone enthusiastically invites you to provide the last all Lancastrian side to play for Lancashire (and never mind the boundary changes), or to name the only transvestite ever to appear at an Old Trafford AGM.

Of course, I couldn't answer that question - but there definitely was one. Having gained full membership in his natural-born state as a male person, he turned up at the meeting in the late 1990s dressed as a woman and caused consternation, nay panic, when he joined in the voting. Just a trick, as he admitted afterwards, to show up the club's hypocrisy in refusing to give women equal rights. Afterwards, he fluttered gorgeously long eyelashes for the photographers and invited the Press to interview him. I was careful with my questions - I didn't want to repeat a previous experience when I had interviewed a trans-sexual who had been charged as a woman with soliciting for prostitution on a street corner in Whalley Range, Manchester, only to prove, by virtue of a birth certificate, that she had been born a man and, therefore, could not be convicted of said offence.

James, as she had been christened, had dyed ash-blonde hair, thick hairy eyebrows and thick hairy wrists. 'Trannies' then were big news. I said: "Do you consider yourself a man or a woman?"

Crossing her legs with a Kenny Everett flourish, she flicked cigarette ash at me and snapped: "I'm a woman. I've had the op. I've got a fanny. I'll show it to you if you want." At which, in the style of the old Sunday People sex scandal investigators, I made my excuses and left.

In drawing up my average Member identikit, I also have to admit that I am black, and that's definitely not *average* Membership material. I can remember only a handful of non-whites at Lancashire's AGMs through the years, and that at a club where every effort has been made to encourage support from all ethnic groups. Lots of younger fans from the Asian communities of Manchester and East Lancashire are seen at one-day matches, and one of the most popular food stalls at Old Trafford sells a mean curry, but the face of the Championship crowd throughout England remains that ageing, tanned white.

Editor's footnote: Evans is not black.

*****

HISTORY of any sort meant little to our gang in the Swinging Sixties. It was all about now, because, for the first time, a generation believed it could do virtually anything it wanted.

The writer Philip Norman said: "It was the summer when British life broke up and re-arranged itself in a kaleidoscopic array of seeming brand-newness."

Bob Dylan put it like this: "The dominant myth of the day seemed to be that anybody could do anything, even go to the moon. You could do whatever you wanted - in the ads and in the articles, ignore your limitations, defy them...anything was possible. It was almost like a war against the self."

We put it like this: "It'll blow your mind!" (Because our vocabulary was limited). In fact someone once reckoned that an average teenager used only 20 words for 60 per cent of their everyday speech. Surely an exaggeration. It's nothing like 20. My grandchildren can now get along with a daily output of four - 'yeah', 'nah', 'cool' and 'whatever'.

The life of the Western world was being turned on its head, social boundaries pushed to the wire, over it, and through it, whether for good or bad. Yet Dylan himself went too far for his fans, who booed him off stage at the 1965 Newport Festival on one of the most notorious nights in the history of popular music.

Dylan was a rebel folk singer with a cause. Or so we thought. With his acoustic guitar, straining voice, and sometimes an almost incomprehensible language, he shouted for freedom and equality and, for a while, we sat back, soaking up the streams of strange sentences, letting it be known through the occasional nod of the head that we understood perfectly, that here was our Messiah, giving us The Word and we were ready to follow. But true disciples were to be betrayed when he went electric. Newport became the folkies' Gethsemane. He swerved onto a different path, playing with a 'pick-up' band for the first time in public. For many, Dylan was a lost cause.

A year or so later, when he did an electrified set at Manchester's Free Trade Hall, one of the audience, John Cordwell, rose from his seat and yelled at him: "Judas". Unfair, really, because Dylan had never agreed to anything, had never promised anything. Cordwell, in fact, claimed many years later that his action was borne out of frustration with the ineffective sound system, taking his cue maybe from the folk singing guru Pete Seeger, who had raged during the Newport gig that the audience couldn't hear the words properly because the volume was turned up too high. "That's the way Bob wants it," he was told. Seeger shouted: "If I had an axe I'd cut the cable." Cordwell, though, was totally out of order. You don't insult someone in that way simply because his words are a bit fuzzy, otherwise I would have suffered a dreadful life.

From his youth Dylan had always listened to, and had been influenced by, all forms of music, literature and art. Now he needed to throw off the shackles. Wasn't that what we were all doing? Yet, on July 23 1965, after hearing of the Newport controversy, I also charged Dylan with betrayal.

Which, in retrospect, is worrying. If I hated the prospect of Dylan abandoning his folk roots, maybe I wasn't as tolerant, nor as progressive, as I believed. Perhaps the little conservatism of the council estate and grammar school was more deeply ingrained than I had assumed. Dylan was a brave musician, determined to go his own way, but he never made a better album than his early vinyl LP 'Another Side of Bob Dylan', containing, among others, 'Blowin' In The Wind', 'Don't Think Twice', and 'Mr Tambourine Man', 45 years old now, the dog-eared cover showing him collar turned up, looking wistfully towards the horizon.

Although 'Like A Rolling Stone' was a big UK hit, Dylan's music was rarely heard in The Twisted Wheel and other Manchester clubs during that summer. The main attraction was R and B and soul music, to dance to all night. No alcohol, maybe one or two Purple Hearts to keep you popping, although you had to be careful. A big chemists had been broken into and drugs - amphetamines - stolen. The city's police were on red alert...Heroin was also available. A tall, lanky dirty looking peddler from the North-East was regularly seen offering cheap shots in the alleys around various clubs. He got enough takers to make it worth his while, but heroin was definitely out of bounds for most of us. If we took anything it was to keep us awake through the all-nighter rather than to get a high.

The Twisted Wheel Club, run by the Abadi brothers, has a special place in the hearts of British teenagers of that era. At one point it had 14,000 members, most from the North-West, but also with a large contingent from West Yorkshire and regulars from London and Glasgow. This was the 'in' place for rhythm 'n' blues and then, as the Mod scene blossomed, for the soul music which originated in the States but had been successfully taken up by some British groups.

Its D Js, particularly Roger Eagle, got their hands on the latest and the best records, young stars to be like Rod Stewart played live on stage, The Rolling Stones once went along to taste the atmosphere after a gig in Liverpool, and heard Eagle rag them as a 'great backing band'. He then went on to play the originals of all the songs they had covered on their LP, a daggered reminder of what they owed to lesser known American artistes.

This is how Eagle remembered it, when he gave his last recorded interview to Paul Welsby of the Mod magazine The New Breed.

"Yeah. I'll tell you exactly what happened. The Stones came down to the club and they were standing in the coffee bar having a cup of coffee. The kids were standing round them - just looking at them. Not talking to them - just looking. And I played all of the original tracks off their first album, which had just come out.... 'I'm A King Bee' by Slim Harpo, 'Walkin' The Dog' by Rufus Thomas, ... They knew exactly

*what I was doing... I played them in exactly the same order as the LP.
It was just me saying there's a North/South thing. I'm a Southerner
by birth - but a Northerner by emotion. I prefer the North. I'm not
saying I don't like Southerners, but they tend to be so temporary down
there. To me if something's solid then its worth looking after. Whereas
they're into it and out of it. Which is really not the Northern style.*

*"I actually got on OK with The Stones. Brian Jones bought a copy
of R&B Scene* (Roger's own magazine from the early/mid-60s) *from
me when I was in London. Mick Jagger once bummed a cig off me.
That sums up The Stones for me! But joking aside, I'm one of the DJs
that publicised the music, but when The Stones went to The States they
got Howlin' Wolf onto primetime national televison. Fucking Hell.
That's the thing to do. I admire them for doing that."*

Eagle wasn't a Mod, and didn't have the patter nor the ambition to become
a star. But he became a major influence on the music scene just by playing the
music he loved, hours and hours of it, notably in The Twisted Wheel and later
in other clubs like The Three Coins in Manchester's Fountain Street.

*"I'd be playing tunes in the club and those guys would be listening.
You know Rod Stewart and those guys. Pete Stringfellow used to come
over and write down the name of every tune that I played. I didn't
really know what was going on. I wasn't sharp enough business-
wise to realise what I had going. I'm not bitter about it because I am
absolutely totally committed to the music. It means so much to me.*

*"I was originally a rock 'n' roll kid until I heard Ray Charles. The
'In Person' and 'Live At Newport' LPs from around 1958/59 really
converted me. Rock 'n' roll died in 1958. Ray Charles was the first
to see the possibilities of mixing different types of musics. He mixed
R&B, rock 'n' roll and even Country. There were other acts at the time
that were a great influence. Fats Domino, a lot of the R&B releases on
London Records, Gary US Bond's 'New Orleans', Arthur Alexander,
LaVern Baker, Chuck Willis' 'The Sultan of Stroll' - that was a very,
very important LP.*

*"There were various coffee bars in Manchester, like The Cona
Coffee Bar (in Tib Lane near Albert Square) where you could take in
your own records to play. You would take your own in and also listen
to other people's and pick it up from there. There were a few like-
minded people around and you would bump into them or meet them
in places like The Town Hall pub. Before I got the job at The Twisted
Wheel, my only DJ experience was taping tracks on one of these reel-
to-reel recorders and taking them along to parties to play. One day I*

received a parcel from the US that contained all of the Chuck Berry and Bo Diddley back catalogue LPs. I took them down to The Left Wing Coffee Bar, just to have a look at them. I was approached by the Abadi Brothers, who said: 'We're buying this place and turning it into a night club - do you know anything about R&B?' I said 'Yes' and they offered me the DJ job there and then.

"The only other club anywhere that was playing anything like what I was playing at The Wheel was The Scene Club in London. I was getting hold of some records before their release even in the States, things like Stax and so on. We weren't consciously trying to create a movement or anything like that. We just liked to have a club that played the right kind of music.

"I used to be friendly with Steve Winwood. He would come round to my place and listen to records when The Spencer Davis Group played the club. Georgie Fame did some good things - very King Pleasure influenced. The important thing is to take the influence and then add a twist and take it on further. It's important to remember that there is a big big difference between club groups and pop groups. Eric Clapton was a good friend at that time. I remember one Sunday morning after he had played at the club, he brought a good-looking young Mod girl round to my place and she got completely pissed off because all he wanted to do was listen to Freddy King records."

Regular acts at The Wheel included Georgie Fame and The Blue Flames, Graham Bond Organisation, John Mayall's Blues Breakers and Alexis Korner. Eric Clapton had been the lead guitar with The Yardbirds, formerly the Metropolis Blues Quartet, but later he linked up with Mayall and their first album, 'Bluesbreakers', sold well. Some of the most popular acts came from the States, John Lee Hooker, Inez and Charlie Foxx, Screaming Jay Hawkins, a crazy guy, who, it was rumoured, fell out with some of his associates and, after having a pistol held to his head, fled back to the States, never to be seen in Britain again.

Music critic Chris Lee wrote: "Manchester kids have always had an obsession with black American music, ever since the mid '50s when both black and white musicians from Burtonwood (near Warrington) US Air Force Base began living and playing in the city."

This love of soul and R and B music unwittingly enabled Manchester to play a small part in the race struggle. The North-West kids bought deeply into the Stax label, a Memphis recording studio which based its output on black musicians, like Otis Redding, the Sharples Singers, and later Isaac Hayes. But its most significant achievement was that, for the first time in the American south, blacks and whites actually worked together, not just in the studio but in the offices, collaborating to produce great music and to build a successful business, supplementing the efforts of men like Martin Luther King and the Rev Jesse Jackson to bring about racial equality.

One major musical debate of the day was whether British artistes could play blues as well as the Americans. Usually the answer was No. How could they, we thought. Our bands didn't have the life experience to express themselves in the same way as Howlin' Wolf, Muddy Waters, etc. But there were exceptions. Mayall was one. Originally from Macclesfield, he worked in advertising in Manchester before emerging as the leading British light of blues. He played keyboard, 'harp', and a peculiar nine string guitar. Mayall was in his mid 30s when he persuaded the 20 year old Clapton to join the Bluesbreakers early in 1965, and in May they headed the all-nighter gig at The Wheel. The place was crammed - Clapton's reputation as a guitarist was spreading rapidly. Many of the fans already revered him as an anti-hero, partly I think because he sometimes turned his back on them while on stage, although there was a technical reason for this as it enabled him to pound out the riffs while exposing the electronic pick-ups on his instrument closer to the amplifiers, thus achieving better 'sustain'.

You stood and watched the live act, and danced to the disco grooves, a strange type of dancing, with thumbs hitched into your lapels, and lots of nifty criss-crossing footwork. Dave Godin, who coined the phrase 'Northern Soul', said: "The dancing is, without doubt, the finest I have seen outside of the USA - in fact I never thought I'd live to see the day where people could so relate the rhythmic content of soul music to bodily movement to such a skilled degree in these rigid and armoured Isles."

You couldn't buy booze at The Wheel, nor at any other of the Manchester all-night venues, but you didn't need it. The clubs had a special quality which drink would have tainted. And it was the Mecca for wannabe stars.

"If you wanted to make it as an R and B band in England, you had to be accepted by the kids at The Wheel in Manchester first," said Elton John.

Certain sections of society, however, thought The Wheel and its rivals had no quality at all. Were dens of iniquity. Parliament, a year earlier, had passed the Misuse of Drugs Act and Manchester had a campaigning Chief Constable, a James McKay, who was determined to stamp out the 'moral decay of the innocents', as one commentator put it. McKay was helped by stories like the one in the Manchester Evening News, January 4 1965, which said: "Drug peddlers are believed to be behind a raid on a Manchester chemist in which more than 3000 'pep pills' and sedatives, including Purple Hearts, were stolen."

McKay ordered his Vice cum Drug Squad to investigate, gather evidence which could be used to clean up the city. In 'Central 1179, the Story of The

Twisted Wheel', the authors Keith Rylatt and Phil Scott, talking of the club scene in general, claimed: "That some form of control was needed there is no doubt. Poor conditions - bad ventilation, inadequate lighting and sanitation - were commonplace, and ignored by a lot of club owners. But McKay's ultimate intention was to completely close down the teenage coffee dance clubs."

It is true that there was a degree of lawlessness in the city. To the extent that the notorious Kray twins were rumoured to have visited Manchester to give it the once-over, see if there was anything they could get their dirty mitts on. The story went that that they were met at Piccadilly station by a welcome committee comprising members of Manchester's own criminal top dogs, the so-called Quality Street Gang, along with certain police officers who entertained the brothers at a city centre hotel before escorting them back to the train station. Only a story but easily believable as, during the 1970s, I and other journalists dealt with many Manchester court cases involving the Quality Street Gang. We also got to know several police officers, who had served in the city throughout the 1960s, and who inhabited shady corners.

Chief Constable McKay authorised raids on some clubs, and the Drugs Squad sent in young bobbies, disguised as Mods, to obtain first-hand data. One, codenamed Eleanor B, spent an interesting night at The Wheel, reporting: "In the largest room a group was playing ...it was very dark and crowded and couples were lying on the floor. It was impossible to pass through because there were so many people asleep or couples kissing and cuddling."

There was a bit of a fight in one of the rooms, leaving a youth with a cut face, and an unpleasant smell from the gents. And some of the 250 who stayed all night at the club, mostly male, looked a bit young. Maybe 15. Other than that, little to report, sir. The all-nighter ended around 5.30am and everyone drifted into the pale, chilly morning streets, tired and quiet. Eleanor B didn't say, in her written statement, whether she and her colleague had enjoyed themselves! I suspect they did.

But, with concerns that some youngsters went missing from home to attend these all-nighters, the police had the Press on their side. A police report amplified the 'moral frenzy', as Rylatt and Scott described it in Central 1179, when it claimed some clubs were owned by criminals. It went on to say: "Older women and *many coloured men* (my italics) were frequenting the clubs." And you couldn't have that, could you? Drug peddlers, prostitutes, absconders, tramps - all could be found operating or hiding in the clubs. Of course, a roll call at most would have also turned up bank employees, hairdressers, factory workers, apprentice plumbers, insurance clerks, sales reps, counter assistants, and even the odd journalist. But, eventually, McKay and his cohorts convinced the powers that be to take radical action. The result was the Manchester

Corporation Act of 1965, which gave the city's authority full control of all the clubs, allowing the police to enter and search without a warrant, and threatening the owner with jail if drugs were discovered. This Act of Parliament received Royal Assent that summer, became law on January 1 1966 and led to the closure of many of the original 200 plus coffee bar-clubs. The Wheel, though, survived.

*****

DAVID GREEN earned an extra £50 in mid July 1965 by smashing the West Indies' feared fast bowler Wes Hall all around Lord's. Green hit an unbeaten 23 off 18 balls in the first tie of the Charrington Single Wicket Competition and dismissed Hall for 22 off 19 deliveries. The crowd were perhaps disappointed, they had wanted to see Hall charging in at Mushtaq Mohammad or Basil D'Oliveira. Richie Benaud also slipped out of the first round.

Having beaten Kent's Alan Dixon in the quarter-finals, Green lost a thrilling semi to Mushtaq, who went on to pulverise D'Olly in the final, hammering 76 not out off the allotted eight overs with two sixes and 11 fours. The Pakistani, who was living in England to qualify for county cricket with Northants, clattered one six onto the canopy above the Tavern, but his best trick was to turn from right-hand to left-hand for the final ball, beating Kevin Pietersen by 43 years.

'Much lively cricket was seen on both days,' said Wisden. But it wasn't crash, bang, wallop. Kanhai, for example, took 16 balls to make nine in his first round win, and Jack van Geloven toiled for almost all his eight overs to score 17 off D'Olly's bowling.

After picking up his £50 cheque, Green returned to Old Trafford, where on Saturday July 17 Lancashire took on Glamorgan and brought in another new face, 24 year old Ken Snellgrove, who had asked the committee to pay him 14s petrol expenses for his daily trip from Bootle to Manchester. He didn't get the cash, but he did get a debut against the title contenders who had jumped to the top of the table in late June and stayed in the race to the end of the season. Snellgrove quickly asserted himself at number five, making Lancashire's top score of the game - 39. Lancashire were undone, first by Don Shepherd's off-cutters, and then by the pace of Jeff Jones, and Glamorgan only had to score a total of 21 runs to win by 10 wickets.

It was the start of a decent career for Snellgrove, who played in over 100 championship matches between then and 1974, chalking up almost 4000 runs and making significant contributions to the one-day successes of 1969-73, particularly in the Sunday League. Yet, in a 2008 unofficial Lancashire supporters' forum, he was branded as one of the county's worst-ever players!

Other players were also unjustly named and shamed, but, of course, the accusers remained anonymous, disguised by their user 'tags'.

Of Snellgrove, Green said: "There were lots of players coming through. Some made it, others like Gerry Knox did well initially but didn't train on, but the good thing was that, whether by design or accident, there were opportunities."

With so many championship fixtures to get through, Lancashire were easily able to play three of them at their outgrounds, Liverpool, Blackpool and Southport. Most counties moved around, taking the game to as many parts as possible. Middlesex and Surrey stayed put at Lord's and the Oval respectively, but Derbyshire's home matches could be seen at Derby, Chesterfield, Buxton, Ilkeston and Burton on Trent. Essex travelled to every corner of their county - Brentwood, Ilford, Romford, Colchester, Westcliffe, Clacton and Leyton - and Glamorgan, as well as playing at Cardiff and Swansea, climbed up and down the valleys to Neath, Ebbw Vale, Llanelli and Pontypridd. Kent, with nine grounds, wandered to and fro. Wherever you lived, county cricket wasn't far away.

'Southport. A paradise for sports lovers' proclaimed one advertising poster for the West Lancashire resort. First-class cricket at the Trafalgar Road ground, top golf at Royal Birkdale....

And, said the bill, there were 'beautiful gardens, elegant boulevards, Continental cafes, and lots of evening entertainment.'

Certainly from a reporter's viewpoint, Southport was my favourite destination. Whatever the game, it always produced a story. Wasim Akram, having already taken a hat-trick, just failing to add a century with a pull which fell five yards short of the rope; Muttiah Muralitharan's perplexed look after failing to avert a Lancashire defeat despite taking a record 14 wickets on his bowling debut; the famous 10 wicket win over Warwickshire after Lancashire had been thrashed in a stand of 470 in 290 minutes between Alvin Kallicharran and Geoff Humpage. But, for me, the most vivid memories of Southport always centre on Colin Croft.

The West Indian fast bowler had an inauspicious start with Lancashire, the chairman Cedric Rhoades having boasted to the Press of signing a 'left-arm paceman'. After Croft's first session in the nets, a series of brutish bouncers delivered, of course, with his right arm, the captain David Lloyd turned around and said calmly: "He could be useful when he starts bowling properly."

From then on, Croft had a chequered career with the club, sometimes unplayable, sometimes nowhere to be found. Looking for him after one game at Trent Bridge I located him stretched out and sparkers on the dressing-room bench, yet he had only been off the field for five minutes. On another occasion I asked a team-mate where Croft might be. "On another planet" was the quick as a flash response.

I remember him in two games at Southport. One against Essex when Lancashire were on the brink of a two day defeat. The extra half hour had been claimed, and 10 minutes through it, the ninth wicket went down. The evening gloom was thickening, a breeze kicked up mini sand storms, and the fans sensibly had sloped off long before, leaving just players and officials, who all wanted to get it over with and enjoy a day off. Well, not quite all. Out of the pavilion strode a giant of a man determined to save his side single-handed. Croft pushed forward to off-spinner David Acfield and continued to push forward with a big stride down the pitch to each delivery for the next 15 minutes.

Suddenly it hit home that we might have to return the following day for just one wicket. I imagined the mutterings in the flapping Press tent were similar to those in the dressing-rooms. Then, as Acfield lobbed down another ball, our batting hero stepped away from the crease, towards square leg, appearing to rub his face. Too late for the umpire to stop the delivery, the ball was on its way and hit the unprotected stumps.

Out! The bails were whipped off at the bowler's end and everyone shot off towards the pavilion. Except Croft. Obviously he hadn't fully realised what had happened, but as players and umpires streamed past him, he suddenly cottoned on, and the everlasting image I have is that of a tall West Indian chasing two umpires, waving his bat and protesting that he had been unfairly bowled while blinded by a speck of sand.

The other face of Croft was that of a ferocious fast bowler who, when he decided to give it 100 per cent, was truly scary. Against Somerset at Southport he bowled down the slope with unmanageable pace and bounce. Despite a lot of ducking and diving, several batsmen were hit and Lancashire's keeper John Lyon saw ball after ball fly overhead to land a foot short of the rope, leaving a series of red rimmed dents in the sightscreen. While Croft took only three wickets that day, he shook them up so badly that they were unable to cope with Peter Lee from the other end and they collapsed miserably. Unfortunately for them, they had someone even more frightening than Croft to deal with when they got back into the pavilion - their manager, Brian Close, who, of course, would simply have taken Croft's assault on the chest, arms and chin, and laughed about it. I felt sorry for Somerset. One of them had a broken finger, others were bruised, and then they were locked in the dressing-room for 40 minutes for a lashing from one of cricket's tough guys.

The Press facility at Southport was a large tent, well placed behind the bowler's arm, a couple of trestle tables, a dozen chairs and a phone connection. On a nice day, nothing better. As long as the ground staff had erected the tent and the phone was connected. Usually, one or the other task had not been completed, sometimes it was a double whammy. Communications were the biggest problem. Twelve reporters into one phone just didn't go. The priority list was agencies, evening newspapers, nationals. Others had little hope.

By tea on the first day, the phone is red-hot. Tension grows. "When can I get on? I've got to call the desk," asks the Daily Telegraph man.

"No chance, maybe in 20 minutes."

"What about me?" chimes The Times.

"After him, but you'd better make it quick."

A meek voice from the back of the tent... "Would it be possible...?"

"Who are you?"

"Radio City."

"Sod off."

Yes, the camaraderie was one of the things which made working at the out grounds so worthwhile. Another Southport memory is a Benson and Hedges Cup tie where a familiar figure, with a B and H badge on his lapel, approached the Press tent before stumps were pitched, smiled warmly and asked whether we would all like a drink at lunch-time. "Anything you want, it's on the sponsors." Unused to this sort of hospitality - it was in the very early Benson and Hedges Cup days - we all got our orders in quickly, a pint here, a double G and T there, but not the Press Association man. Oh no, he was made of sterner stuff. "I'll not sell my soul for a bottle of lager," he said. You had to admire his honesty and his principled stance. Me? I sold my soul for a pint of shandy. The familiar figure, incidentally, was Alan Wharton, who, like far too many other Lancashire players, had left Old Trafford prematurely, joining Leicestershire and then adorning league cricket. Back in 1965, with Lancashire still struggling to find their feet, Wharton was the Lancashire League's top amateur batsman, playing for Colne and making 770 runs. Ken Grieves, the county's former captain, was also in the Lancashire League and finished bottom with Accrington.

Lancashire's visit to Southport in 1965 came two days after Lord Derby had opened the Trafalgar Road ground's new pavilion, replacing the original which had stood since 1881, and Lancashire celebrated with an innings and 14 runs win over Derbyshire. Green's 53 led the way with the bat, Geoff Pullar helped him put on 89 for the opening wicket, and Harry Pilling (46) and John Sullivan (38) gave solid support. Green said: "Noddy and I had a good understanding. I enjoyed batting with him. It was never easy against their opening pair, Rhodes and Jackson, so to put eighty odd on the board gave us a head start."

There is a grainy black and white photograph of Green turning a Rhodes delivery to leg for a four early in that innings. In the background are the white perimeter fence, deck chairs, a white marquee for the VIPs, men in grey suits and ties, women in summer frocks and sun-glasses. Green looks powerfully built, perfectly balanced, shirtsleeves rolled up exposing his elbows, and there is the hint of a smile as the ball skips away over the turf.

"We knew if we made a decent total, then we had the attack to put Derbyshire in trouble," he added. "Their batting wasn't great. We had Statham, Higgs and Peter Lever and, later in the game, Tommy Greenhough would come into it."

Which is exactly how it went. The seamers demolished Derbyshire for 80, and it would have been even worse but for an entertaining last wicket stand of 25 between Jackson and Rhodes. Derbyshire put up a little more resistance in their second attempt, but Greenhough nibbled away at them to ensure Lancashire didn't have to bat again. As well as 10 points, it earned them a full day off. Very helpful, as they had a little trip of almost 300 miles for the next match at Hove.

Statham, for one, would not have relished that journey. "Some grounds I really enjoyed playing at, like Warwickshire and Leicestershire. With Sussex it seemed to work in reverse. I never bowled badly down there, but often got little for it."

The upside was that Lancashire had just notched their second win in six matches, he was bowling as well as ever, and younger players such as Pilling and Sullivan were making their way.

*****

'FOR no accountable reason,' said a report, fewer women were watching Lancashire in 1965 than ever before. About 1500, almost 500 less than the previous year, subscribed to Lancashire, paying a total of £3,400. Maybe the weather and Lancashire's decline of recent years were not entirely to blame. Perhaps the stay away ladies had been persuaded that their place was at home, where they belonged, busying themselves about the house, rather than sitting in deckchairs, sipping pretty drinks and watching cricket. There was still a lot of that sort of advice around. As in: 'How To Be The Perfect Wife', an extract from Helen B Andelin's 1965 book, 'Fascinating Womanhood'. Now listen up, girls......

The Plan

● Keep an eye on the clock. Finish tasks or interrupt them an hour before he is expected. Your anguished cry, "Are you home already?" is not exactly a warm welcome;

● Take 15 minutes to rest so you will be refreshed when he arrives. Turn off the worry and be glad to be alive and grateful for the man who is going to walk in. Touch up your make-up, put a ribbon in your hair and be fresh looking;

- At the time of his arrival eliminate noise of washer, drier, dishwasher or vacuum. Try to encourage the children to be quiet...let them be a little noisy beforehand to get it out of their system;
- Have him lean back into a comfortable chair or suggest he lie down in the bedroom. Have a cool or warm drink ready for him. Arrange his pillow and offer to massage his neck and shoulders and take off his shoes;
- Never complain if he does not take you out to dinner or to other places of entertainment. Instead, try to understand his world of strain and pressure, his need to be home and to relax. If he is cross or irritable, never fight back.

The Goal

To make your home a place of peace and order where your husband can renew himself in body and spirit...

There is more of it, but sorry, I can't go on. I'm laughing too much. Thing is, this book was a best-seller in the States. Even that enchanting singer, Dionne Warwick, got in on the 'You're the man, I'm the slave' act. In her 1965 song, 'Time To Get Ready for Love', she warbles:

> *'Hey, little girl, comb your hair, fix your make-up,*
> *Soon he will open the door,*
> *Don't think because there's a ring on your finger,*
> *You needn't try any more.'*

My favourite verse was:

> *'Day after day there are girls at the office,*
> *And men will always be men,*
> *Don't send him off with your hair still in curlers,*
> *You may not see him again.'*

I would sing that to the missus sometimes, while watching her prepare my picnic lunch for the match. Until I began finding strange things in my sandwiches.

The advertisements in the Lancashire Year Books of the mid sixties harden the chauvinistic image. Only two per cent of the advertising was directly aimed at women, unless you were a pie-eating, beer-guzzling gal, mad about cars and the abrasive and super refractory goods churned out at the Carborundum factory in Trafford Park - certainly not the domestic heroine envisaged by Andelin and Warwick.

One advert in the Year Book boasted that Seymour Mead and Burgons was the leading North-West grocer's with 250 branches. But your local Seymour Mead's was a traditional store, and shopping was about to be transformed. A new shop opened in our town that summer. Bright and busy looking with a wide, glass frontage, long counters, smartly uniformed assistants and display cabinets heaving with ready-made, cellophane wrapped sandwiches, to be taken away and consumed in the park, the office, or while walking down the street. Before the arrival of the specialist butty shop, lunch-time grub for us in the newspaper office was one of the following:

- Set three course in one of two old-fashioned cafes: Pros - goggling at young waitresses in 'Allo 'Allo type uniforms. Cons - price, 3s 6d, expensive on my wages;
- Coffee bar salad roll and Coke: Pros - price, 2s. Cons - smell of greasy burgers and icy stares from the proprietor Mrs B, who knew Mum and kept threatening to tell her what I was 'really like';
- Ploughman's and half pint in the Lion. Pros - chatting up licensee's daughter. Cons - icy stares from the licensee, who also happened to be the Town Mayor and kept threatening to tell the Editor what I was 'really like';
- Warm meat bap from butcher's in the square: Pros - cheap, 1s 3d. Cons - dodgy position of butcher's slaughterhouse (next to undertaker's Chapel of Rest).

The new place, bright and snazzy, won hands down. As for general shopping, you were spoiled for choice. Let's take a 1965 stroll down one of the two main streets in our town and see what's on offer from: 5 butchers, 3 general grocers (including Seymour Mead), 3 greengrocers, 2 sweet shops/ tobacconists, 2 sweets only shops, 1 fishmonger, 2 cake shops/cafes, 2 toy shops, 1 cycle/mower repairer, 1 watch repairer, 3 gents' outfitters, 1 ladies and gents outfitters, 1 ladies only outfitters, 1 glassware shop, 1 ironmonger's, 2 florists, 1 chemist's, 1 shoe shop, 1 art salon, 1 barber's, 1 antiques store, 3 pubs, 2 hotels with public bars, 1 coffee house, 2 newsagents, 2 electrical shops, 3 banks, 1 estate agent, post office, newspaper office, accountant's and solicitor's offices, and a number of cottages/houses.

Nowadays the street is dominated by cafes, bars, restaurants and designer clothes shops. But don't try to persuade me that hypermarkets and out of town retail parks have destroyed the good life. Oh no. Doing the weekly shopping was a pain. You had to carry it miles, got sopping wet when it rained, and it took hours because old Mrs Whatsername was gassing for ages to Jean or Hilda or whoever was behind the counter at Seymour Mead's. Surprisingly Tesco's, which opened in the square a few years later, fell by the wayside. FW

Woolworth's also came and went (many years before the wholesale collapse of Woolies in 2009). Yet the Co-op lives on. That pleases me. Even now I can remember Mum's 'divi' number, 114666, the tin with the broken biscuits sold at knock-down prices, and the big, red slicer which cut all manner of meat such as pork luncheon, 11d a quarter, and only needed the occasional wipe clean with a rag - the slicer, not the meat, although…The Co-op was friendly. Ours. The manager of the gentleman's clothing department who sold me my Stanley Matthews Continental soccer boots in 1957 was, half a century later, still cheerfully riding his bike around the town.

Most intriguing of the Lancashire Year Book adverts - ignoring the fishnets of the shapely showgirl who tried to entice you into Gaythorn Filling Station in City Road, Manchester, where extra Green Shield stamps were on offer - was the claim of the District Bank that its forerunner was the IGIBI, 'a private bank in ancient Babylon' operating in 575BC.

"What sort of service those far-off customers got we'll never know," read the blurb. "But one thing is certain. It could hardly have been more friendly and more personal than the service you get from us at District Bank."

Number one spot, though, goes to the marketing men from The Bakery, Stelling Street, Gorton, Manchester, who described their best-selling product as:

'Ellis's Pies. The Pie of Golden Opinions.'

*****

John Lee Hooker is clawing his way through 'I'm a Boogie Man'. It's after midnight, the best time to listen to someone like Hooker. The Wheel is full, but not crowded, and it can't be the night of PC Eleanor B's spying mission, because, while there is a pong from the gent's, and there are a few kids knocking about, there are no couples cuddling on the floor. I've not had a single alcoholic drink, nor any 'uppers' tonight, but I feel as though it can't get much better, that this is where I want to be, letting the vibe soak in. Someone says: "There's a blues festival at Richmond. Let's all go down there." And you can feel this ripple of excitement. And, later, staggering out, heavy-eyed, into the Manchester morning, heading towards Oxford Street for a fry-up, we are all thinking: "Blues *festival*" and wondering exactly what it is because we have never been to one before, in fact I've never heard of such an event. I'm not the only one. Many, even some in the music industry, haven't even heard of the blues, never mind putting it into a festival. "Blues, what the hell is that?" asked one London based record producer when the chance of recording some British groups was put to him. Fortunately there are a number of enthusiasts, like Roger Eagle, who push and push for the genre to win wider appeal in the UK, and, of course, there are musicians like Clapton, who just cannot be ignored. Anyway, we are up for it. A Blues Festival. Richmond - isn't that in London?

SEVEN

YOU are having a chat about the old days and the name of Harry Pilling crops up. And what happens? Everyone smiles. We all loved Harry, the little 'un with a cheeky grin and a big heart. Women wanted to mother him, fearing for his well-being as he faced up to some big horrid fast bowler, at least a foot taller. Men, including Neville Cardus, viewed him as a proper Lancashire lad. He dressed smartly, was convivial company in the bar, and rather enjoyed being 'mothered'.

Pilling, 4 feet 7 inches when he joined Lancashire's groundstaff at the age of 16, grew to almost 5 feet 3 inches, but remained one of the smallest players ever to appear in first-class cricket. That alone made him popular, a titch successfully making his way in a hard game. He also had a playful, sometimes disarming, sense of humour. Having a drink with a supporter after close of play one evening he said: "Would love to squeeze your wife's cheek before I go." The fan took it in good part. "Better ask her first," he replied, laughing.

Lancashire's coach when Pilling launched his Old Trafford career was the redoubtable Stan Worthington, who didn't take to any larking about. 'Like being back in the Army,' complained one player. A few weeks after signing, Pilling found himself on the carpet - because of the way he spoke. "Stan called me into the office and told me I was saying 'aye' and 'eee' too much. I'd never given it much thought - it was just the way I'd always talked, but he wanted me to have some elocution lessons. Thought that as a representative of Lancashire I should talk properly. He went on at me for half an hour and then asked me: 'Has all that sunk in?' I said: 'Aye, coach.'"

David Green provided another example of Worthington's sergeant-major style. "Before a Roses match, Alan Wharton was having a net with around 600 people watching. Yes, 600, that's what a Roses game meant then. Stan, who wore a bowler and stiffened collar wings, came into the nets and stopped the bowling to show Wharton how he should play a particular shot. Wharton, at that time, was one of the country's leading batsmen and didn't take kindly to it. He tucked his bat under his arm and walked out of the nets."

Worthington had first-class technical credentials as a coach. In 1936, in one of his nine Tests, he shared in a fourth wicket stand of 266 with Wally Hammond against India at the Oval, and his all-round abilities were a major factor behind Derbyshire's Championship triumph the same season - achievements for which Wisden acclaimed him as one of its Cricketers Of The Year. But it appears that man-management was not his strongest suit.

Despite, or partly because of, his broad accent, Pilling became one of the big favourites at Lancashire and the admiration I had for him had nothing to do with his height nor his cheeky comedy. The fact is Pilling was a class act where it counted - out in the middle. He played from 1962 to 1980 in 323 first-class games for the county, scoring almost 15,000 runs, and surprised many people by adapting successfully to the one-day game, where he built a prolific partnership with Clive Lloyd and featured prominently in the Gillette Cup and John Player League triumphs 1969-74. He was the man of the match at Lord's in 1970 and was the first to score 1000 Sunday League runs - that, in an era of Lloyd, Barry Richards, Rohan Kanhai and Garry Sobers.

Like another charismatic Lancashire figure, Jack Simmons, Pilling was never picked for England, although he fielded once for them. When 17, still playing league cricket and then only a shade over five feet high, he happened to be at Old Trafford during a Test against South Africa and was called on as a sub for Brian Statham for the last 30 minutes.

"Freddie Trueman escorted me onto the field and after touching the ball I was all right and not nervous," he said. "Afterwards Colin Cowdrey said I had fielded very well. But I was due to play for Oldham that night and, all the time, I was wondering whether I would still have time to get home for m' tea."

Pilling never made it to Test level, but he was a clever, efficient player, this diminutive batsman, and earned his accolades the hard way, not through some sympathy vote. Sheer determination made Pilling the good little 'un that he was. There was no cricketing pedigree in the family. He just knew he had what it took, was taken on at the Staley club where a mate of his dad played, and spent his spare time practising by himself with a MCC coaching manual at his side. And he used the jibes that he heard in club cricket like - 'Is this your mascot coming out to bat?' - to push himself further.

"Harry Pilling believed in Harry Pilling - that's all there is to my story, certainly in the early years," he said.

In 1965 he came of age as a county batsman, passing 1000 runs for the first time and winning his cap and, although he had already made a century, perhaps it was an innings at Hove in late July which really embedded him as a Lancashire star of the future. Lancashire had just beaten Derbyshire inside two days at Southport, giving them extra time to make their longest journey of the summer, and they arrived at Hove in confident mood with Statham, Higgs and Lever aiming to dismantle a fragile Sussex batting line-up, missing the injured Ted Dexter and England's Jim Parks. Alan Oakman, in his benefit year, was struggling for top form and John Langridge - the batsman Statham usually had most problems dismissing - was also a little off colour.

Sussex opener Ken Suttle enjoyed being on the same field as Pilling. "He was 5 feet 4 inches and I was the only player he could look down on," he explained. Suttle, the ex Chelsea footballer who had just played in his 300th consecutive game for Sussex, was also one of their few batsmen scoring runs that season, and he made 49 on the first day, sharing in a partnership of 92 with the Nawab of Pataudi, Mansoor Ali Khan.

Hove was not Statham's most profitable hunting ground. Although he came good in the second innings with 5-38, he made little impression in the first, and, as a result, Sussex made a useful 286-9 dec. Mike Buss and the promising John Snow combined to bowl Lancashire out for 171, and on the last day the Red Rose men faced a challenging target of 247. It looked impossible with half the side out for 63, but Pilling mounted a stirring fight back with Peter Lever, and at 161-6, they had a chance until Buss and Snow ripped through them again, leaving Pilling stranded on 88 not out, and Lancashire 39 short of victory.

Green, as ever, had batted with enterprise for 50 and 34. "Pilling showed that day he could take 'em on. Hove had some pace and bounce, especially after a spot of rain. Chesterfield, too. Slow turners at Swansea and Northampton. We enjoyed playing on a variety of pitches. It helped with technique, and made life different.

"During one rain break at Hove, there was a big cards game going on, a few of our lads, one or two of theirs. Ken Higgs cleaned up. The Nawab was the biggest loser. He owned large tracts of land in India but ran out of cash during that session. So when Higgs bet 'all in', the Nawab said: 'OK - I bet Bhopal.' Bhopal! One of the biggest cities in India. He lost. After that we called Higgs, who came from Staffordshire, the Nawab of Kidsgrove.

"Pilling, I think, finished with an average of over 30 (31.06) that year, which, in a bad season for the batsmen, was good going. It was obvious then he was going to make it."

Pilling, however, was, in hindsight, to take a surprisingly different view. "In some ways 1965 was my worst season," he said. "It made me a bit complacent. I thought I had made it, didn't keep working at it and I got caught out. I was only 22 and felt I had made it to the top, but even before that season ended, I came to realise I was only just starting off in the game. As a capped player, everyone expected regular performances from me and it meant extra pressure."

In 1966 he had a shocker, but he battled his way through that crisis to score over 1600 in 1967 and he rarely looked back after that. He could play shots, Harry, but he admitted: "By nature I was a nicker and a nudger. I think I hit eight sixes in the whole of my time with Lancashire." Maybe, but he savagely cut anything short, and his whipped on drive was a classic. Fast bowlers held no fear for him. Bouncers usually sailed high over his head, Bob Willis once promising him: "I'll find your bouncer length one day."

"He never did," smiled Pilling.

Kent's Alan Brown was outraged once when umpire Charlie Elliott turned down a loud lbw appeal against Pilling. "Too high," said Elliott, after Brown had rapped him on the pad. "Too high?" exploded Brown. "It would be going for the stumps if it hit him on the head!"

Pilling's ability to keep the scoreboard ticking over proved invaluable in one-day cricket where, at the start of many stands with Clive Lloyd, he would score the quicker. "I thought the one day game might mean the end of my career," he said. "I was quite worried initially that it wouldn't suit me, but I decided not to try any crash, bang, wallop stuff, just kept on nudging and rotating the strike. In Championship cricket I wasn't always a number three. I started out at six, but the batting was a bit fragile at times and I went in at 20 or so for 4 on a fairly regular basis. My job was to stabilise things, then I moved up."

Pilling could also hold his own in the sharp riposte stakes. During a difficult innings at Hove once, someone muttered mischievously: "The ball keeps hitting the edge, doesn't it Harry?"

"So what?" he said. "You pay for all t' bat, don't you?" But he had to laugh, when, after getting entrenched on a tricky Old Trafford pitch, a fan held up a copy of the Manchester Evening News and shouted: "Pilling, you were eight not out in the first edition and you're still eight not out."

Denied by the England selectors after his best ever season in 1976 - some critics thought his size counted against him - Pilling gave Lancashire loyal service. He loved the life, and although his benefit yielded only £12,000, he never complained. "Nobody should criticise county cricket in my presence," he said.

*****

PROTESTS over slow scoring, dilatory over rates, the preponderance of seam bowling, throwing, walking, umpiring, ground facilities, apartheid - the cricketing pages were full of protest. I'm surprised there wasn't a song about it all. After all, protest songs were all the rage in 1965, indeed throughout most of the 1960s. Protests against war in general, specifically Vietnam; protests over civil rights; protests about individual freedom, hundreds of protests, all put to music. Some of these songs became iconic of the era. 'Blowin' In The Wind', 'Where Have All The Flowers Gone' and my favourite 'Eve of Destruction'. Not just because it was a great song, but because of the way it was made, recorded in one take by Barry McGuire, reading the words of composer PF Sloan which had been scribbled on a scrap of paper. McGuire couldn't make out one of the words, so he filled in the gap with a grunt, a sort of Aah which you can hear on the record. Meant to be a 'rough mix' to be polished up and released later, it was leaked to a radio DJ in mid July and put on air within 24 hours of recording. The record producer went berserk, but shut up quickly when it became an instant hit, and carried as a banner by the anti-war movement. It also produced a counter protest from the conservative hard-hats who believed America was doing the right thing in Vietnam, and a right-wing rock group named The Spokesmen quickly brought out their version entitled: 'Dawn Of Correction'.

McGuire had longish hair and a bit of a beard, but hardly came across as a rebel of any sort. He had sung with The New Christy Minstrels - remember their daft song 'One Wheel On My Wagon'? Exactly. Someone said he had all the personality of a rock. But 'Eve Of Destruction' was a heavy puncher.

It has been argued that protest songs influenced events in Vietnam. Not the decisions of the generals and the politicians, but in the way the foot soldiers conducted their war. This was a battleground where music was readily available, either through the army's own radio station - subject of that brilliant movie 'Good Morning Vietnam' - or on cassette. Infantry, preparing for battle, tuned in, turned up the volume and lost themselves for an hour or so before going out to kill or be killed. They listened to the latest pop hits, a bit of jazz, some of the old crooners and, maybe now and again, one of the protest songs that got through the censorship. They certainly heard 'Eve Of Destruction', as they painted the title on the side of one of their gun trucks.

Might it have affected them, listening to McGuire chiselling out: 'You're old enough to kill but not for voting.' Did it make some of them a little less gung-ho on their jungle missions against the Viet Cong? Perhaps. But I'm sure there was ample compensation in those whose appetite for the war was re-energised by the equal number of patriotic melodies issuing forth from America's Country and Western heartlands, where they believed that fighting the Cong and keeping the Reds at bay was a heroic and entirely necessary action to take.

One intriguing question is why the protest song died. It's not as if war went away, tail between its legs. People have been dying a plenty in this terribly bloodied start to the 21st century, and, in the same period, popular song-writing has mushroomed. But no protest songs. Certainly none which have burrowed into the public conscience.

Like others of the genre, 'Eve Of Destruction' was scrutinised by the censors, escaping a total BBC ban, but being placed on their 'restricted list' - that is, not suitable for a general entertainment programme - by the Beeb's Dance and Music Policy Committee. Tough guys, these, hard to get past. Even George Formby had to bow to them. Asked for clarification of their attitude towards some of Formby's songs, the committee noted in an internal memo: "We have no record that 'With My Little Stick of Blackpool Rock' is banned. We do, however, know, and so does Formby, that certain lines in the lyric must not be broadcast."

It's possible to look back now and take a more objective view of some of the lyrics which anti-war and civil rights campaigners took so much to heart in the mid sixties. Joan Baez, one of the leading lights of the protest movement, claimed recently that 'Blowin' In the Wind' and 'With God On Our Side' really said very little at all. "The answer is blowing in the wind," she said. "But what was the answer?" Okay, we're all a lot older now, with the experience to cut through the crap, but, at the time, we didn't necessarily want the answer. Laying down the question was enough. Baez must have believed that, too. Whenever Dylan invited her on stage for a 'With God On Our Side' duet, she was there like a flash, and singing with all her heart.

Censorship never killed the protest song, indeed, in some cases, it helped to popularise it. So why has it vanished? Might it be that we see so much of war that we have become inured to it? Watch the death and destruction on the box while having lunch. The broken bodies, the mothers wailing - pass me the ketchup - the rolling tanks, the falling rockets, and then a quick half-hour on the laptop before getting back to work, because that latest war game is real cool, and, having gunned down and bombed your way through to level 20, you are catching up quickly with Pete in Accounts. And there's a new version out soon, which gives even more detailed close-ups of exploding bodies, brains, guts, the lot, dead realistic. And, despite the recession, life in the West is still so comfortable. Protest song? What about?

Mind you, if I sat down now to pen a protest, it would probably be to howl against some of the garbage that was recorded as pop music in the mid 1960s. Contrast 'Eve of Destruction', for instance, with this 1965 classic, 'Choc Ice'.

Chocolate ice - very nice
Hey, hey, hey, hey
Peaches and cream - know what I mean?
Hey, hey, hey, hey
Strawberry pie - oh me, oh my
Hey, hey, hey, hey
Peppermint twist - goes like this
Hey, hey, hey, hey.

Repeated twice, those are the complete lyrics. Mercifully it was a very short song. Many were in those days, partly because radio stations would not play anything longer than three minutes. When they relaxed this rule, Dylan's 'Like A Rolling Stone', just over six minutes long, shot into the charts and would have made No 1 in July 1965 but for The Beatles' 'Help'.

*****

LIFE at the newspaper was, well, let's just say pleasant as we drifted into the height of summer, and the 'silly season'. We didn't have a great number of pages to fill, and, lacking competition, didn't feel under any pressure. Advertising revenue was good, circulation steady, and The Editor disappeared for long periods, gunning his brand new sports car around the country lanes, leaving us free to saunter down the street for a coffee, usually the caff with the jukebox, sometimes on a really lazy morning, the old fashioned Coffee House where they ground the beans and brewed it freshly and Mrs O, in her smart black and white waitress outfit, would smile and say: "Mum all right, Colin?" as she plonked the cup and saucer in front of me.

Timetable of a summer's Thursday for a 17 year old rookie reporter in 1965:

9am: open up office;

9.15: enjoy first Maxwell House brew with morning paper, starting with cricket scores;

9.30: open pay packet - six £1 notes and a handful of shrapnel;

10.00: call at police station and fire brigade for latest news; ring hospital for injury details of latest M6 crash (there was carnage on the de-regulated motorways);

11.15: swagger down the street for elevenses , eyeing the well endowed female assistant at Johnson's greengrocers;

12.00: check latest edition of our paper, cut out and file relevant articles;

2.00: focus hard on writing six pars re Mrs Williams, the winner of the WI's monthly competition for home-made scones (fruit):

3.00: read a chapter of 'On The Road';

3.30: ring local churches, hoping not to catch the fiery Father Kelly, who has threatened to 'beat me with a stick' over a story about worshippers' cars causing an obstruction in the street;

4.00: darts practice in the file room;

4.30: write 500 words of latest novel 'A Rural Lust For Life';

5.30: pluck up courage to chat up greengrocer's assistant, fail miserably and end up taking home a pound of bananas.

Compare that with a working Thursday 40 years later as a 57 year old cricket writer during the Ashes summer of 2005:

6.30am: Wake up, try to remember location - i.e. which hotel, which city. Clues - crash of waste bins being emptied outside, smell of rotting rubbish, East European voices. Got it.'Discomfort Inn', London. Therefore, Lord's Test

7.00: Check call to Sports Desk. "Ring back later."

7.30: Check call to Sports Desk. "We're busy. Sod off."

8-9.00: Scan cricket reports, get embroiled in stilted conversation with homesick Russian room cleaner, arrive late for buffet breakfast to find an inch thick crust on the scrambled egg;

9.30: Arrive Lord's after two miles, 20 minutes bus journey down Finchley Road featuring, would you believe it, a female Aussie conductor with a mouth capable of swallowing The Great Barrier Reef;

9.45: Check call with Sports Desk: "Where the hell have you been?"

10.30 - 7.30 pm: Watch every ball (helped copiously by TV replays, and colleagues sympathetic with my increasing number of comfort breaks and failing eyesight) and grind out a total of 3000 words for evening and morning newspapers;

8.00: Last check with Sports Desk: "Yes, we've got your copy - unfortunately. Ron's subbing it now, trying to make sense of it. Keep your mobile on. Now sod off, we're busy."

8.30: Back at hotel;

9.00: Flask Inn, Hampstead. First pint of Young's Bitter and a feeling that you can't take much more of it. The life, not the beer.

One job in the early days that I wasn't so keen on was the daily police call. True, it produced the juiciest stories, but it could be personally embarrassing.

"Anything doing today, Sarge?" And, with a big sigh, he opens the ancient, hard-backed incident book, slides a thick finger towards the interesting bits and reels them off, making sure you realise how bored he is.

"Window smashed in an empty house."

"That'd be Dave," I'd think.

"Hmm. 11.45 pm, officer called to a domestic in Shaw Street. No arrests."

"That'd be Geoff and his missus," I'd think.

"Oh, and there's a report of youths causing a bit of a disturbance outside the Keys. Can't take their ale, these kids."

"That'd be us," I'd think.

Truth is, it wasn't easy balancing on the rim of respectability. Basically, I was still a kid from the old council estate and had inherited Dad's (and Dylan Thomas') liking for beer - 'its live, white lather, its brass-bright depths, the sudden world through the wet brown walls of the glass, the tilted rush to the lips, and the slow swallowing down to the lapping belly, the salt on the tongue, the foam at the corners.' I love Thomas' description. But I craved acceptance in 'higher' circles, to be seen drinking with the town's high and mighty in the bar of the Angel, vainly promising them, like Thomas, to 'put you all in a story by and by.'

*****

LOOKING through the cricket scoreboard each morning was a good way to kick off the day, much more enjoyable then than now. With a full board every day you knew exactly where you were. Sixteen of the 17 counties were in action, all in the same competition, with the games starting on the same day, Wednesday or Saturday. All the names were familiar, too. Far more complicated nowadays. Which competition? Second or third day? Who's that playing for Northants - never heard of him. Who's that playing for Lancashire?!

My board reading routine was Lancashire first, naturally; then Yorkshire; then Surrey; followed by the rest in no particular order. Usually there was a lot of detail to take in, because even on the first day there would be at least one innings completed. Lancashire's progress needed careful scrutiny and analysis, while Yorkshire and Surrey demanded at least a wicket by wicket appraisal. The remainder got a good once-over, with the exploits of favourite individuals commanding particular attention. Players like Tom Graveney, Arthur Milton, Alan Oakman, Colin Cowdrey, John Murray, Derek Shackleton and Tom Cartwright. Then there were those who were just names to me, but which I looked for simply because I liked the sound of them - Nicholls, Livingstone, Millman, Reynolds, Julian.

And Inman, Clive. Leicestershire's Ceylonese batsman who created a world record that summer by hitting 51 in eight minutes against Notts at Trent Bridge. It was a farce, a single off the last ball of one over, and then 50 in two overs of declaration filth from Norman Hill. Inman took 18 off one, and 32 off the second - 4, 6, 6, 6, 6, 4 - all slow full tosses, pulled to or over the midwicket rope. The previous quickest half century belonged to Jim Smith of Middlesex, who needed 11 minutes against Gloucestershire at Bristol in 1938.

Steve O'Shaughnessy took advantage of a similar situation at Old Trafford in 1983 to equal the world record for the fastest century, 35 minutes, set by the illustrious Percy Fender 63 years earlier. O'Shaughnessy, a young Lancashire whippersnapper, was suitably embarrassed to see his name in the record books alongside that of one of England's most famous batsmen after slamming a succession of long hops and invitingly slow full tosses from Leicestershire's David Gower and James Whitaker to a leg-side boundary, in front of the pavilion, only 55 yards from the wicket. Leicestershire were hoping for a declaration in a rain ravaged game, and O'Shaughnessy and the left-handed Graeme Fowler slammed 201 in 43 minutes of crazy cricket.

O'Shaughnessy would have been far more embarrassed had he beaten Fender's record. And so would the game of cricket. Actually, he did beat it......

Interest grew in the Press Box as ball after ball crossed the rope, some zooming over it, others bouncing over it, with one or two mis-hits trickling over it, carefully shepherded by fielders ready to poke it further should it threaten to roll to a halt too early. Utter nonsense, yes, but here, after two days of nothing to write about, was the story of the season. Wisdens were out, records checked, and when O'Shaughnessy reached his century, my colleague Stan grabbed the internal phone to get the 'hits' (fours and sixes) and the official time from the scorer.

Stan, a brilliant freelance journalist, knew this could be a big, money-making story for us. He was excited. So excited that, when the scorer Amos Lowe answered the phone, Stan called him Moses. When this momentary confusion was cleared up, Amos gave the duration of O'Shaughnessy's innings as 34 minutes, and Stan, even more excited, said: "Moses, do you realise that's a world record?"

Moses - sorry, Amos - obviously didn't. He was a true cricket lover, the Lancashire scorer, a bluff, heavily built man, an accountant by profession, with whitening hair and cherry red cheeks, which grew deep crimson when upset or angry. And was he angry at this moment. This sort of cricket was sacrilege, and to think that it had created history...We could hear him spluttering into the phone, ...world record, no, that's not cricket. Not having that. He needed more time to check. Would ring back. We waited anxiously. Then..."Official time, 36 minutes, not a world record."

But we were not prepared to accept that. We understood Amos' attitude, but this was a story and we couldn't have cared less whether it damaged the image of the game or not. By my reckoning, O'Shaughnessy's duration was as low as 32 minutes. Eventually, after some argy-bargy, a compromise was reached, very reluctantly on Amos' part - OK, let's settle for 35, equalling the record. He would not go any further. A few days later O'Shaughnessy, at the expense of the Manchester Evening News, went down with Brian Bearshaw to spend a day with the 91 year old Fender at his home in Horsham.

Fender, who apologised for not being able to get about, invited them to have a cup of tea - 'but you will have to make it yourselves.' He recalled his record century in 1920 when Surrey were chasing the Championship, saying: "When I went out to bat, I was about halfway to the wicket when I looked at the clock. It was seven minutes past four. There were 23 minutes to go before tea and, in that time, I hit 91 runs. But Podgy Peach had the strike after tea so I slowed down a bit. But, you know, I always thought it was 34 minutes."

O'Shaughnessy kept quiet about the controversy over the timing of his innings. He asked Fender whether he still had the bat he used that day against Northants. "No, that was destroyed in Hitler's war. A lot of stuff went, a great shame." O'Shaughnessy had taken his bat with him and Fender picked it up, carefully ran his hands up and down it, and said: "It hasn't got much of a backside, has it? Mine was much lighter and the meat was higher up." He hung onto it, and as O'Shaughnessy prepared to leave, Fender said: "Thank you. It is very good of you to come all this way to give me the bat." The Lancashire youngster went pale until he realised that the grand old man was having him on. "I think I had him worried then, didn't I," said Fender, with a wink.

"He was a true gentleman," said O'Shaughnessy, whose joint 'record' was later accompanied by the rather sneering note of 'in contrived circumstances' and then dropped altogether.

Perusing the scoreboards daily meant that I was extremely familiar with the name of DM Green. I knew what he looked like from photographs, and I must have seen him play - but when? I cannot for the life of me recall it. Strange. It wasn't as though he was an easily forgettable figure.

His Lancashire career began in 1959, at the age of 19 while still at Oxford University and while I was 11 and preparing for my first year at Altrincham Grammar School, just up the road from his family home. I remember that sun-kissed summer vividly. We watched Nottingham Forest beat Luton in the Cup Final, replayed the match on the field at the back of the local paper mill, and then put the soccer kit into store to concentrate on cricket. Twenty over matches in the late afternoon sun at the beautifully kept boys club ground, longer games there on Saturday mornings, knock-abouts in the street or on the mill field with home-made bats and stumps, and as many trips to Old Trafford as possible, depending on the cash made from the Sunday morning paper round.

1959 was the best summer of my childhood. I watched the Tests on TV, carefully filling in a ball by ball scorebook (which I never did as a reporter) and, on the back garden, where in the winter I had pretended to be Tom Finney or Stan Matthews, I was Statham with a ragged tennis ball, or Peter May with a bat hewn out of an old plank. Dad was handy with a saw, hammer and chisel.

At Old Trafford, maybe in the Roses match that year, I must have seen Green, going in at number six. Powerfully built, fair-haired, and nervous.

"I hated hanging around for my turn," he added. "I was playing for Oxford University once and got so wound up I ended up hiding in the showers, crying. Our captain AC Smith found me. Opening was no problem, it was good to get out there and get on with it, but when I started with Lancashire I was at six and getting more and more worried the longer I spent in the dressing room."

It is possible that I only had eyes for Statham, Washbrook and Pullar, who had a great season in 1959, and that a young middle-order batsman held little attraction. Green had four years with Oxford and began to play regularly for the county in 1962, so I must assume that I watched him several times, although by then our visits to Old Trafford were decreasing. Girls were entering the equation. We had launched a rock group (me on drums, or rather, biscuit tins - until they found someone with a proper set and kicked me out). And Lancashire were struggling in what turned out to be their worst campaign on record.

In 1964 Green, still at six, bagged four ducks in five innings, a pair against Glamorgan, 0 and 26 against Worcestershire, and 0 and 1 against Yorkshire. Cyril Washbrook asked him: "Are you always like this?"

"After the fourth duck they strapped my pads on and locked me in the toilets. When they let me out, it was 38-4, but I did a lot better after that."

Green had fallen under cricket's spell 'rapidly and completely' as a six year old, and at the age of nine made his first trip to Old Trafford, just a few miles from his home in Timperley.

"My father, a high-class rugby player for Sale and Cheshire, had little interest in cricket at that time but he made me a junior Member of Lancashire. Since I was under-sized and bronchial he was probably pleased that I was interested in sport at all. For the next four or five years I spent my summer holidays on the old Hornby Stand, below the present Press Box, watching from behind the bowler's arm, with my cheese and tomato sandwiches and my screw top bottle of pop, happy to watch the second team if the first was away. In good weather I couldn't have been happier, in bad I would hang around all day on the off chance of seeing a few overs.

"Cricketers were my heroes. I was hugely impressed by their creamy flannels, sparkling white pads and their beautiful bats, which were characterised in those days by a black triangle on the back of the blade below the meat. This was caused by gardening, using that part of the bat to repair the scars the ball had left on the soft surface. It wasn't until I started going to Old Trafford that I realised the reason for the dark triangle.

"Cricketers of that era were rarely demonstrative. They went about their business in a cool, purposeful style and this control of emotion, combined with their expertise, made them appear - to me at least - remote, god-like figures, and it was clearly impossible that such beings would belch or go through other normal bodily functions. Not many years later, when I found myself practising alongside these very same men in the Old Trafford nets, I was startled to find them flesh and blood, earthy, humorous and irreverent."

In Green's first summer as a Lancashire fan, he saw a strong batting line-up led by Washbrook, let down by lack of bowling resources. "I remember watching them play Derbyshire and rejoicing as they made over 400 with Washy making a very rapid 36, most from hooks off Les Jackson, who had the last laugh by having him caught at long leg by a man in a weird cap. This was Dick Sale, an Oxford Blue in 1939 and 1946, wearing his Harlequin cap of maroon, red and buff segments. I was cock a hoop as Lancashire took some early wickets, but then Sale came in, still wearing that stupid hat, and creamed it around in that casual style that so many left-handers have, making 146."

Green continued to visit Old Trafford as much as possible, dropping in on the way home from school to watch the last couple of hours, undeterred by threatening weather. "You knew if play was at all possible, the players would be out there. Nobody seemed to think it necessary to wait until conditions underfoot were perfect. Almost as soon as the rain stopped, the groundsman would be out chucking sawdust onto the muddiest patches. He'd leave a huge cone of sawdust at each end. With the run-ups left uncovered - in fact only the crease and the bowlers' landing area up to a couple of yards behind the wickets were protected - it wasn't easy for anyone. It was often too slippery for the fast bowlers so the slow men had to bowl with a wet ball. But they just got on with it."

Green learned from watching the likes of Washbrook, his opening partner Winston Place, Jack Ikin, Geoff Edrich, Ken Grieves and Alan Wharton. Washbrook, short but powerful with thick forearms, a deep chest, and a classic sideways on stance. "I can remember his cuts bouncing 20 or 30 yards off the stone coping in front of the pavilion."

Place, tall and graceful; Ikin, an elegant left-hander, and resolute against fast bowling; Edrich, the ex POW who was congratulated after withstanding a battering from Frank Tyson, and said: "What's the fuss about? The ball's not a bullet. It's only on you for a second," Grieves, a powerful back foot player with a two eyed stance, Wharton, who went close to a Test cap…Green enjoyed them all.

He witnessed Statham's entrance to first-class cricket. "He made a deep impression on me. I loved it when he bowled his yorker - it always seemed to knock at least two stumps out of the ground."

Of the spinners, Bob Berry, Malcolm Hilton and Roy Tattersall, 'Tatt' was his favourite. "Tall and very lean, he ran in briskly off a longish approach, his left shoulder pointing at the batsman and his bowling arm hidden behind his body, the ball held near the back pocket to conceal his grip. Not a big spinner, he made the ball pop on damaged wickets and on flat pitches his flight and subtle change of pace got him plenty of wickets. His artistry was plain to see, even for a kid.

"Although I was unaware of it at the time, those early years at Old Trafford were imbuing in me a fascination with the game which has endured a lifetime. My recollections of the players I saw and the pleasure they gave me are as clear now as if yesterday. I don't think he was talking about cricket, but the Irish poet Tom Moore put it much better than I can:

> *'Oft in the stilly night*
> *Ere slumber's chain has bound me*
> *Fond memory brings the light*
> *Of other days around me.'*

At the newspaper, we were into Irish poetry, too. Not as elegant as Moore's. H, one of my colleagues, was an unusual and courageous reporter, who overcame the handicap of a heavy stammer to carve out an impressive career. An inspired limerick writer, he could whip one up in an instant although reciting it took a while longer. He found that inserting the odd swear word or profanity helped to lever open his reluctant vocal chords.

"There was an old lay lay lay, fucking lady, f f from Ch Ch Ch Christ! Chester...

Who left her n n n knickers to f f f fucking fester"...

And so forth. In December 1965 Roger Daltrey only pretended to stammer - "Why don't they all f f fade away," he sang when The Who recorded 'My Generation'. And, as it stormed to number two in the charts, we sang with him: "Why don't they all f f fuck off?" - only not too loudly because we didn't want to be barred from the pub, did we?

Alcohol was another useful tool for H. After a couple of pints, he was almost loquacious. The flip side was that, after too heavy a night, he could hardly force a syllable out. As a hangover also reduced me to a few grunts, it didn't make us the best company on the Saturday morning shift, as our new reporter Yesdi discovered.

Yesdi was a Ugandan with an Indian heritage and probably the first non-white journalist in the North-West. He spoke the Queen's English (only trouble was that it was Victoria's, not Elizabeth's) in a lovely modulated accent, smiling in bemusement at our slang, getting ragged by our photographer Les - "Yesdi, it's raining elephants and giraffes out there"- and generally permeating the office with sunshine. Striped jacket, striped shirt, striped tie, striped trousers, and a permanent wide smile below his stripe of a moustache.

So here we all are, a Saturday morning after a triple X category Friday night. H, hardly able to talk, sits at the desk, head down using his arms and typewriter as a pillow. I'm perched on the storage heater feeling strangely shivery, head pushed back against the wall, wondering if I can make it in time to the toilet. Yesdi, who doesn't drink and so is full of the goodness of life, refuses to take that stupid grin off his mug and to keep qw qw qw fucking quiet.

"Y y y you can m m m m."

"Yes?" says Yesdi, smiling sweetly and all much too innocent.

"Make some k k k k...."

"Yes?" even sweeter than before.

"M m make some k k k k...."

"Would you like some coffee?"

"...fucking coffee." And, turning belligerently to me: "He n n n knew w w w what I fucking well m m m meant."

While Yesdi is out in the kitchen at the back of the building brewing up, H and I are rattled by an extraordinary noise. After a few seconds we realise it is the phone ringing. H pushes it away from him, gestures towards me. I close my eyes and stay rooted. It is an old black, bakelite phone, with an insistent ring tone. Eventually H throws out a hand, picks it up and clamps it to his head without moving anything but his right arm from the elbow down.

"Er, er, er."

"Hello, is that the Guardian?"

I can hear a woman's voice. Cultured. The sort with ice-cubes as well as a plum in the mouth.

"Hello, hello."

"Er, er, oh shit, er."

"Pardon, what was that?"

"Er, erm, erm, er..Jesus Christ."

H is waving at me frantically by now but I can't help. Can't even move.

"Hello, what, for Heaven's sake, is going on?"

One last valiant effort. "K k k k bloody hell, can we h h h h."

But he gets totally stuck on the h. At that moment Yesdi appears with a tray and mugs of coffee to have the phone thrust at him. The woman sounds very agitated. I hear something about 'imbeciles'.

Yesdi, co-operative as always, takes the phone and gently enquires in his warm Afro-Asian way: "Guardian office down here, what is that we may be doing for you?"

The outraged letter of complaint lands on the Editor's desk on the following Tuesday morning. We blame Yesdi. He smiles.

H overcame the speech demons. What I also admired about him was the way he worked his contacts, frequenting the haunts of councillors, traders and farmers, picking up gossip and some decent stories. His biggest scoop however came right on his doorstep, and it was one which shook the nation.

J was a nice 10 year old girl who lived 100 yards or so from him. One Sunday morning she went for a ride down a nearby lane on her 'Pink Witch' bike. Her family never saw her again. The bike was found abandoned on the verge. Dozens of volunteers, armed with thick, long sticks helped police search the surrounding, crop-filled fields. We edged our way forward in long lines, pushing the barley aside with the sticks, occasionally stumbling against the rutted soil. Slowly, carefully at first, and then with growing, desperate haste as the sweat glistened down into our eyes. I remember my toe making contact with something soft, gasping with surprise, looking down and seeing something that could be…no, just a bundle of farm sacking. Days of searching. Interviews with police, relatives and friends. Lots of stories. Appeals for information. Garbled tales from would-be witnesses. A car, maybe with a girl crying in the back seat. But nothing substantiated. Nothing solid for the family to hang onto. They had told her not to be late back for lunch. The days became weeks. She had vanished.

Children disappeared. Several had gone missing in the Manchester area and, in October 1965, the great horror of the Moors Murders began to unravel with the arrests of Brady and Hindley. But this was a quiet country lane, just outside a little rural town where nothing happened. What could have happened to her? How could anything have happened to her? Somehow there was a collective tinge of shame, as well as a great sense of loss.

Massive publicity is important in cases like this. The quicker the better, while people's memories are fresh. But there were no instant communications. No internet, mobile phones, local radio, or 24 hours TV news. Newspapers were the main source and, while her picture was circulated throughout the local, regional and national Press, they would not print it day after day, week after week, month after month. The story never completely disappeared, but it did fade, and, with no clues, the police investigation wound down. J's family tried to get back to normal. Her father was seen playing snooker in a local club. How could he? whispered some. The McCanns could answer that. You have other children and they deserve as near to a normal life as you can possibly provide. But you also have a responsibility to yourself. Somehow you've just got to carry on.

J's remains were found several years later, on an embankment near the North Wales coast. H was the first reporter to get to the scene. Her mother identified the buttons from her cardigan. Can you imagine the horror of that - being asked to identify your long lost little girl from a set of buttons? At least the family got closure of a sort. And, for what it's worth the police got him. Just a man, a stranger to the area, happens to be passing through, happens to spot a nice looking kid, follows her bike down the lane, stops, pushes her off, pulls her into the car, drives away. On a lazy Sunday in our town.

That story had readers in tears. However, the content of our paper rarely varied from the humdrum. Hard news for the main inside page came from the Urban District and Rural District Councils, and the courts, with bits and pieces from the usual suspects, churches, Round Table, Rotary Club, Chamber of Trade etc, while gossipy snippets from various sources went into the By The Way column. Obituaries were important. Occasionally, for a big funeral, the undertaker asked for two reporters to help with the taking of mourners' names and inscriptions on the floral tributes. He gave us a quid each, so we always looked forward to the death of one of our civic dignitaries. He might have a half pint of bitter with us, a tall, sharp-featured man, sipping his beer carefully like a long beaked bird, eyes darting here and there as he brought the glass to his lips, chatting matter of factly about the problems of laying out. "Had a terrible job with that one - had to break all sorts to fit him in." You had to be careful with obits, make sure that every name was in and correctly spelled, every wreath and its donor included. No-one liked to be omitted from a funeral.

On a Tuesday afternoon I'd nip along to the Clerk of the Courts office to peruse the Magistrates Court charge sheets for the following day's hearing. The Clerk's name was Mr Clarke, tall, dark and Bryclreemed. On a Friday night he would down four pints of mild, usually standing alone at the bar. In his dark, wooden panelled office he'd push the court sheets over to me and hardly say a word.

"Thanks Mr Clarke."

"All right young man …how's your mum?" He lived 50 yards from us but the families didn't mix.

Presiding over the magistrates' court, held in a historic building with stone pillars and polished oak fittings, was one of the local squires, Mr W, who puffed and ranted like Captain Mainwaring in Dads' Army and who constantly had to be kept in check by his sergeant, in this case the Clerk. A typical exchange went along these lines:

"This defendant is an out and out ruffian - six months."

Up pops the Clerk, from his station under the elevated Bench. "Sir…"

"Yes, Mr Clerk." (Here, I have to admit, for the sake of accuracy, I'm not sure whether it was 'Mr Clerk' or 'Mr Clarke').

"Sir, I have to advise you that that is not possible."

"Why not?!" cheeks reddening, fists clenching.

"Because, sir, the law does not allow it. In fact on first offence you have to consider probation before a custodial term."

"Absolutely ridiculous."

"Agreed, sir, but at this moment in time, that is how the law stands."

As some of the out and out ruffians who appeared before Mr W happened to be friends and acquaintances of mine, I was more than grateful for the Clerk's knowledge of the law. Outside court, Mr W changed into the most amiable of men. President of one of the out of town cricket clubs, he helped to inaugurate a successful and long-running sixes tournament. Watching the first event from a deckchair by the white marquee and in something of an alcoholic haze, I saw him walking by, brown brogues topped by grey flannel trousers and tweed jacket, and tried to get up to greet him, only to fall back helplessly into the chair, half expecting him to bark: "Two years for drunkenness."

My three years indentureship with the Guardian Series was settled and only had to be signed and sealed. They agreed to train me for journalistic stardom, and I agreed that I would uphold the reputation of the company, carry out all legal and reasonable demands, and behave appropriately at all times. Some hope! If anything had fallen behind the times, it was our version of The Local Rag, a broadsheet with its front and back pages obliterated by adverts. Inside, sport was mixed with news. Only the sports reports carried a by-line, so I began my cricket writing career as Bob King.

As befitted such a venerable and august organ, the newspaper's indentureship contract was embodied in a manuscript resonating of pure Victoriana, bound in red ribbon. The Editor, who liked a pint, insisted that it should be signed by all parties (himself, me, and my parent/guardian because I was under 18), at a formal ceremony in the Angel. Eight o'clock sharp. Dad, long out of the Parachute Regiment and now a postman, had been up since 4 30am, sorting mail and then delivering it to the farms and cottages on his country round. As the evening wore on, the Editor dragging it out as long as possible, Dad grew noticeably more tired. "Well, Mr Evans," said the Editor rather pompously, "I suppose it is time to get this signed so that your son can start his career in earnest." No answer. Dad had dropped off. Mum, who had done her best to keep the conversation flowing, gave him a hard dig. "What the blood..." Dad, jerking upright, stopped himself just in time. His hands had flexed momentarily but ominously. His shoulders had hunched. "Er, if you could sign here," said the Editor, with just a little less authority.

EIGHT

LIVING directly under the flight path of Manchester Airport, only three miles from the edge of the runway, we were used to aircraft noise. And the rumble of long freight trains, rolling down the Manchester-Chester line just 25 yards from the back door, scarcely bothered us. Occasionally, we suffered the double hit, an ICI 'hopper' - a line of huge limestone filled trucks - pulled by a big, black steam locomotive, and, simultaneously, a Comet flying in less than a couple of thousand feet above. Sometimes the house trembled. Then we learned that Concorde might be soon seen, and heard, overhead. And felt.

"That'll be it, this place will collapse," warned Dad, who had seen houses collapsing before. In Wales, due to mining subsidence, and during the war, due to the Luftwaffe. Concorde was getting ready to roll and, in the summer of '65, as engineers worked on the prototypes in Bristol, the government carried out market research into the effect of the plane's sonic boom.

This so-called research was one of Baldrick's cunning plans. It consisted of a jet fighter plane hurtling over built-up areas of the country at supersonic speed and a note made of the number of subsequent complaints. But here's the sneaky bit - some of the flights were over Bristol, where, of course, many Concorde workers lived. As their livelihoods depended on it, they were unlikely to complain. Problem solved.

But you couldn't fool the British public quite so easily. Campaigners demanded more precise scientific data, referring to tests on sonic blasts in the USA where 4000 complaints in a month had been registered, although not all were treated seriously. One woman blamed the bang for snapping her bra straps. Eventually, it was agreed that the noise levels would be too great and Concorde was barred from supersonic booming over urban areas. This remarkable aircraft, however, collared our imagination. Ugly or beautiful? Worth the money? It didn't matter. It was new and fast. That's all that counted. And, hopefully, we would see it at close-hand, before the house fell down.

Being an avid train/plane spotter, I had thrived on our proximity to the railway and airport, but many in the town muttered bitterly about the adverse effects, particularly that planes interfered with 'telly'. You could hear the gossip at the front gates. "Watching Coronation Street last night and Elsie was just about to let fly at Len Fairclough and picture goes all fuzzy. Bloody planes. And when picture comes back, they're in the Rovers and we don't know whether she's belted him or not. Bloody planes - don't talk to me about Concorde."

In the late 1970s flights were increasing and plans to further develop the airport were met by withering fire from residents on our estate. As a Town Councillor for the ward, I was asked, no, instructed, to do something about it. Otherwise they would tell Mum what I was really like. So, at the next council meeting, I raised my hand in a token vote against the development. Afterwards, a colleague took me to one side, put his arm around my shoulder (much in the way Malcolm Allison had done a few years earlier), and said: "You're a Labour councillor. Labour support the development. Next time stick to the party line, or else." I've never trusted politicians since.

Back in '65 I produced my version of a sonic boom, gunning my little scooter downhill, and despite a faulty and explosive exhaust, getting up to 45mph, only to lean too hard into a left-hand bend and fall off, sliding down the road with the scooter on top of me. Luckily it was very late at night, no-one around. Even luckier, I escaped with cuts and bruises, despite having no helmet. In fact, I got off lighter than John Edrich had done when hit on the head by Peter Pollock at Lord's.

What saved me, I guess, was the relaxed way in which I slid off the scooter, helped, no doubt, by slugging six pints of bitter during the previous two hours. Scootering was so un-regulated! You only needed to be 16, with a provisional licence and a second-hand dream machine, costing between £20 and £30, and away you scooted, putting yourself and the neighbourhood in immediate and real danger. After bombing around the streets for half an hour, just to get the feel of the kick-start, twist grip throttle and gear shift, you could have a few pints and, as long as you could stay in the seat and steer a relatively straight course, no-one could touch you. Of course, if you came off, no-one would want to touch you, because usually your helmet-less head would be in such a mess, but we didn't worry too much about that.

We had races. Dave, a daredevil, won most, screeching around tight corners, with the platform scoring the tarmac and sparking against the kerb. But, on a straight run, Robbo's new streamlined Lambretta TV175 was unbeatable. He took me on his pillion to Blackpool, urging me along the way to scream obscenities at any Rockers we saw. He was middle class, an only child, and as well as having the fanciest scooter, he became the first of the group to own a car, a sporty Triumph Herald. He went into oil.

Smudger, who had ambitions, eschewed scooter transport. Expelled from grammar school for an incident involving an air pistol, he grabbed the opportunity to make an earlier than expected start in business. In 1965 he alternated between our mob and a trendier set who wore striped blazers and crimson polo shirts and shared a Mini Cooper, which sped them to resorts in North Wales and Lancashire's West Coast and was safer than a scooter for shouting obscenities at Rockers. Within a few months he had an old van which seated two, but in the way we arranged it, could accommodate at least nine if some didn't mind their legs dangling through the open rear door. (One night we had to backtrack a mile or so after realising one had fallen out.) But what he really wanted was a smart car. One evening in 1965, a knock on our front door. "Come on, we're celebrating. I've won the pools."

It was a small fortune. We climbed into his van, had a few, and accidentally ran over a cat on the way home. Next day I wrote the story, omitting the bit about the poor moggy. 'Firm's Pools Syndicate Celebrate Massive Win', but we rarely went out together after that. He realised his ambitions. He got the motor he had dreamed of - a Cortina - the girl he had always fancied, and enjoyed a successful business career.

Scootering was a summer sport. For warm, sunny weekends when you could show off, tearing up and down the local streets. Sometimes there would be a long, leisurely meander into the countryside, perhaps as far as the coast, along quiet B roads, but, usually, it was all about beating up the town, screaming to a halt in front of a gaggle of girls, standing astride the scooter, executing a quick pelvic thrust as you revved the throttle, wallowing in the attention. Because even an ugly, lanky pen pusher was worth a giggle and a provocative twist of the hip, if he would take you for a spin.

Admittedly, my scooter wasn't the best puller around. Robbo's Lambretta stood head and handlebars above all the others. The 175TV machines were slimmer than the outgoing, somewhat bulbous bikes, with a narrower body and sleek side panels. In many ways they were ahead of their time, featuring a disc brake, weight-saving fibreglass mudguard, multi-function ignition/light switch, and a funky hexagonal headlight. Improvements to its carburettor helped make it a deal quicker than any other.

The TV was launched in the UK in 1965, and Robbo was one of its first owners. Soon, however, speed addicts were demanding something even bigger and better. The Italian manufacturers responded icily, suggesting that if the Brits wanted to go faster they should buy motor-cycles, perforce, become Rockers! But, being Italian, they then threw up their hands in mock despair and set about designing a 2 litre model.

Other lads had Lambretta 150s and 125s, or Vespas. Mine, though, was a red and white Agrati Garelli Capri, unusual in that this scooter, from Milan, was never officially imported into Britain and possibly came via Germany where it had sold well. Smaller than the other more popular makes, it had a simple 50cc engine, producing 8 hp, and a supposed top speed of 50 mph. It stood, a little forlornly, as Bargain Of The Week £15 on a garage forecourt and I didn't hesitate, only spotting the rough paintwork and the rusting leg shields - on account of water gathering under the rubber mats - when I got it home. No matter. Just a bit of work on the kick-start and the two-stroke spluttered into life, and I was away, not having checked brakes, tyre pressures and electrics, but, within seconds, discovering that, thankfully, the horn worked, enabling me to warn the little girl who was playing in the road on a pair of stilts that we could be on a collision course. I think her mother, watching from their front door, screamed a warning - or she might just have been screaming - and a second later, I was safely past, honk honk like Toad of Toad Hall, glorying in the power and freedom, even while knowing that back home, the girl's mum would be confronting mine to make the first of many complaints about my road sense, or indeed, any sense.

I was told, firmly - fatherly finger pointing you'll do as you're bloody told or you won't be keeping your bloody silly little scooter in this house firmly - that before taking it out for another ride, I should read the Highway Code and the smeared DIY maintenance manual that came with the Capri.

"Okay, but no, I'm not buying a helmet. Do you want me to look like a big girl's blouse?"

"What do you bloody think you look like anyway, with hair like that?"

Breezing through the Code, I turned to the manual and digested the Capri's inner parts while not having a clue what it all meant. For instance: 'Check for little end play by holding the connecting rod firmly and trying to move the piston up and down. Side play is unimportant but up and down play indicates that the bush is due for renewal.' Huh? If it had been a sex manual, I might have guessed what it was all about. But such was the extent of my mechanical inclinations at that stage, I had already spent an embarrassing 15 minutes at the filling station, trying to locate the fuel tank. A wizened old attendant, having enjoyed the show, put me out of my misery by suggesting I lift the seat. Twenty years on, another cricket writer, Mike Stevenson, encouraged me to read a book, 'Zen And The Art of Motor Cycle Maintenance', for its philosophical content, I presumed, although what really impressed me was its insistence that attention to detail and correct organisation was the basis for success, especially if you had a scooter.

The Capri developed into a cult model. Mine developed rust. Other defects appeared due to a lack of maintenance and a lack of sobriety. It kept buzzing along, but, unlike the others, shiny and beloved by their owners, it seemed pointless decorating it with accessories like extra wing mirrors and a chrome back-rack. Not surprisingly, the number of pillion riders I was able to attract dwindled.

*****

ENGLAND'S selectors had work to do. Coming up was the second Test against South Africa, and they also had to think long and hard about the squad for the winter Ashes tour. Their options were limited. No great problems over the batting. Geoff Boycott was struggling for runs on Yorkshire's under-prepared pitches, but his Test form was good, and the likes of Bob Barber, John Edrich,

Ken Barrington, Colin Cowdrey and Peter Parfitt would automatically go into the hat, along possibly with Tom Graveney. But the bowling caused some furrowed brows.

By the end of July the top 25 in the national averages included just two spinners, Fred Titmus and Ray Illingworth. The others were seamers. And, considering Fred Trueman's Test career was over and that veteran Brian Statham was unlikely to tour, none of that 25 offered two opening bowlers who, in the opinion of Bill Bowes, would "satisfy the demands of international cricket or were so obviously ahead of all challengers that one could say with conviction - they are the best we've got."

Bowes felt that Warwickshire's David Brown might have edged ahead of David Larter (Northants) and the left-armer Fred Rumsey (Somerset), but, generally, he was again pessimistic about the country's bowling resources. Glamorgan's left-armer Jeff Jones was unlucky in having to bowl on 'the sands of Swansea'. Others could pick up wickets at will on seamers' wickets. "It seems to me, and the all England averages bear it out, that all you have to do to be a successful bowler is to trundle at little more than medium pace and have an ability to bowl just short of length. The pitches do the rest."

One man capable of upsetting any batsman sat at the top of the averages, but Harold Rhodes was also deemed capable of upsetting umpires as well. Robin Marlar, writing in The Cricketer, accepted that Rhodes' controversial action made him ineligible: "Bowlers must be snow white," he declared. But he was very unhappy about some aspects of the Rhodes Affair and said so in deliciously rich language. "The lunatic fringe have already been snapping over the sad case of Harold Rhodes, a delightful person with cricket thick in the blood. Crusading Princes of Ignorance have given battle with full quivers of verbal diarrhoea. Having hurled their ammunition, no doubt they are happy that the situation is now more acrimonious than it need be."

As for snow white, what about the bowler at number 25 in the averages. John Snow, said Marlar, hit the keeper's gloves as hard as anyone, but his action was 'curious'. "He kicks himself away to the edge of the firing line in the critical final stride." Marlar thought Statham should be invited to tour under 'grand old man terms', to be kept oiled but under cover until the Tests. And his Lancashire partner Ken Higgs might well go with him.

Higgs had little chance to impress the selectors before the second Test to start at Trent Bridge on August 5 because Lancashire's home game with Surrey was ruined by the weather and they lost the Roses match at Sheffield by seven wickets. After being put in by Surrey on a green, drying Old Trafford pitch Lancashire were tumbled out for 96, with only Green (36) and John Sullivan (30) making double figures. Surrey reached 100-1, Green getting in a bit of bowling practice and claiming his one and only wicket of the season, and that was it, although Surrey at least earned six points for first innings lead.

Sullivan maintained his form at Sheffield, but the Roses match was a disaster for Lancashire, with Trueman ripping through their top order. His book, 'The Freddie Trueman Story', was on the shelves. In it he proclaimed: "I must have success. I thrive on it, and if I'm not getting it, I'm down a bit. In recent seasons I've been bitterly hurt when people have tried to write me off if things haven't gone my way."

Harry Pilling said: "Every Roses match when we were just getting ready for battle, Fred would come into our dressing-room. It was his big psychological job. He went around asking: 'Tha' playing today? Tha' playing? Tha' playing? Tha' playing? That's four wickets I'll get today then.' More often than not he was right."

On that basis, Trueman obviously spoke that morning to Green, acting captain in Statham's absence, Gerry Knox, Ken Snellgrove and Sullivan. He got them all. And Tommy Greenhough, although he wouldn't have even bothered trying to wind up a tail-ender. Sullivan, though, defied him until he had 53 under his belt. And Pilling gave the fast bowler a cheeky grin and went on to make a superb 60 after going to the crease at 31-4. Jimmy Binks held onto five catches behind the stumps, underlining Yorkshire protests that the England selectors did not consider anyone wearing gloves north of Watford, and Lancashire stumbled to 175 all out. Yorkshire declared 19 ahead and although it was into the final day, Lancashire could not hold out, dismissed for a miserable 75 by the spin of Don Wilson and Ray Illingworth.

Trueman had made history a few days earlier when bowling Brian Taylor of Essex, his 2000th first-class victim. He was only the fourth Yorkshire bowler to achieve the feat following Rhodes, Hirst and Haigh, although few fans in the crowd at Bradford realised it. Trevor Bailey also made it to 2000 when dismissing Jack Bannister of Warwickshire at Clacton. Bailey was the first Essex player to do it.

*****

JOHN SULLIVAN, formerly a good amateur boxer, was at Old Trafford for 13 years, 1963-76, and in 1965 was just beginning to make an impression with his hard middle-order hitting. His championship career looks disappointing on paper, 154 games with an average of 20.5, but Jack Simmons reckoned he wasn't given enough chances at this level. Where 'Sully' came into his own was the one-day game. If Lancashire needed quick runs, he would be pushed out to get them. And, as he always put the team's requirements above his personal ambitions, he was often the 'sacrificial lamb' as Simmons put it. But he became a key member of the Kings of One Day cricket line-up, particularly in the Sunday League.

In 1969, their first League triumph, he hit 56 not out with a six and seven fours as Lancashire beat Yorkshire in front of 30,000 fans in the decisive game. And in 1970, he scored 364 runs at 40.4 to take third place in the county's averages, behind only Clive Lloyd and Harry Pilling. Sullivan went back into league cricket after leaving Lancashire and, sadly, hit the bottle. He died in 2006 in dire circumstances, a lonely figure.

*****

DAVID GREEN and I were both in London on August 4, him at the Oval, me in St James' Park. Both of us had been in a row, him with the Lancashire selectors, me with the Metropolitan Police. Both of us were a mite tired, him after three days of Roses cricket and a long trip south from Sheffield, me after a rough night in the middle of a large bed of rhododendrons.

I've said previously that I had little chance of watching Lancashire that summer because of work commitments, but that week was an exception. Lancashire were just a hop away over the Thames, but I have to confess that cricket, at that juncture, was not an option. Priority was to persuade the Met not to arrest us for vagrancy.

We had chosen St James' Park because it was close to Trafalgar Square, where we had all gathered after reaching London, en route to Richmond, and also to Soho, where we had spent the evening gawping at the sex shops, being taken to task by some of the ladies for not being up to it (we were so obviously from the North), and being ripped off in a dingy café-club where: "Sure there's striptease, sir, but later, much later - now that will be a quid for your Coke." I'm glad we didn't protest too much, later I found the club had connections with a criminal gang linked to the Krays. Freddie Mills, the former world light heavyweight champ, who went into Soho club life after retirement, had been discovered dead in his car not too far away earlier that summer, and while suicide was recorded, many questions had gone unanswered.

The Krays were on trial for various offences, Great Train Robber Ronnie Biggs was on the run after escaping from Wandsworth Jail's high security wing...crims were constantly in the headlines, and they sounded nasty and daring, so you paid 15 per cent of your week's wages for a Coke, smiled nicely and legged it.

It goes without saying that we had no intention of looking for proper digs. Not at London prices, and not having just spent a fortune on warm pop, so we headed into the nearest park, crawled into the middle of the shrubbery where there was enough damp, but clear grass on which to roll out our sleeping bags, chatted a little about the festival and what Richmond would be like, and drifted off. Just a happy band of Northern lads, up for the cup, so to speak. Dawn filtered through the rhodeys, the dew rose and there was a musty, almost swampy scent in the air. And something else, wet, around my ears. A sort of lick: "Stop it, it tickles." Aargh, Christ, a bloody dog. A big, bloody dog, with a chain and something at the end of it, oh, shit, a copper at the end of it.

In fact, a few coppers. Two with dogs. All with nasty looks on their faces. Two panting with tongues hanging out. They were concerned, they explained, because:

One - Her Majesty lived just up the road and would be wondering why eight dirty, smelly thievin' tramps were lying in wait just a couple of hundred yards from her front gate, and, don't try to be clever son, she might be at Balmoral but that's hardly the point is it?;

Two - their dogs normally used this spot as a latrine and we couldn't expect the poor beasts to hang on just because we were there, and therefore, we wouldn't mind if they pissed on us, would we?;

Three - they would like to inform our parents that they had found us in distressed circumstances, but they knew we didn't have any (parents);

All in all, they considered the best thing would be to lock us up as vagrants, or give us a good kicking, or both, or just let the dogs have a bit of fun. Tough choice. We didn't have quite enough cash to bribe them, and eventually they let us go with a warning. First the crims, then the cops. London wasn't exactly throwing open her arms to us, but we were happy. We had a story to tell and Richmond was just over there, and wasn't it going to be some weekend.

Green's entanglement with the Lancashire selectors was borne of his continuing frustration over the way some players were treated, and, to an extent, his rather fiery disposition. For the game at the Oval, he was again the acting captain and he felt that, with Statham absent, he needed as much experience and quality as possible at his disposal. Therefore he needed Geoff Pullar. The selectors thought differently. Pullar was short of runs - 33 in his last five innings. He needed a rest, they said. Green exploded.

"It's true Noddy was struggling a bit, but he was a class player and it wasn't that long since we had put on 89 at Southport. The secretary Jack Wood gave me the team as picked by the cricket committee and I couldn't believe that they had left him out. I had started getting into a bit of trouble with the committee, a lot of it stemming back to the sackings of 1964. 'George' said: 'You can't win, you just have to get on with it.' But I couldn't accept them leaving out Noddy. I said it was ludicrous, that they were asking for trouble."

Green got his way. Pullar travelled to London and hit a magnificent century. Some members of the committee curled up in embarrassment, but perhaps it was a Phyrric victory for Green if he held an ambition to succeed Statham to the permanent captaincy. He had rubber-stamped his credentials on the field, and had the respect of the dressing-room, but standing up to the committee carried a penalty. Green was coming to be viewed as difficult to handle. Statham, it seems, would have taken the easy way out in accepting the committee's verdict on Pullar. He would have been wrong to do so. For reasons previously stated, I find it difficult to criticise him, but this definitely exposed a flaw in his make-up. A captain has to stand up for his players, on and off the field, and he was prepared to sacrifice the team's only Test batsman to avoid confrontation.

In fact, Pullar usually rose to a challenge and Statham knew this. Pullar fully justified Green's defiant stance, hitting a magnificent 112, his first Lancashire century at the Oval, although it was there that he had hammered 175 against South Africa five years earlier. He was at the crease for five hours, helping Green put on 125, the side's best opening partnership of the summer.

"It was a triumph for determination, skill and spirit...and without it Lancashire would have been in a very sorry state during the last few years," said one report. "It is much easier for a batsman to look good in an outstanding team of batsmen. But it is much more difficult to shine when with every game you know your failure could lead to a collapse. This has been the problem facing Pullar and Green. When, in years to come, people start to talk fondly of Lancashire's outstanding batsmen, and names like John and Ernest Tyldesley, Cyril Washbrook and Harry Makepeace are brought up, it will be as well to remember that their eras were with outstanding teams. Pullar's efforts have been during adversity."

His hundred did not inspire a Lancashire win, but it did lay the platform for a great game - unfortunately, one which again underlined Lancashire's vulnerability in the field. With Higgs demonstrating his England potential, they had Surrey against a wall, only for three catches, all off Peter Lever, to go down. This after Surrey had effected three run-outs to wreck Lancashire's hopes of a rare 300 plus total. With quick runs needed on the final day, Pullar was kept back and Gerry Knox slammed his second century of the season before Green declared, setting Surrey a target of 282 in 225 minutes, and they were only five short with three wickets left at the close, Higgs and Lever bowling unchanged for the last hour and a half to keep them at bay.

At Trent Bridge, England had joined battle again with South Africa. The opening day was overcast and Tom Cartwright, that adept exploiter of English conditions, seamed it around to claim 6-94 in his first Test of the season. But even he failed to dim the brilliance of Graeme Pollock's stroke-play. The left-hander hit 125 out of 160, including 21 fours, in a breathtaking 140 minutes, and, as a result, South Africa recovered from 80-5 to make 269 all out. Wisden described Pollock's performance as 'one of the finest Test displays of all time.'

Reviewing the best left-handers he had seen, Cyril Washbrook said: "Perhaps the greatest of them all is Frank Woolley, who made batsmanship look so easy, and strokes to every part of the ground were produced with an elegance which can never be forgotten." But Pollock, he added, "is probably the greatest batsman in the world today."

The Trent Bridge Test proved as dramatic as the first at Lord's. A great Colin Cowdrey century, a Geoff Boycott controversy, a furore over the use of 'nightwatchmen' and sensational bowling from Peter Pollock - 75,000 fans enjoyed four days of cricketing theatre.

Boycott was a bowling hero, a batting villain. After Cartwright had broken his right thumb late in South Africa's first innings, Boycott manfully plugged the gap in the second, recording 26-10-60-0. But, with 319 needed, England's victory bid was undermined right at the start on Saturday evening when, with 35 minutes of play left, Bob Barber and the nightwatchman Fred Titmus fell in quick order. England surprisingly sent another nightwatchman, John Snow, to the crease, which meant that the hard-hitting Jim Parks was relegated to number nine. Snow survived until the close but didn't last long on Monday morning, while Ken Barrington slipped up hooking a Pollock bouncer, and England found themselves at 13-4.

Boycott's response was to make six in an hour, and when he was bowled for 16 he had been there for 140 minutes - 'a dreadful effort when courage was needed,' said Wisden. Yet, what was Boycott supposed to do? Still early in the fourth day, with Cowdrey, Peter Parfitt, the captain Mike Smith and Parks still to come, surely it was his duty to stick there as long as possible, blunt some of the South African fire, and hope that the others would make runs? If that was his plan, it didn't work out. Boycott, Cowdrey and Smith were all back in the pavilion and England 114-7 when Parfitt was joined by Parks. They, too, began slowly, only to go on an all-out attack, cracking 80 in an hour before Parfitt, on 86, was bowled by Peter Pollock trying to hit across the line. Pollock wrapped up the tail quickly to claim his second 'five fer' of the match and a match haul of 10-87.

It was South Africa's first Test win in England for 10 years, England's first defeat in 15 games under the captaincy of MJK Smith and the moment when the talent of two brothers blossomed and illuminated a wet English summer.

*****

LONDON'S bright lights were dimming for us. Back in Trafalgar Square after our eviction from St James' Park, we found a bench to squat on, only to be pushed on our way again by a policeman who refused to consider the argument that other benches were also occupied, albeit by those from higher echelons of society, and so, for a lark, we decided to honour the steps of the National Gallery with our presence, until a gentleman from one of the higher echelons demanded to know why I was wearing a cross and chain - "Are you a Christian - I think not. Fucking poseur." And, although I ignored him, one of the others grabbed his hat and a policeman came over, and he asked what our plans were, and we said: "Going to Richmond for the festival," and he said: "Well, lucky old Richmond, - tube station's over there. Now fuck off."

We hit Richmond mid-morning, linked up with a couple of Yorkshire lasses, and swished into town. Word was that the festival organisers were putting up a huge marquee for us ravers to doss down, but there was no tent. Fans, who had already arrived, had been sleeping rough. The golf course, with its springy turf, was a favourite haunt. Greenkeepers kept tripping over soggy sleeping bags. The riverbank had sordid tales to tell. The streets and lanes were filling up with the great unwashed, provoking the local newspaper to label them as "People of all ages with a penchant for vagrancy and little use for all the conventional paraphernalia of beds, changes of clothing, soap, razors and so on."

Not exactly true. In the hood of my bag, I had some spare underpants, T shirt, toothbrush and paste. We used the washbasins in public toilets to keep reasonably fresh. And there was always the river....

The poster advertising the festival always strikes me as extraordinary. So matter of fact, so under-stated. Yet promising such riches. We gaped at it. So this was, as it said: 'The 5th National Jazz and Blues Festival at the Richmond Athletic Association Grounds'. It forecast, on the first night, Friday, The Yardbirds, The Who and The Moody Blues along with The Mike Cotton Sound. Price - 10 shillings.

The Yardbirds were at number two in the charts with 'Heart Full Of Soul' and, with The Who and The Moody Blues, made up three of the UK's top groups, so along with one which we knew well and liked from our Twisted Wheel experience, it wasn't a bad line-up for starters. Incidentally, these guitar threshing heroes were groups, not bands. Bandsmen blew silver and brass instruments, gripped in fingertips rendered permanently grubby from working at the pit. They drank brown ale and bitter, scoffed hot-pot and black pudding, and led the Whit Walks in mill towns where, not so long ago, people had sold the contents of the household chamber pot to the urine wagon-master who trundled along the streets, collecting the precious liquid for use in the cotton dyeing process.

Despite the big names at Richmond, what grabbed me most about the advertisement, and still does, was the simple illustration in the top left corner of a trumpet standing upright on a wooden chair. This, I supposed, was a back marker to earlier Richmond events, which really were all about blues and jazz. This one was to major on rock. However, the festival's traditional fans were still out in force. They were older, knew the town, hung out in the corners of its pubs and cafes, rolling their own, screwing their eyes to focus through the smoke, and drinking slowly without intent. We stood out, awkward, hesitant, looking for a base, and, when we found an unoccupied table, drinking quickly and never feeling comfortable enough to stay long in one spot. Gradually we made our way to the golf course, found some bushes for cover by the perimeter fence and snugged down for the night, in the full realisation that someone with a long, pointy stick, or a dog, would give us an early wake-up nudge.

The morning began, as expected, with an encouraging shout to 'Get the hell out of here before we get the police.' We had a greasy breakfast in a café. I'd read Hemingway's 'The Sun Also Rises', envying newspaperman Jake, sitting in a Spanish café on the square in Pamplona, sipping a fino, greeting friends, waiting for the bull-running fiesta to start. I'd imagined that was a little of how it might be in Richmond, except for the bulls of course. Hmm. It was damp and we were rammy and tired, gorging on sausage and egg, swaddled in fat and accompanied by skimpy toast with thin, industrial coffee. And still two hours from opening time. No fiesta in sight yet.

These were the early days of such festivals. Richmond's debut was in 1961, concentrating on what it said on the tin, jazz and blues, until, in 1963, The Rolling Stones appeared - for a fee of £30. Next year the Stones topped the bill, girls screamed, and the British rock festival was born. Richmond's organiser Harold Pendleton kept faith with its traditions where possible, but in 1965, the rock and blues groups dominated, with jazz demoted mainly to the afternoon sessions. There had been another festival that summer, at the Hillingdon Showground, featuring The Who, Zoot Money, John Mayall's Blues Breakers, Spencer Davis Group, Marianne Faithful, The Byrds and Long John Baldry. Some cast. However, it was a one day show. The Richmond weekend, where you could pay £1 for an all-in ticket, or pick and choose from a total of five sessions, was unique and paved the way to Glastonbury et al.

The 1965 event was the last to be staged at Richmond. Complaints grew over the behaviour of festival-goers, the golf club raged about damage to their course, and the Athletic Club bowed to the pressure and banned it. In 1966 it moved to Windsor and eventually to Reading. Not only did the venue change, so did the content. Soon there was no demand for the likes of jazzmen Chris Barber, Johnny Dankworth and the Clyde Valley Stompers. Some of the R and B groups also faded into the background as flower power blossomed. Compare the austere Richmond 1965 poster with that of the Love In Festival at London's Alexandra Palace (Ally Pally) in July 1967, which depicted two naked torsos (difficult to say exactly of which gender), decorated with a garland of flowers. And instead of the 'boys from next door' type groups like Graham Bond Organisation, Mike Cotton Sound etc, there were the exotic sounding Pink Floyd, The Crazy World Of Arthur Brown, The Nervous System and The Apostolic Intervention.

We caused problems at Richmond, no doubt. Some damage to the peripheries, some drunkenness which caused publicans to cut opening hours, and I can understand why the local toffs were a little unhappy. But I do not remember any extreme violence, or major street disturbances, nor have I since found evidence of such. Drugs, yes, but generally 'poppers' and 'roll-ups' rather than the hard stuff. One incident, however, lit a fuse.

In the Friday night set, The Who stoked up the excitement. Lead singer Roger Daltrey sashayed across the stage during one number, kicking out the stage footlights as he went along. Barbara Pendleton, wife of the organiser, was so angry that she deducted the cost of the damage from The Who's cash fee, but the crowd loved it. Rock fused with physical violence - it was the first time we had seen anything like it. The Who's stage act expanded from there, burning guitars, wrecking drum kits, etc., and others followed suit. Shock culture thrived, and still does, although so much of it masks artistic ineptitude.

Some of the work of street theatre groups of that time was branded as 'avante garde shock tactics'. But, despite Establishment reaction, a middle-class counter culture was gaining ground. Poetry readings - 7000 had turned up at London's Albert Hall to hear verse from international poets and unknowns - new magazines and theatre pulled together a well-educated, fairly affluent and leftist mass of beats, hippies, free thinkers and nerds, from which emerged a string of London based anti-Vietnam political organisations such as The International Marxists and the International Socialist League.

Vietnam was the litmus paper of the Left, so it was said. You could only be a leftie if you were against the war. Which put Harold Wilson's Labour government in the dock. Wilson needed the USA. When Frank Cousins of the Trades Union Congress asked him why he had not taken a firmer stance against Vietnam, Wilson replied: "Because we can't kick our creditors in the balls."

But Wilson was a canny politician. He doled out MBEs to John, Paul, George and Ringo, he supported Huddersfield Town, confessed to liking brown sauce on his chips and puffed a pipe, and he remained popular although his right-hand man Jim Callaghan, who had beaten Ted Dexter at the last election, had raised taxation and was planning to cut public spending. None of our set was greatly concerned about the counter culture movement, but we revelled in the kick-ass antics of Daltrey and The Stones.

It was late when we found a spot to kip on the Friday night. A slightly sloping lay on the river bank. Most of us had companions. Sleeping bags then were rectangular and roomy enough for two at a squeeze. Mine was quilted in a bright red tartan, not quite neon but easy to see in the dark. In the early hours, I woke up to find a figure bending over us. Thankfully, not a copper. A tramp, traditional at that, with overcoat tied by string and a hat. I'm not sure what he was planning to do, or hoping to see, but she screamed and he scarpered. I didn't get any more sleep. In the morning, we paddled in the muddy edges of the Thames and she and her friends said they would be on their way, had other people to meet, and wasn't Richmond something else, and no way did they want to go back home tomorrow to boring old Sheffield. Yeah, what a dump - you should get over to Manchester, it grooves, said we from the little town known only from its proximity to the new motorway. Anyway, we were happy to see them go - it meant we didn't have to offer to buy them breakfast.

*****

BRIAN STATHAM returned from injury to lead Lancashire against Essex that Saturday, August 7, and promptly provided another captain's performance with 5-51. Trevor Bailey was run out and Tommy Greenhough dismissed the dangerous Barry Knight, an all-rounder in splendid form, as Essex struggled to 184 all out. Greenhough had 3-45 from 29 overs. The leg-spinner had had little success so far, with 31 wickets in 16 matches, and, with only seven games left including the one with Essex, he had little time to make an impact. His had been a chequered career. A 1950 newspaper story tells of his first great misfortune.

'Tommy Greenhough, the 18 year old Lancashire County colt, had a 40 feet fall yesterday, and broke a wrist and dislocated an ankle. Both his feet were badly injured. Greenhough was working on the top floor of a Rochdale printing works near a hoist when he fell through a door which opened onto the street.

'Clifford Carter, another employee who was working below, said: "I was the first to get to him and I expected things to be far worse than they were. He is the luckiest man alive." Last night Greenhough was reported to be comfortable in the Rochdale Infirmary. He was due to be called up (for National Service) next week.'

No Health and Safety rules, then. And no compensation. All Greenhough received was a badly mis-shapen foot, a year out of cricket, and the cancellation of his Lancashire contract. Greenhough, from Rochdale, was a cheerful, but determined bloke. Specially made boots helped him to overcome his handicap, and he persuaded the Old Trafford committee to give him a weekly deal to prove himself. He went on to play for 15 years, collecting 751 wickets at an average of 22.3 and four Test caps.

His career was beset by problems. Playing in a Lancashire League match, he had a finger so badly smashed by a fierce drive from Frank Worrell that surgeons discussed whether they should amputate it. "You can't - I'm a spinner," he told them,. Another hand injury stemmed from his habit of smacking it against his thigh in delivery. He tended to run onto the pitch and had to remodel his action. And, of course, he was a leg-spinner. Why should that be a problem? Let John Kay, of the Manchester Evening News, who wrote an emotional article in the early 1960s denouncing the lack of appreciation for players like Greenhough, explain:

"Leg spinners are the gamblers of cricket. They are also the artists of a game that has lost much of its charm in recent years by the constant covering of the pitches and the development of the deadly dull seam bowler. Any man with an ounce of cricket ability can become a mechanical seam bowler but it takes brains, skill and artistry to become a spin bowler. It takes more. A serene temperament and a happy go lucky attitude to punishment are essential to the make-up of any spinner - especially the man who specialises in leg breaks and googlies. Such a man is Lancashire's Tommy Greenhough.

"Such cricketers are often expensive luxuries. Doug Wright was one and Greenhough is another. They promise so much and generally produce so little but in the process they bring to cricket something that few other sports can command. The leg-spinner is the game's gay deceiver. On form he is a brilliant, sometimes memorable, match-winner. Out of touch he is expensive and exorbitant...but who would have it otherwise? Cricket would be deadly dull if all was plain sailing and the orthodox triumphed over the unorthodox.

"In many respects Greenhough was born a generation too late - or one too soon. In the great days of old, when results were not the be all and end all of the game, Greenhough would have been welcomed for what he was, a cricketing artist. But today unless you bowl 'em out, you drop out. Tomorrow, it might be very different."

Kay was pointing the finger at selectors who failed to keep faith with Greenhough on numerous occasions. As an example he used the Roses match of 1962, when Greenhough bowled superbly and with great heart and endurance on a perfect Sheffield wicket and against in-form Yorkshire batsmen, only to finish with 2-90. He was dropped for the next game.

"It is always the same with a spin bowler," added Kay. "No records can tell of the discomfort endured by batsmen who have been beaten but not dismissed by Greenhough's deliveries. In the privacy of the dressing-rooms up and down England, I have heard batsmen pay tribute to him and on the hard and fast pitches of Kent, Hampshire and Sussex, he is often Lancashire's best bet, yet often he is omitted."

Greenhough bounded in, cradling the ball in both hands. He bowled it quickly, mixing 'leggies' and googlies, and could be devastating on any pitch with a hint of bounce, but in the first half of his Lancashire career he had to contend with soft wickets, as well as competition from other high-class spinners, Bob Berry, Malcolm and Roy Tattersall. In 1958 he decided to quit, only to be persuaded to stay by the then captain Cyril Washbrook, who promised him a regular place.

"A lot didn't like Washy," said Greenhough. "He was a hard taskmaster, but all I ever got from him was a fair deal - and an order to get my hair cut."

Responding to Washbrook's encouragement, Greenhough won four England caps in 1959-60 and toured the West Indies. Against India at Lord's he took 5-12 in 31 balls, despite wicketkeeper Godfrey Evans fluffing a series of stumping chances. He also took two weeks out of the game to rectify his faulty follow through, but in the next five years, hard though he worked, his career went into a long, slow decline. Injuries, poor wickets, and Lancashire's captaincy merry-go-round, all contributed. And David Green added this factor: "The big problem was that he had to bowl into the wind all the time. Remember, we had Statham, Higgs or Lever operating at the other end, and none of them wanted to bowl into the wind. It affected Tommy's googly. Some people didn't seem to appreciate that."

When Sonny Ramadhin joined Lancashire in 1964 EW Swanton enthused about this pairing of two Test spinners. "Between them they muster the skill to make a notable partnership." But the West Indian quit in 1965, and the following year Greenough lost his last Old Trafford battle.

Green recalled: "We were in the nets one day in late August and a girl from the office came over and told Tommy 'they' wanted to see him. When he came back, he was white-faced, very emotional and said: 'I've got the bullet.' It was totally out of the blue, because he was still a great bloke to have in the side and a very good bowler. I was disgusted at the way he was treated."

Greenhough found it difficult to return to Old Trafford for some years after that, until a later Chairman Bob Bennett paid a conciliatory visit to his neat terraced home in Cronkeyshaw, Rochdale where he had always lived. And, what of leg-spinners, John Kay's 'gay deceivers'? Lancashire signed Nasir Zaidi, nicknamed Zebedee. He played 19 matches in two seasons, 1983-84. Then they produced Chris Schofield, who was offered fame far too early and left in a huff after a contract kerfuffle. There was another named Atherton, who decided, for obscure reasons, to concentrate on his batting!

Lancashire beat Essex by nine wickets, their most convincing win, with solid batting down the order led by Green (62) and Gerry Knox (74) hauling them to 309-9 dec. Statham, Higgs and Greenhough again bowled well, and David Lloyd picked up the vital wickets of Bailey and Knight, leaving Lancashire an easy target for victory. Pullar had not figured in this game, through injury, but Duncan Worsley was a useful replacement, and Knox again showed what he could do - and perhaps what he could not. This innings, coupled with his centuries against Yorkshire and Surrey, gave him

283 runs from three knocks. In 33 others he aggregated 416 at an average of 13.6. Worsley, who made his debut in 1960, was to have another two seasons at Old Trafford, finishing with a record of 62 matches and 2508 runs.

*****

RICHMOND was warming up. The weather remained iffy but more fans arrived, boosting the crowd to around 30,000, and the atmosphere was lively. We hung out. Someone claimed they had seen Eric Clapton in a pub up the road, Rod Stewart was spotted crossing the street and Paul Jones getting out of a car. Saturday afternoon's gig didn't look that attractive to us. Headed Modern Jazz, it presented, among others, Ronnie Scott and The Albert Mangelsdoff Quintet - 'the first appearance of this world famous group from Germany.'

The evening concert 'Modern Beat' looked more our style. Manfred Mann, Georgie Fame, The Graham Bond Organisation. We had seen them all in Manchester over the previous few months, knew they would get the place hopping. But we had several hours to kill. We were invited to a party by a well-spoken young lady who said Julie Driscoll would be there. It looked promising, a white Georgian fronted house in a road straight out of Mary Poppins, but nothing was happening when we arrived. Some of the lads grew impatient at the lack of action, wanted to move on. Find some Rockers to bait. What about Brighton?

The music was good, the crowd big and enthusiastic, but fatigue was seeping in. We had not taken a great deal of alcohol on board, but neither had we slept or eaten well for several days. A few pills were handed around. Another night on the riverbank beckoned. The beach sounded a better deal. Brighton here we come.

NINE

ONE hot afternoon in the middle of 2005, I was parked in a lay-by on the approach to Brighton, trying to work out from a street map the best way of getting to my B and B a couple of miles further on in Hove. Suddenly came a tap on the passenger door window. A sun-burned guy, dressed casually in black, gesturing for me to open up. I leaned over, wound down the window and reeled back from the stench of stale beer and sweat. But he was well-spoken, polite, and, according to him, in desperate need of a lift into the town centre.

"I've spent the night in a cell and I've been walking for an hour, I can't walk any more."

I'm not saying my mind went back 40 years to our minor brushes with the authorities, the tiredness, and the slog to Brighton, but somehow he struck a chord. "Get in."

He was getting divorced, a drink-fuelled spat with the wife had led to police intervention, and he had a nice house which he would have to sell, and wasn't Brighton becoming a mess? "Look," pointing to a young man, prostrate on a roundabout, "degenerates, all over the place. Drugs, drink, it's not the place it was."

I laughed. "Difficult to justify that, in your position, isn't it?"

"Oh, yeah…but that was a one-off, I promise you. These people are swarming over Brighton, they've wrecked it."

"We were called degenerates when we came to Brighton in '65."

"Oh? Oh yeah, the Mods and Rockers. The battle on the beach. But that was '64, wasn't it? They made a film about it, Quadrophenia, Sting was in it. What was the name of that character, he played?"

"Ace Face. Apparently it was modelled on a local bloke. Alan Morris, I think his name was. But he became better known as King Jerry, he was a DJ."

"Yeah, I've heard of him. He's still knocking around."

I dropped him off on the prom. As he clambered out, thanking me profusely, I noticed his expensive tan Timberland boots. He suddenly appeared re-energised because he sprinted across the road and down a side street. I wondered if I had just helped him to escape.

Forty years earlier, having left Richmond behind, we arrived in Brighton. It hosed down. A constable stopped us for a chat. "Hope you're not here to cause trouble, because if you are, we'll have you."

The previous summer, the Mods-Rockers clash had shocked Britain. Fighting on the beach spilled into some streets. Windows were smashed, weapons brandished. Bicycle chains whirled through the air, spanners glinted, a blade was spotted, stones hurled. Mods chased Rockers, Rockers chased Mods, and in Brighton and other south coast resorts, peace loving folk recoiled in horror.

Of course the Press lapped it up. In terms of injuries and damage, it all proved to be small beer. But the headlines told a different story, embellishing the violence, warning the nation that a new youth sub-culture was ready to run riot over the land. The moral panic, famously identified by the sociologist Stanley Cohen, set in. But, although there had been some trouble during the 1965 Whit Bank Holiday, by August things had quietened down. The Mod phenomena was soon to fade away, and all we knew was that we were sopping wet, had nowhere to sleep and had the police on our case. We slopped onto the beach and got a shock. It was all pebbles. No soft sand to make a bed. The West Pier at least offered shelter from the downpour. We burrowed down, getting as comfortable as possible, listening to the rush of the pebbles under the tide and the rain beating down.

*****

HOVE was host that weekend to the cricketers of Sussex and Derbyshire as well as a gang of Northern hoodlums seeking action.

Sussex had beaten Lancashire a couple of weeks earlier but, desperately missing the injured Ted Dexter, had since lost to Middlesex and Worcestershire and seemed destined for a lowly spot in the Championship. Derbyshire, thanks to their bowlers, could relax in mid-table.

Sussex's match with Middlesex had turned into a weather-hit farce, like so many around the country that summer. Some, though, were worse than others. Here are the bare bones of this one: Sussex 54-3 dec, Middlesex 15-1 dec, Sussex 103 all out - Fred Titmus claiming the first seven wickets at a personal cost of eight runs - Middlesex 146-1, winning by nine wickets. Well, it's a result isn't it? But, as Titmus once admitted: "If I were not a player, I wouldn't find time very often to spend a whole day at a county match."

And what about this, the late August clash between Hampshire and Worcestershire at Bournemouth. Perhaps the most vital game of the season, Worcestershire needing to win to stay in contention with table-topping Northamptonshire, who had completed their list and were back in the clubhouse waiting for their rivals to finish the course. A draw seemed inevitable, with rain cutting the game by half and Hampshire a comfortable 217-6, 146 behind, but with Peter Sainsbury and Brian Timms, having added 47, looking in command, and with captain Colin Ingleby-Mackenzie among those waiting to bat. Well into the final day, Worcestershire's dream of retaining the Championship in their centenary year was all over. Suddenly,

Ingleby-Mackenzie called his batsmen in. Obviously a deal had been struck to forge a finish. Don Kenyon responded by declaring at 0-0 after Ingleby-Makenzie's first ball of the second innings, leaving Hampshire to get 147 in 160 minutes.

Now all that might well have been accepted as a reasonable way of beating the weather if Hampshire had made a real shot at it. Unfortunately, trapped on a quickly drying pitch, they collapsed to 31 all out, only the second lowest total of the season, demolished by Jack Flavell and Len Coldwell. You might say that, whatever the motivation, it didn't look particularly good. Ingleby-Mackenzie cherished his reputation for the sheer joy of playing the game, over and above winning, but this, felt his critics, was going a bit too far. Not that Northamptonshire complained - after all, they had benefited from a similar agreement at Clacton where, after three declarations, they dismissed Essex for 88 to win easily.

What sort of game was this? The obvious answer was that, in such a wet season, at least they were providing some excitement for the fans - what fans would be left after two days of rain. But cricket's image was in question, and Wisden's Editor admitted: "The general grievance was that Worcestershire were given a chance to get 10 points when their main rivals Northamptonshire had completed their programme." After 1965 captains were allowed to forfeit an innings, to avoid the circus of two batsmen facing one ball to enable a declaration.

Sussex and Derbyshire didn't need declarations, because their batting was so feeble. The teams scratched out a total of 493 runs over the three days, for the loss of 39 wickets. And there was a genuine, dramatic climax.

I heard it. Or at least I heard the shouts and applause as Derbyshire, needing 124 to win, reached the last over on 119-5. A single and one good shot, or a lucky edge, would do it. But Mike Buxton was run out, and Tony Buss grabbed a sensational hat-trick with the last three balls, leaving Derbyshire on 120-9. I was walking past, sodden sleeping bag over my back, head down, not even realising that the ground was so close, when I heard a muted roar, stopped, heard more applause, then saw supporters exiting, chattering excitedly. One told me what had happened. It was Buss's second hat-trick of the summer, following one against Cambridge University.

I had to wait until 1978 to witness my first Championship hat-trick, Jack Simmons obliging against Nottinghamshire at Aigburth. Jimmy Anderson's against Essex in 2003, including Nasser Hussain, was the best I ever saw. I didn't see Dominic Cork's for England against West Indies because I arrived a little late at Old Trafford. But, as I walked towards the entrance, I heard it.

*****

NO Rockers appeared, but the weather relented a little, enough to play cricket, and enough for us to dry out, lying back uneasily on the pebbles, watching early morning bathers run into the sea. My quilted, tartan sleeping bag held the water and would stay wet forever, and the heavy combat jacket would give off a musty sniff for the rest of its shelf life, but the Levis and T shirts steamed nicely under the sun. One of the bathers approached, towelling her hair, stepping gingerly on the stones. Rog chatted her up. Within half an hour their conversation had become more intimate, wrapped up, as they were, in his soggy, stinking bag. We left them to it. Didn't see Rog again for a long while. They became attached to each other and he spent the rest of the summer in Brighton.

The group was dispersing. Some fancied hitching it to Weymouth. Something about the quality of the draught cider. One was off to Cornwall to try his hand on the trawlers. What?! How could you be a Mod on a trawler? It was as if something was ending.

In 'Quadrophenia', a year or so after the Brighton battle, Ace Face has returned to 'normal' life. His Mod days well behind him, he is seen working at the very hotel he had once vandalised, the act of ultimate betrayal to Jimmy, still wearing his fish-tailed Parka, still on his scooter, still believing, still *having* to believe because being a Mod was the only way out of his humdrum existence. None of us were Faces. Neither were we like Jimmy. There were one or two exhilarating rides left, but the fairground exit sign was blinking brightly.

As for the other Ace Face, aka Alan Morris or King Jerry, well, he also returned to a fairly normal life, if being a top DJ in Brighton comes into such a category, only to suffer an extraordinary demise.

Brighton's evening newspaper The Argus reported in December 2007 how news of his death filtered through the town, and how a group of his fans, some in disco gear, turned up at the Downs Crematorium to pay their respects at his funeral. Only when they noticed a woman's photo, placed at the front of the chapel, did they realise something was wrong. Apologetic, they learned that the deceased lady was Gerry King, a grandmother who had taught at the local primary school. In the paper, the death notice, placing, in the usual manner, her surname first, gave it as: King Gerry.

"Oh dear," said Milton King, the fan who had spread the rumour. "I can't believe it. I'm in shock. I really thought he was dead. I'm just pleased he's still alive. Everybody loves him, he's a great guy."

King Jerry, co founder of the aptly named group Soul Survivors, had been a DJ since the age of 16, had played alongside The Who when they were known as The High Numbers, and was accepted as the King of the Mods. At least, down South he was. He might have won such acclaim in Manchester, too, had we known about him, although he would have faced some stiff competition from the boys in The Twisted Wheel.

Ken Snellgrove who, in 1965, launched a useful career with Lancashire, making a significant contribution to their Sunday League successes under Jack Bond. He scored 443 Championship runs that season in 13 matches, finishing fourth in the club's averages.

David Green turns one around the corner in the Southport Championship game against Derbyshire in July 1965, marquee and deckchairs in the background. 'Southport', proclaimed an advertising poster, was 'a paradise for sports lovers'.

Harry Pilling and coach Stan Worthington in the Old Trafford pavilion at the onset of 'Little Harry's' career. Worthington had an early rebuke for the 4 feet 7 inches youngster, warning him to speak properly and to cut out 'aye' and other expressions. "Understood?" said Worthington. "Aye, coach," replied Harry.

'Meeting of the world's two fastest bats' said the Manchester Evening News headline. Steve O'Shaughnessy equalled the world record of the illustrious Percy Fender of a century in 35 minutes, and then went to Sussex to meet him. "He was a true gentleman," said O'Shaughnessy.

John Sullivan, seen here in action, had his best season so far in 1965. He developed into a vital member of the Lancashire squad - often used as the sacrificial lamb in pursuit of quick runs. But, although always the team player, the popular 'Sully' found life hard after his career ended and died a lonely figure.

An early picture of Tommy Greenhough. He didn't realise it but the former Test leg-spinner was coming to the end of his career in 1965. The following August he told his colleagues: "I've got the bullet." David Green was disgusted at the way Lancashire treated him.

Ken Higgs, from Staffordshire, was labelled the Nawab of Kidsgrove after winning the pot in a cards game with the Indian prince, the Nawab of Pataudi, then playing for Sussex. Higgs, a fine fast bowler, made his England debut in the last Test of 1965.

Ken Higgs shows the letter calling him into England's
party for the Ashes tour of 1964-65. Looking on are
Lancashire team-mates Harry Pilling, Geoff Pullar,
Tommy Greenhough and David Green along with
(centre, in whites) David Larter of Northants.

County cricket coaching has changed drastically in the last
20 years. This was how Harry Makepeace, dressed in cap
and mac, did it in the 1950s, carefully watching some
youngsters in a cold, damp pre-season work-out in the nets.

Two intriguing adverts from the Lancashire Year Book. How could you resist the scantily clad young lady boasting treble Green Shield stamps at Gaythorn filling station, or indeed the pie of 'golden opinions' baked at Ellis's Pies, Gorton? Marvellous!

Brian Statham captures his 250th Test wicket, winning an lbw appeal against South Africa's Tiger Lance. Statham, recalled by England for one final fling, celebrated with five wickets in the first innings of the last Test at the Oval. It was his 70th Test and he finished with 252 wickets.

Ken Shuttleworth began to push his way into the Lancashire line-up in 1965, taking 10 Championship wickets including 5-38 against Gloucestershire at Bristol. A tall, lean, and naturally quick bowler he was to form a superb partnership with Peter Lever when Brian Statham called it a day.

Another example of Brian Statham's Principle of Accuracy - "If they miss, I hit." The victim is Don Wilson of Yorkshire in Statham's career finale - the Old Trafford Roses match of 1968.

David Green, early in his career. Green, who had sometimes been at loggerheads with the Lancashire hierarchy, left Old Trafford after the 1967 season and joined Gloucestershire. He burned his Lancashire blazer but years later was happy to accept a replacement - even though it didn't fit him!

While peace reigned on the Brighton beach, not so in the committee room at Hove cricket ground after one Sussex member, a Mr W Foster Horsfield, had written a furious letter over being charged extra to get into a Gillette Cup game, as recommended by the Advisory Committee of county cricket.

"Who constitutes this body I do not know, but I am fairly certain it is made up of members of that last bastion of feudalism in this country, the MCC," he raged.

Of course, there were a few 'last bastions' knocking about in those days. Indeed, there was one in Manchester until as late as 1998 when the ladies of Old Trafford were at long last given the vote. But that's by the by. Returning to Hove, where Mr W Foster Horsfield was also apoplectic about the lack of a members' enclosure, a members' lunch and tea-room, or "any of the other amenities one finds in the Pavilions of other County Grounds." And what about the subscription of £5 5s per annum? Higher than any other club. Disgraceful.

Of course he was wrong, as sternly pointed out by the Club Secretary Mr PC Williams, who presented a long list of facilities and £80,000 worth of ground improvements in recent years. "We are certain that the great majority of our 8230 members are more than satisfied ..."

I'm sure they were. But you always get one, don't you? During a brief employment with Lancashire, I dealt with Members' Complaints. Most cropped up after a Test Match, a One Day International, or a rock concert. Like...

Complaint 050706-67CE

"I bought pie, mash, peas and gravy from the Wigan Pie Stall at the One Day International. The sign said £4.50. I gave him £5, but he wouldn't give me change. He said the sign said pie, mash and peas £4.50, and I'd had pie, mash, peas and gravy and that was £5. What I'm asking is what about my 50p?"

Reply:

"I'm afraid Lancashire CCC cannot help you. This is a contractual matter between you and the owner of the pie stall. However, if, on your next visit to Old Trafford, you care to contact me, I will personally refund your 50p, without prejudice to Lancashire CCC or the Wigan Pie Stall."

Signed Colin Evans, pp Lancashire CCC.

I have tried to estimate the time taken by Mr Williams to deal with Mr W Foster Horsfield's complaint. His first task, on a preliminary reading of the letter - a fairly lengthy one riddled with issues - was to sort out exactly what he was going on about. Then to place it before the club committee, who would no doubt debate it at length. Then to draft a full reply, checking to ensure everything was covered before taking it back to the committee for amendments and approval. Then to write the final, approved version. And, in between, to hold a face to face interview with Mr W Foster Horsfield. In all, I reckon at least one full working day, possibly two. For one wildly inaccurate letter from one member.

At Old Trafford in 2006, I fielded over 100 Official Complaints. Some ridiculous (and I swear on Archie MacLaren's grave that the pie controversy was genuine), some tetchy, some serious. I tried to give time to each one before responding, making an enquiry with the Catering Department or maybe with a steward: "Why did you confiscate this member's camera?... Because he threatened to snap you hitting what kid?!" (I won't swear on Archie's grave this time, but you get the picture).

The 'Why No Chips In The Pavilion After 3pm' complaint was a real hot potato. How to reply? A simple: "Because the chef ran out of cooking fat." No, too flimsy. "Because the chef ran out." Far too flippant. "Because the Catering Manager says it is not profitable enough?" Huh-huh, on the right track. Let's try this: "Because there is not enough demand, but if we find that more members want chips in the pavilion after 3pm then, of course, we will seriously consider it." Got it - with fingers crossed that it isn't leaked to the Daily Mail Sports Diary.

I failed badly over Complaints. They piled up on the desk. Complaints about complaints not being dealt with flooded in. They made another pile. I gave up. Mr PC Williams would have had my utmost sympathy and respect.

*****

KEN HIGGS was named in the England squad for the Ashes tour. The other seamers were David Larter of Northamptonshire, Jeff Jones of Glamorgan and David Brown of Warwickshire. Fred Titmus (Middlesex) and Gloucestershire's David Allen were the spinners, Jim Parks (Sussex) the keeper, with John Murray of Middlesex his deputy, and the batsmen were Colin Cowdrey (Kent), Bob Barber (Warwickshire), Geoff Boycott (Yorkshire), Ken Barrington and John Edrich (Surrey), Eric Russell and Peter Parfitt (Middlesex), and the captain Mike Smith (Warwickshire).

Smith had been criticised during the summer for being too defensive at times, and he had not scored a weight of runs, but he had a successful record as captain and no outstanding rivals. As for the rest of the party, it seemed well-balanced, strong in batting resources, with massive experience in the spin department, and we all had to hope that the new ball attack would do the job.

Higgs, who was to make his debut in the third and last Test against South Africa, was the surprise, albeit a minor surprise. Cowdrey thought Higgs would do the job - 'an Englishman who bowls like an Australian'.

But he had this message for the seamers: "I would beseech them to be prepared for a hard slog. This is not in any way defeatist; it is better, in my mind, to be realistic. In this country they become so used to beating the bat, beating the stumps, appealing and generally thriving on a general sense of supremacy over batsmen. In Australia they are not going to beat the bat so often, or look so menacing, yet they may be just as successful overall. Brian Statham used to accept these conditions philosophically and his example I would commend to all young bowlers touring Australia."

Statham's name was missing. His Test career was almost at an end, just one last hurrah to come against South Africa at the Oval. For the first time Statham found himself overshadowed by another Lancashire bowler. And, at Edgbaston, when they teamed up against Warwickshire, it was Higgs who took the honours with 4-57 from 28 hard-working overs. Warwickshire were not the force they had been in 1964, when they chased the Gillette Cup and the Championship. Six Tests meant that Barber and Mike Smith each missed a dozen matches, but Dennis Amiss was progressing. The Warwickshire correspondent said: "He possesses a correct technique and can shrewdly mix aggression with caution."

However, Barber and Smith both played against Lancashire, and contributed heavily, while Amiss fell cheaply twice to Statham. A neat combination of pace and spin did for Warwickshire as Lancashire racked up a notable victory over the Midlands side. In the first innings, it was Higgs and David Lloyd, in the second Statham and Tommy Greenhough. Green and Pullar put on 131 and 76, and Lancashire eased home by nine wickets.

Green said: "We felt that if we could play so well and hammer a team like Warwickshire, that maybe we had turned the corner and the club could look forward to a new era."

He was right, but perhaps not in the way he envisaged then. And, by the time Jack Bond had transformed Lancashire's fortunes, virtue of their one-day successes, Green was well away from Old Trafford.

*****

NORTHAMPTONSHIRE, bottom of the table at the start of June, were hoping to mark their Diamond Jubilee by winning the Championship for the first time. Captained by Oldham-born wicketkeeper Keith Andrew, they produced few memorable individual performances, with only four centuries between them and just one bowler passing the 100 wicket mark, but they worked hard for each other and very nearly achieved their ambition.

Andrew, a good keeper, played two Tests against Australia and South Africa, some years apart. Godfrey Evans, Jim Parks, and John Murray all got the nod before him, but at least it gave Northants full use of his services, and he led a tightly-knit group of players which included the Watts brothers, Jim and Peter, and cousins David Steele and Brian Crump.

When they took on Lancashire at Old Trafford in mid August, they had three matches left, the middle one being against Worcestershire. They knew they had to beat Lancashire - and did, convincingly, despite one of Brian Statham's best ever performances - 26.2-10-47-7.

With only Colin Milburn standing up well to the opening spell from Statham and Higgs, Northants were reduced to 85-6, until revived by a stand of 124 in 150 minutes by Lightfoot and Crump. The Guardian's cricket writer complained that Lancashire should have picked Peter Lever as an extra seamer, having laid out a 'fast bowler's pitch'. If so, Northants would have been shot out for less than 100. However, Higgs thought he had Crump caught off an edge before scoring, but the umpire shook his head and Crump stayed at the crease. There had been a similar incident with Steele earlier in the innings, although Statham sent him back before he could do much damage. It left a bad taste in Higgs' mouth.

"He was livid," said Green. "Northants went on to win easily, but it might have been a lot different if Crump had gone. After the game, Higgs and Crump and Steele found themselves on the same platform at Piccadilly station. They were all from the Stoke-on-Trent area and were going home. Crump and Steele saw Higgs and began walking towards him, I suppose thinking they would travel home together, but Higgs ignored them. As far as he was concerned they were guilty of poor sportsmanship and he didn't want to know."

Lancashire's batting line-up remained unstable. Harry Pilling had been promoted to number three, Jack Bond was again in the shadows, and John Sullivan was missing from this game. They slumped to 80 all out, and that after Green and Geoff Pullar had put on 39. Following on, they made a better fist of it, but off spinner Haydn Sully took his match figures to 11-87 and Northants stayed on top of the table with a 10 wickets success.

It was to be their last win. Luck deserted them. They lost at Worcester after their main strike bowler Larter had broken down with hamstring trouble and were thwarted by rain when held to a draw by Gloucestershire. That last game produced one of the season's most spectacular batting displays, with Colin Milburn trying to make up for lost time, blasting 152 not out in 210 minutes with seven sixes and 15 fours. Two of Milburn's big hits landed on the nearby bowling green, two finished on the adjacent football pitch and three flew into a garden, narrowly missing a greenhouse. But his side were thwarted by the weather and an unbeaten 86 from Arthur Milton.

There was also the contrived finish at Bournemouth to consider, but Andrew refused to whinge. He said: "We lost it (the Championship) at Worcester. In that match Worcestershire played the better cricket. Jack Flavell's bowling and Tom Graveney's batting were too good for us. If there is a better player in the country than Tom Graveney I should like to see him. It is true that Larter broke down…just as he was beginning to look lethal, but that was our misfortune. Certainly it was no discredit to Worcestershire. It was up to us to field 11 fit men.

"As far as Worcestershire's match with Hampshire is concerned, obviously it was a bit galling for us but don't blame Don Kenyon. He did what he could. Colin Ingleby-Mackenzie must have thought he had a better chance, or else he would not have done it. I have no grumbles."

Andrew also dismissed claims that Worcestershire and Northamptonshire had won games on bad wickets at home. "I refute these suggestions," he said, "by recalling the following facts. 1: Last year Worcestershire won 12 of their 20 wins away from home; 2: This year we have won only three out of our 13 wins at Northampton."

Intriguingly, he added: "The most boring sight in modern sport is the mediocre batsman getting a big score. Good cricketers thrive on good cricket wickets. What better example is there than Tom Graveney? True, fast wickets are what we really want, but they are heaven-sent, like winning the toss - and the rain!"

There were few batsmen of any standard making big scores that summer. Graveney, however, scored 1684 Championship runs, including four centuries, at the age of 38. As for the toss, the cricketing gods smiled on Andrew, who won it 11 times in their last 13 games.

Northamptonshire, Worcestershire and Glamorgan, the top three, all faced accusations about the quality of their pitches. Maybe it provided losers with a ready made excuse. Glamorgan's skipper Ossie Wheatley explained: "Whenever a side does well in contemporary cricket a moan usually goes up about home pitches. Worcestershire are under criticism, Yorkshire always are, and Glamorgan are a favourite Aunt Sally. Most of our critics have never been to Wales." Wheatley reckoned Cardiff was a good pitch, when dry. Trouble was that the only time it had been dry that summer was for the game with the New Zealanders!

He added: "Swansea is a slow turner on which *good* players can get runs, and quickly, because the bounce and turn of the ball is consistent. Happily most visiting sides have given up the contest before they arrive - at least the Press have done us this favour for which I most sincerely thank them."

If that was a dig at the cricketing Press, how about this from businessman Laurence Weidberg, an MCC member who earned some notoriety for taking his shirt off while watching cricket at Lord's. Mr Weidberg was in mock despair over reporting errors in The Guardian:

"I was born and brought up in Manchester. However, there were compensations. It is not always easy to think what these could have been, but one springs readily to mind. The Manchester Guardian, as it was then called....

"Certainly, to a Lancashire schoolboy (before the county cricket team fell on evil days), there could be little that was calculated to give greater pleasure than reading the work of Neville Cardus. I suppose Carduses don't grow on trees but for the many years since his departure, readers of The Guardian have been confronted with some startling offerings on the cricket page. I am not referring to the typographical errors, which I believe are called literals and which readers of The Guardian have come to love and cherish as part of the price we must pay for a whiff of our native health. No! The errors I refer to are much grander. They are often splendid accounts of events which either did not happen at all or which happened in a way completely different from that described. Sometimes, too, the words used to describe those events are beyond belief. Certainly they are beyond the Oxford English Dictionary."

Mr Weidberg gave a series of examples, confessing that one of his pleasures in life was to pore through the paper each morning over breakfast looking diligently for mistakes. I hope he didn't blame the writer every time. Possibly he would have been more sympathetic if he had had detailed knowledge of the way a cricket report was transmitted from ground to sports desk.

Picture a typical scene at a Lancashire out-ground, approaching lunch on the first day, well before the buzz of laptops and the William Tell Overture ringtone. In the crowded Press tent, reporters are vying to use the one phone to dictate their reports, some of which are scribbled in notebooks, some typewritten, and some, by the more experienced and confident hacks, to be 'ad libbed'.

Our evening paper correspondent has to send over 300 words. Each one of immense wisdom. He grabs the phone at 1pm, and has to be off on the button of lunch at 1 15pm, so that the Exchange Telegraph and the Press Association agents can use it for their progress reports which are flashed around the country. Timing is crucial. Fifteen minutes should be enough for our man but...wickets suddenly tumble. As he is waiting for the switchboard to put him through to the copy room, he has to quickly amend his report accordingly. Then the copy girl - in fact a mature lady of around 50 - answers.

"Hello, copy room."

"Ah hello, Mabel." (He has recognised the rather relaxed, couldn't give a monkey's drawl, and curses under his breath because he knows this could be difficult and why, out of the eight copy girls on duty, does he have to get Mabel?)

"Mabel, got to be quick with this one, pressure on the phone."

"Okay, just get the carbon in. Oh, drat, it's ripped. Hang on...yes, have a good time Mary. Sorry, that was Mary, she's going on her hols, now. Spain, should be lovely, shouldn't it?"

"Er, yeah. Right, Mabel, here we go..."

"Is this for the next edition, or for The Pink?"

"Edition, and I'm running late, so..."

"Edition, then, but it is for the Sports Desk?"

"Yeah, it's the cricket, Mabel."

"Course, it is. Silly old me. Be no good sending cricket to News, would it? They wouldn't have an earthly of what it was about. I don't, either. Right, cricket for the edition, off you go..."

"Right - Lancashire slumped into trouble... at Southport today.... when three wickets crashed just before lunch."

Silence.

"Mabel? Mabel!!"

"Sorry, luv, just having a slurp of me coffee. Don't get time nowadays to have a proper brew break. Right, where were we? Lunch. Right."

"Got to get a move on now, Mabel. David Lloyd - that's double l o y d, and Graeme - Graeme with an a e - Fowler ...f o w l...yeah, that's it - hammered a half century opening stand ...before Fowler was caught off bat and pad..."

"Off bat and pad - that's a funny one. Off bat and pad, don't they use some daft expressions? Oh, look at that, it's just started raining. I've got to go out in a minute and I haven't got a brolly. Irene, have you got a brolly I could..."

"Mabel!!"

"Sorry. It's OK, Irene says I can borrow her brolly. What's the weather like there? Bet it's nice at the seaside."

At 1.20pm, with murderous shouts coming from all corners of the Press tent and still with 50 words left - "Oh, the Sports Desk want a word with you."

An exasperated male tone buts in. "Bloody hell, we're late with the edition, waiting for you. How long are you going to be? The Editor's doing his fruit."

"...and, after 34 overs, Lancashire had crumbled from 57-0 to 94-5. Right, that'll have to do it, Mabel luv."

"Oh, that wasn't too bad then, was it? I don't know what the sports desk lot are screaming about. After all, you're doing your best."

He plonks the phone down, exhausted. Someone says: "About time. You'd think he's the only one who needs to use the phone."

And someone else groans: "Hell, they've just changed Fowler from caught to lbw. Scoreboard is wrong, too. Should be 92-5."

Mr Weidberg would not, I am sure, have taken such matters into account in his one-man campaign against newspaper inaccuracy. Cardus cast his shadow over many cricket writers, particularly those in the North-West. Lancashire created a Cardus archive at Old Trafford. His framed photograph looked down on my designated seat in the Press Box. Probably just my inferiority complex, but I always thought he was sneering as he looked over my shoulder.

*****

FOR the last time that summer, we are in London, again, with nowhere to stay. We meet a couple of girls from South Norwood. They know a dive where you can stay all night and get free soup and tea. It's for tramps, really, but we'll be okay.

A narrow doorway, just off Leicester Square. Stairs leading down. Halfway, we are confronted by a man, probably in his mid 20s, in a neat, light grey suit. (Damn, this race thing again. I was going to write 'black man' and now I have, but only to illustrate how easily it is to get sucked into it all. If it had been a white man, the thought of writing 'white man' would not have entered my consciousness).

Anyway, this man smiles then pulls a knife and points it at my throat. He wants to know who do we think we are, and that's not easy to answer. "Just come for a cup of tea." He smirks and brushes past us, still wielding the knife. In the room below, rows of chairs, most occupied, and not by tramps. There are all sorts, some sipping tea, a few trying to snatch some shut-eye, others leaning forward listening intently. The little stage at the front of the room is dominated by a handsome man (white), in a smart suit. We know who he is, Terry Dene, a pop star who mysteriously disappeared from the TV screens and the music charts a few years previously.

Dene, first spotted in the same London coffee bar as Cliff Richard and Adam Faith, made a number of records for Decca, some of them minor hits, until a drunken escapade was latched onto by the Press and used as an example of how rock music could devastate Western society. Now, after a nervous breakdown, he is back on stage, but spouting religion, his once jet black hair streaked with silver, his eyes shining with belief, his face configured into a look of wonderment and love. We listen for a few minutes, so that we can justify a dry spot for the night, and a mug of soup from the tureen which sits on a trestle table in the corner.

Dene might have made it a as a major rock star. He had the looks, and a decent enough voice, but lacked the temperament and was crucified by the media. After recovering from his breakdown, here he is, saying how much he loves God, and how much he loves all of us. I make sure my non-religious cross and chain is tucked safely away.

Cliff and Adam had fared rather better than poor Terry. A table of the most popular artistes of the 1960s makes surprising reading.

1 Cliff Richard
2 The Beatles
3 Elvis Presley
4 The Shadows
5 The Rolling Stones
6 The Hollies
7 Manfred Mann
8 Roy Orbison
9 Adam Faith
10 The Kinks

Tom Jones, Billy Fury, Cilla Black and Englebert Humperdink were also in the Top 20. This table was constructed on the back of how many singles, as opposed to LP albums, were sold in the UK, and that made a big difference to the positions. So no Bob Dylan, The Who or The Moody Blues - and why Cliff outscored The Fab Four and Elvis The Pelvis.

The Shadows, Cliff's backing group, made a series of highly successful instrumental singles and their 'Wonderful Land' was second only to The Beatles' 'She Loves You' in the UK's best-sellers chart 1960-69. 'Wonderful Land', with its green Columbia label, was in my early collection, the 'B' side was 'Stars Fell on Stockton' (Hank Marvin's hometown). Third place in the singles chart went to 'I Remember You' by the Australian yodeller (yes Australian, not Austrian) Frank Ifield and, fourth, 'Sugar Sugar' by The Archies, but biggest surprise of all was 'Tears', by Ken Dodd in eighth spot.

British pop was maturing by 1965. Radio Caroline was beaming non-stop music and there were TV programmes like 'Ready, Steady Go', 'Top Of The Pops', and 'The Beat Room'. Radio One was just two years away. Solo singers and groups were writing more of their own stuff, rather than covering other artistes' work. America waited for the latest UK hit to arrive on its shores, reversing the previous trend.

Terry Dene missed out on pop stardom, but he seems happy in Christ now, and blesses us all before leaving the stage. We are bored stiff, - 20 minutes of Terry is more than enough to earn a berth for the night and some thin home-made broth. Next morning we break up into twos and singles for the hike back north. Up the M1, around Birmingham, onto the M6, back to cow country, and doesn't it look so green?! A succession of lifts in cars, trucks, vans, anything that will stop for a bedraggled, teenage tramp trying to get home.

"Where the hell have you been?" Dad is trying to remove the blur on the TV picture by hammering the top of the set with the palm of his hand. Satisfied, as Hughie Greene sharpens into focus, he turns to look at me. "Huh - looks as if you've been dragged through a field. Thought you would have sent a postcard, your Mum's been worried. There's some potato hash on the stove - ask her to warm it up for you."

*****

PS:

September 2007: Good Heavens! Terry Dene is back. I can't believe it. But there he is, in leather coat and hat, long hair - all silver now - plonking away at an acoustic guitar and singing Elvis numbers. He is 69 years old. And the reviews of his performance at London's 100 Club are extremely favourable. Says one: "Terry was extraordinary. When he appeared on stage wearing his Italian long leather coat, leather wrist band and hat, he looked as much the authentic rock 'n' roller that he has always been."

Dene, say the long list of fans' websites, turned to religion in the 1970s, but as I witnessed, it was in fact much earlier than that. He went into gospel music, was described as a street singing evangelist, was the subject of a book called 'I Thought Terry Dene Was Dead' and then staged his rock 'n' roll revival.

TEN

LANCASHIRE'S cricket coach in 1965 was Charlie Hallows, who had been with Worcestershire for their Championship triumph of the previous year, but accepted an offer to return to the Old Trafford stamping ground where he had enjoyed a fine playing career.

Hallows was 69, with an athletic figure and active mind. He was old school, as previous coaches Harry Makepeace and Stan Worthington had been. Like them his playing record was to be respected, and his roots were deeply entrenched in Lancashire soil.

Eighteen year old David Lloyd found him a tough taskmaster. But Hallows had championed the youngster's cause, and in turn, Lloyd 'happily indulged his eccentric coaching methods'. These included a lesson of how to go down the pitch to spin bowling, stealthily, rather than like a bull at a gate, by placing a pad on Lloyd's head and insisting it stay there until he had played the shot - "a sporting version of a deportment class," explained Lloyd.

Lloyd made an encouraging start to county cricket in 1965, but was shoved into the second XI for the start of 1966, at which time Hallows said: "We think he is potentially a first team player of uncommon talent. Last season, though, his bowling opportunities were restricted and he was not used as often as he should have been. We want to develop his spinning and he can do that better with the second team."

Lloyd's under-employment in 1965 was partly due to a finger injury, which kept him out for three weeks, but Hallows' comment about limited chances was significant. Within a few months, leg-spinner Tommy Greenhough was fired. David Green, knowing that Hallows was one of only three batsmen to hit 1000 runs in May, listened to his advice intently, which, basically, was to blend a little more caution into his instinctive, attacking play.

"I knew about his prolific partnership with Frank Watson and that he was a very fine batsman," said Green. "The story goes that he never played an attacking shot before lunch, while I was a bit of a helicopter, so you can imagine what he thought of my batting. He was always asking me: 'What type of plucking shot was that?'

"He wanted me to bat at five because I was hammering away. I remember one match against Middlesex at Old Trafford and John Price was bowling. I usually enjoyed batting against him, because I could get back and hit him. That day I got three fours over slips off him and we got to 53-1 and I was 39. He called it 'disgusting batting'."

Green laughed. "It reminds me of a game later on when Barry Wood ('Sawdust') was opening. I was captain and had put myself at five. Sawdust got a century, but it took him five and a half hours and we needed to get the score moving, so I went in, had a go at everything and made 25 in three overs so we could declare, and someone says: 'Christ, you're a real hacker.'"

Hallows, a left-hander, had starred in Lancashire's successful post First World War side. In 1928 he and Watson put together first wicket stands of 200, 202, 107 and 118 in consecutive matches. You could say he knew how to open an innings. Lancashire's plan in those days, so the story goes, was to win the toss, bat on a good wicket and make 300 in the day as the platform to push on for victory. At 20 or more overs an hour, it wasn't exactly fast scoring, but it did the job. Harry Makepeace, the team tactician, would order: "Wicket's lovely. No fours before lunch!"

Hallows followed orders, batting stubbornly, but occasionally unleashing classic straight drives. He made 55 centuries but, with Hobbs and Sutcliffe barring the way, played only twice for England. After ending his playing career when 37, he held professional posts all over Britain and then emerged as one of the game's leading coaches. He never seemed to get old. One commentator described him thus: "He was 74 when he finally declared his innings over, but any stranger would have argued that he was at least 20 years younger. His figure was still upright, his weight never varied from the day he first took guard, his hair showed only a faint tinge of grey and the spirit of the man was remarkable."

Green, knowing his history, held Hallows in deep respect, even if sometimes his advice and criticism fell on deaf ears. But it was more difficult for a teenager, fresh into the game and pulling at the leash.

Lloyd said: "Young players will invariably lack respect for their coach, in the same way that pupils lack respect for their teacher. It's simply a generation thing. It was many years later before I appreciated how good a player Charlie Hallows had been. To me his memories and tales simply came from another era, while I was impatient to be getting on in mine. I never thought of him as anything other than a good coach, yet in the 1920s and 1930s he had been part of a Lancashire side that brought the club its most sustained period of success.

"Charlie would tell us of travelling to places like Somerset and only booking into the hotel for one night because they knew the game would be won in a day and a half. If we won the toss, he said, only the first five would routinely stop at the ground - the rest would sometimes go to the pictures. And, yes, there was always a crate of ale in the dressing room. It was a long way from the Lancashire of the 1960s, languishing near the foot of the championship with a win of any kind precious and elusive and everyone at each other's throats."

That latter sentiment was directed more at his first two years on the staff, rather than in 1965 when he made his debut and when life at Old Trafford had taken a turn for the better under the captaincy of Brian Statham, but it is easy to see why Lloyd found it hard to connect with Hallows' life and times. The 18 year old was driving a mini, liked rock music, and had just been awarded his 2nd X1 cap - which meant a small pay rise, if nothing else - after taking three Glamorgan wickets. He had the whole world in front of him - why bother with history?

Hallows, who had also bowled left-arm spin, certainly played a part in the development of a player young enough to be his grandson, but coaches of that era and earlier were not expected to have the same influence on the team's fortunes as in later times. The captain, his vice and the other senior pros, carried the weight. When the former coach Stan Worthington tried to intervene in a net session, Alan Wharton walked away in disgust. The coach did not travel to away games.

By all accounts Hallows was an exceptional, if demanding, coach, yet it was the dynamic captaincy of Jack Bond and the signing of Farokh Engineer and Clive Lloyd which transformed Lancashire's fortunes in the late 1960s. And something similar occurred in the late 1980s when David Hughes took over as skipper and Wasim Akram was imported. It is impossible to determine Lancashire's best post-war coach/manager. Old stagers like Hallows, Stan Worthington and Harry Makepeace worked in the time-honoured manner of their era, laying down the laws of correct technique for three day cricket and trying to instil discipline into a player's approach.

Thirty years after first hearing one of Hallows' tales of yesteryear, David Lloyd had a shot at county coaching himself. Hallows must have turned in his grave at some of Bumble's antics, morale-boosting slogans plastered all over the dressing-room, rock music blasting out, tapes of Winston Churchill speeches. "Our mad coach," said then captain Mike Watkinson.

But Bumble was hugely popular, of course, and also eager to grasp all the latest coaching help from technological advances. He also had England's most talented squad at his disposal and, in 1995, they did the Lord's double. When England poached him, John Stanworth took over, and Lancashire retained the Benson and Hedges Cup in 1996. Stanworth was a good coach and later became Director of the Old Trafford Academy, but was shocked to learn that the committee had regarded him merely as a 'stand-in'. Lancashire followed that up with another surprise. Like too many other people in English cricket, they thought that Australia held all the cards and brought in Dav Whatmore, who had just tasted World Cup glory with Sri Lanka.

While having a great deal of sympathy for Stanworth, I felt Whatmore was an inspired choice. In the 1996 World Cup, the Sri Lankans had to travel from Colombo to Faisalabad in Pakistan for their quarter-final with England.

Direct travel was impossible because of border controls and their journey took 18 hours. But Whatmore ordered his tired squad to the stadium for a short, valuable practice, more to get the feel of the ground than for anything else. That was commitment for you.

In stark comparison, England strolled out of their hotel to warm up in a desultory net on a private pitch just a few yards away. Mind you, on the day of the match they quickly got the feel of the ground as Sri Lanka's big-hitting left-hander Sanath Jayasuriya forced them to chase to all parts.

Whatmore, though, did not fit in at Old Trafford. He was a top-class coach, but, in the players' eyes, taciturn, moody and 'blew with the wind'. And, of course, he wasn't from Lancashire. From his point of view, medical back-up and other support systems were well short of the required standard, and there were serious issues over the fitness of some players and attitudes of others. Whatmore was scathing in his private criticism of the county scene. It was soft - an accusation levelled a few years later by England's captain Nasser Hussain - and poorly resourced. If Lancashire were the biggest, most successful club of the time, what must the rest be like?

When Muttiah Muralitharan made his remarkable bowling debut for Lancashire in June 1999, taking 14 wickets in the match against Warwickshire yet failing to prevent defeat, the grim-faced Whatmore comforted him with an arm around his shoulders and said mournfully: "Don't worry, that's county cricket for you."

The Sri Lankan born Aussie made many improvements, and did so knowing that, sometimes, he was walking on eggshells. Lancashire were the first county to give their players contracts to cover the whole year, not just the summer. (Too late, of course, for the likes of Harry Pilling, who earned his corn in the winter by selling coffins.) More attention was paid to backroom detail, fitness training changed dramatically and, in 1998, they completed another one-day double. But, when he stood up at the front of the team bus, heading south for a game, to announce that he was going back to Sri Lanka, one senior member of the squad turned around to see how the others were taking it. "I didn't see any tears," he said.

I have to admit that my eyes were fairly moist as Whatmore talked to me over a curry dinner a few days later, but that was only because of his liking for a plate of raw onion, sprinkled liberally with black pepper, as an appetiser. County cricket was pure frustration to him. He needed the international scene. Lancashire appeared to be transfixed by the Aussie factor, bringing in the ever-smiling veteran Bob Simpson - but the ex-Australia captain also looked askance at county cricket's defects. Simpson had a huge challenge, taking over a disintegrating squad whose strongest component, the captain John Crawley, was to become entangled in a painful dispute with the committee. It all went very sour. Simpson quit before he was pushed and Crawley left - a devastating blow to a side which desperately needed his class and strength of character.

Simpson's exit, incidentally, meant that the Manchester Evening News had to find a new columnist. Fifteen months earlier I had introduced him to the Sports Editor, a hard-nosed journo and an unusual type, football mad with not a great knowledge of cricket, yet appreciating its value and prepared to give it tremendous coverage during the summer months. The name Simpson meant nothing to him, except that as Lancashire's new coach he could have a full page every Wednesday to express his views.

Knowing how the Sports Editor refused to bow to big egos, indeed liked to crush them, I declined to tell him that Simpson was one of the game's all-time greats, with strong North-West connections, having scored a ground record of 311 at Old Trafford in 1964, and having appeared for Accrington in the Lancashire League, although I did mention that he had extensive journalistic experience and was, most definitely 'Bob' not 'Bobby'. It was during the following 20 minutes that Simpson's smile sagged - for the first and only time in our acquaintance. This historic clash took place late afternoon in the office, when everyone, work finished, had gone home.

"Well, Bobby," the boss launched off after splashing a plastic cup of lukewarm coffee in front of his guest. "You might not be well known around here right now, but I'm going to make you a star.

"You're going to have your face and name plastered all over the paper. Everyone will soon know who you are. You can write whatever you want, but the thing is, you'll know exactly what's going on in the dressing-room. You'll be our man on the inside. So what we want from you, Bobby, is lots of scoops. What do you mean - how much?!"

When they had finally hammered out an agreed fee, with Simpson suggesting it was about 25 per cent of what he usually charged but he would do it because it was good publicity for the club, I led him away from the Sports Desk, down the aisle of the editorial floor, breathing a huge sigh of relief that it had not developed into an almighty row, with the Aussie scowling and muttering at my side.

"Who the hell does he think he is?!"

I was just about to usher him through the door when a shout from behind stopped us in our tracks. "And don't forget, Bobby. We want scoops, lots of scoops."

A committee member, sickened by what had happened in the build-up to Crawley's departure, told me as Lancashire searched for a new coach: "We have got to have a Lancastrian. This overseas thing just doesn't work with a club like ours. We need one of our own."

And so they returned to familiar ground, with the in-house appointment of former captain Watkinson, who had the full set of coaching qualifications, lots of experience, and was an adept organiser and dyed-in-the-wool Lancastrian. I know that he worked hard and made significant progress behind the scenes, but trophy success continued to prove elusive.

Intriguingly, one of Lancashire's happiest spells in the late 1990s came immediately following Whatmore's exit when they decided to complete the season without a recognised coach. Crawley and the senior players agreed to 'muck in', a system harking back a little to bygone times. The result was an enhanced team spirit and another Sunday League title. But the fact is that no matter how good or bad the coach, or what nationality, Lancashire have failed (1934-2008) to win the major prize, the Championship. The first coach to help lift the pennant will surely be acclaimed as the best.

Hallows won the Championship as a player with Lancashire and with Worcestershire as their coach in 1964. He retired in 1969 at the age of 74 after five years at Old Trafford and with the club just on the verge of their most successful post-war spell, and, at very least, he can take credit for the development of several players who featured in those exciting years. He was 77 when he passed away, looking as young as ever, sitting in front of the fire at home and complaining only that he was a little short of breath.

*****

RICHMOND, Brighton, London ('the most exciting, the gayest city in the world' according to The Daily Telegraph) had faded from view. And back home there was a shocking piece of news. "The Wheel is closing down."

Not quite. What the Manchester Evening News advert said was

Twisted Wheel Members' Notice
Grand Opening Of New Twisted Wheel Premises
Saturday September 18th 1965
Spencer Davis Group
At 6 Whitworth Street Opp Fire Station Manchester
The Club In Brazennose Street Will Close After The
All-night session On Saturday September 11th 1965
Featuring John Mayall

The King of Clubs is dead, long live the King. The Whitworth Street premises stayed open until 1971, but we never went there. There was a new crowd, a new beat.

We had never been truly part of the 'scene' at The Twisted Wheel, not real Mods, not on social terms with the Faces and their sets, but, if you accept that it was a hub of youth culture, and that its spokes of influence stretched far from its rather down at heel centre, you can perhaps understand why it was so vital. If, because of the plan to move to a new site, the Wheel was not broken, it was, in our eyes, badly punctured, and, as the summer days shortened, there was a hint of sadness that things were changing, and not necessarily for the better.

In the book Central 1179, Keith Rylatt says: "The announcement that the Brazennose Street Twisted Wheel was to close...was met with disbelief. Girls cried and it seemed that the scene was over. There was some degree of truth in this. The early Mod crowd at Brazennose Street, the ones who were digging the music when it was truly underground, who had endured the piss-taking and the lack of hip clothes in the local stores, were now swamped by the Carnaby Street brigade (in Manchester it was Brown Street). The Mod scene had gone overground...the exclusivity of the 'in' crowd was fast evaporating."

Rylatt argues that the south coast rioting in 1964 spread and popularised the Mod movement. (More specifically, I think, it was the media reaction to the rioting which had this effect). Adds Rylatt: "It fixed the country's top music clubs in an identical mould." The Twisted Wheel, though, retained its individuality, if with a slightly different character as Motown music began to dominate, resulting in an even greater emphasis on dancing. A Mod danced, yes, but in his original form, he had also been happy to sit, listen and just 'dig' the music.

There was a summer disco at one of the local cricket clubs, and, instead of roistering into Manchester, we danced on the edge of the pitch - our style of dancing. Gradually the older guests stopped their shaking, jiving and twisting to watch us, first with bewilderment, then with smiles. As the booze took a grip, they joined in, led by Pete, a powerfully-built bowler, who usually shunned our lot, but, that night, became one of us, sweat soaking his white nylon shirt as he switched, shuffled and swivelled, elbows jagging out, while staring intently at his feet to make sure he didn't trip up. It seemed to bring him closer to us. A few years later he agreed to manage our football team. He died in a horrific accident, a burning car, and we all said: "Remember the night he danced."

*****

BLACKPOOL was still a Mecca for holidaymakers, with the added lure for us that a sister club of The Wheel had just opened there. It was nothing like the Manchester original, but made a good rendezvous for a trip to the seaside, and we set off on our scooters one Saturday morning, reaching the South Shore a couple of hours later.

Mods, or perhaps 'mini Mods', as Rylatt described the new breed, were all over the place. We gleefully envisaged a rampage along the beach, upsetting deck chairs, kicking over sandcastles, but settled instead for a few tricks along The Golden Mile. A scrap with freshly baked doughnuts. Then a middle-aged man, smelling of drink, was smacked over the head with a hot dog, one half of the sausage flying through the air, mustard and ketchup dripping down the victim's forehead.

Our escape took us into the Tower Ballroom, where they sat at tables surrounding the dance floor and danced through the day on polished wood to the music of The Mighty Wurlitzer organ, made famous in Reginald Dixon's radio concerts. Ladies with sunburned shoulders, in summer frocks and bright lipstick, men in suits with open necked shirts, waltzing and fox-trotting.

Blackpool was a throw-back. Families from the mill-towns enjoying a week at the seaside. "You should come when it's Glasgow week," a bloke in a pub told us. "There's blood in the gutters."

Notwithstanding all our bravado, we weren't into blood. Just ketchup. No, Glasgow week wasn't for us, actually. We knew about Glasgow from a year previously when, on our way to a camping trip in Galloway, we stopped off in the city for a quick drink, breezed brazenly into a bar in Sauchiehall Street, and ordered pints of bitter, only to be totally ignored. After a minute or so of fruitless one-sided negotiations with one scowling barman, we were saved by his colleague, a small, dapper man with a sad moustache, who whispered quietly: "Ye'd do better to ask for a pint of heavy." We did, and were served immediately, if sullenly. We were also told to drink it fast and get out even quicker.

"Why?"

"Because, ye wee piece of horseshit, yer under age, yer not wanted here, and there's a wee mon beyond of ye who's polishing his skean dhu."

"What's that?" said Mogsy.

"Ye'll ken when he sticks it in yer liver."

Knife crime was not unknown in Glasgow. Gangs staged set battles in the streets of tenements. The Gorbals area had a terrible reputation. It was a territorial war based on fierce loyalties. Father fought alongside son, and, in one terrible incident that I heard about, father fought against son. In the 1960s, some of the gangs became known as Tongs, nodding to the Christopher Lee film 'Terror Of The Tongs' with the war cry 'Ya Bass', echoing through the streets.

A Scot who lived in the St Georges Cross area of Glasgow in 1965 recently recalled: "I remember gang names like the Maryhill Fleet, the Shamrock, the Toi, the Cumbie, the Tongs (ya bass!) all being shouted at night when the pubs and snooker halls closed. Me and my brother used to watch from our bedroom window as battles took place right on the Cross, where the weapons of choice usually were flying kicks, blades of assorted types, an occasional swinging chain, and I even remember seeing a sword on more than one occasion!"

No guns. And many of the participants were older than today's street fighters. But knife crime was accepted as readily as your mum's Co-Op divi number.

Around the time of our 1965 trip to Brighton, with the Mods and Rockers theme still gnawing at Establishment nerves, a burly, grey-haired magistrate named Tom Radcliffe ignited a new crime and punishment debate by sentencing four Glaswegian hooligans to be birched. He was able to do that because he was the chief magistrate of Douglas, Isle of Man, the only place in Britain where corporal punishment was still allowed. The youths were convicted of beating up some other holidaymakers and got nine strokes each across their bare backsides. One described the punishment to a Scottish newspaper:

"I was bent downwards over the back of a chair. I cried with fear. My trousers were pulled down and my shirt pulled up. Two policemen held my arms, and a third held my head down. A fourth, a sergeant, used the birch. The pain was terrible. I kept screaming for my parents. I was in pain for hours."

The birch was a switch of three feet long twigs, tied into a 14 inches long handle - light but shockingly painful. Another of the youths said: "I thought they were hitting me with red hot wires." Afterwards, wearing swimming trunks, they showed the scars to a photographer, ragged red lines across the tops of their thighs and, presumably, their buttocks.

Even accounting for a little journalistic licence, it came across as a barbaric form of justice. But Mr Radcliffe said: "The birch might be called medieval, inhuman, even sadistic - all I know is it works. It is a good deterrent." Support poured in from all over Britain. And the Scottish Sunday Mirror proclaimed: "Top officials of The Isle Of Man have given Britain the cure for Mods and Rockers in two terse words - 'Birch Them'."

Hey, hang on. Why pick on us? Why not birch the Krays, or Manchester's Quality Street Gang, and some of the other more 'mature' crims giving our cities such a bad image? But, even in the IOM, the Krays would have been let off with a fine, because the law restricted birching to youths aged 14-21. Perhaps, too, it wasn't such a powerful deterrent. True, one of the four Glaswegians limped away saying: "I'll never do anything that could get me the birch again." But, exactly 12 months later, while he went on holiday to Spain, his 17 year old brother honoured Douglas with his presence, smashed a bottle into a man's face and received six strokes.

Glasgow, of course, was also a city of decent, hard-working and generous folk and is one of Europe's great cities. Dad spent time there recuperating from a serious war wound. Local people visited him and other injured soldiers in hospital, took little gifts, squeezed him into a wheelchair and pushed him to a soccer international at Hampden Park.

"They said there were 150,000 people in the ground, but they shoved us right to the front. One of the nurses gave me a pack of fags. Great people, the Scots. They looked after us, alright. Got fond memories of Sauchiehall Street." Now, knowing Scotland and Glasgow a little better, I would agree wholeheartedly. But, that particular afternoon in the Glasgow bar, I got the feeling that we were definitely not welcome.

Later that same holiday, a Saturday night in the peaceful town of Ayr seemed a better bet. A pub by the dockside allowed us in, and things went swimmingly until Baz emerged from the toilets to say: "I think we've got a problem."

"What?"

"Well, two blokes started talking to me in the bogs and asked me what team I supported and I said United."

"Well?"

"Then they asked me what Scottish team I supported and I said Rangers."

"Well?"

"They were wearing green and white scarves."

"Oh shit!…"

It was the nearest I came, at least in my first 60 years, to violent death. Obscenities and beer mugs followed us through the door and into the street, the swear words sailing out on the wind to sea, the glasses exploding around our feet. The point of a knife pricked my T-shirt. Fear held me rigid, but a noise from behind made my would-be assassin turn and I lurched away, jumped onto the platform of our bus and, as it moved away, vomited.

There was always the potential for fights, broken glass and, no doubt, a blade here and there amid the candy floss and kiss me quick trash of Blackpool, where the back streets were as sleazy and as mean as any, but on the afternoon of our Golden Mile expedition we felt at ease, bouncing up the prom, hanging onto the straps in the tramcar. In the hotel bar on the North Shore, we joined in the fun.

"Now, here's one for Betty from Oldham," calls the bloke on the keyboard. His silver hair is combed over from just above his ear to hide a bald patch. If Peter Kay had been around he would have snapped him up for Phoenix Nights. "She wants Green, Green Grass Of Home. Dead with it, our Betty, aren't you luv? Here we go, then, just hang on while I get me Tom Jones wriggle going…aah, that's it. Like it, do yer?…Eeh you Oldham lasses, reet naughty you lot are. Bet you're all nurses - hope you are. I've given meself hernia with that wriggle! You can have a look at it afterwards, Betty. Reet, Green Green Grass Of Home. Didn't know you 'ad any grass in bloody Oldham! The Old Town Looks The Same, As I Step Down Off The Train…"

*****

LANCASHIRE had been in Blackpool a few days before, playing Warwickshire at the dusty Stanley Park ground. The roller-coaster game was worth a few hours away from the fun and frolics of the prom.

For once, Tommy Greenhough and Ken Goodwin scored valuable runs in the first innings, adding 43 for the last wicket, and Greenhough followed up with 5-46. Lancashire did a lot better in their second knock, Green making his highest of the season, 85, and Harry Pilling his best, 132, with 17 fours, and a challenging declaration left Warwickshire 260 in 210 minutes. At 156-2 they were well set, but Greenhough and Statham persevered and, with four wickets each, turned it Lancashire's way, only for tail-enders Jack Bannister and Tom Cartwright to bat defiantly and, at the close, each side was a whisper from winning, Warwickshire finishing eight short of the target.

"You would have expected George to get Bannister," said Green. "He tried everything but couldn't get him out. A double over Warwickshire, and six wins in all, not many would have complained about that, given the circumstances."

I would have liked Greenhough to have grabbed that last wicket, giving him 10 in the match. The slaps on the back: "Well done, Tommy." A little extra to take with him when they gave him the boot 12 months later. What I've not been able to discover is what input Charlie Hallows had in Greenhough's exit. Hallows had championed David Lloyd's cause with good reason, the club having desperately lacked a left-arm spinner since the departure of Malcolm Hilton after the 1961 season, and perhaps Greenhough blocked the youngster's way.

But the spin department was looking thin. Ramadhin had gone, the young 'offie' Ken Howard failed to make the grade and was also shown the door in August 1966, and Lloyd was still a far cry from the finished article, and, of course, emerged primarily as a batsman. Thankfully it was soon to change with the signings of David Hughes and Jack Simmons, who made his county debut at Blackpool in 1968 and took his maiden wicket with the aid of umpire Cec Pepper, who advised him to bowl around the wicket to Northamptonshire's Hylton Ackeman. Simmons rapped the left-hander on the pads, turned and said: "How's that Cec?" And Pepper replied, raising his finger: "I told you I was right, Jack. That's out."

Simmons loved Blackpool, where Clyde Walcott had taken him and his parents for Saturday nights out during the West Indian's Lancashire League days, and where the fish and chips was to die for. It was certainly good for a night out after the game - a couple of glasses of draught champagne at Yates' Wine Lodge, or one of their 'blobs', warm wine blended with Yates' Scotch, was the conventional aperitif for the Press Gang. But working as a cricket reporter at Stanley Park was a challenge.

For many years, the Press were housed in one half of the main scoreboard, which, of course, meant that you could not see the official score, unless you hung out of the window with someone holding your legs and performed a pike and twist worthy of an Olympic diving pool. Another ill-advised option was to scramble over desks and other reporters to gain access to the scorers' section. The preferred system was simply to thump on the wall partitioning the scribes from the scorers and shout: "Score please Bill."

It worked fine most of the time and, for the Exchange Telegraph, it was absolutely essential that it did work. Extel, as it was known, rang their correspondent every 30 minutes for an update, which would be flashed from their London HQ to media sources throughout the country. They also wanted details of every wicket to fall, completed innings, lunch, tea and close of play scores. Accuracy and punctuality were vital. Other journalists also required an inordinate amount of facts and figures, how long a batsman had been stuck on 111, a bowler's 'wicket to wicket' analysis, how many fours for Hayes, and so on. Invariably, there was a lot of banging on the wall and unfortunately, communications between Press and scorer sometimes broke down.

For the umpteenth time that day...BANG, BANG on the wall. "Score please Bill."

Silence.

BANG, BANG. "Got Extel on, Bill. What's the score?"

Silence.

BANG, BANG, BANG. "Bill we know you're in there, for Christ's sake. Extel are going berserk, we're 10 minutes late as it is. What's the bloody score?"

"You'll have to wait. Bang, bang on the wall, all day. I've got a blinding headache and we're missing a bye."

"I can't tell Extel that, Bill, just give me a score."

Silence.

Reporter hissing into the phone: "Yes, I know mate, I'm trying to get the bloody score now, but...I don't think you quite understand the situation here, we have to bang on the wall and get him to shout the score through...no I'm not pulling your plonker, we have to bang on...what did you just call me?"

I felt sorry for the scorer, trying to do his job and trying to help a bunch of unsympathetic, demanding journalists but, sometimes, it would have been entirely in context if we had sent our copy by carrier pigeon.

*****

OUR minor confrontations in various parts of Britain that August came against the fearful backdrop of the Watts riots in Los Angeles. Six days of savagery left 34 dead, over 1,000 injured and £200million worth of damage. Racial tension, unemployment and its resultant poverty and depression, poor schooling - all were blamed. An American radio DJ who blurted out the infamous 'Burn Baby Burn' catchphrase was also accused of fanning the flames. Buildings were set on fire, shops looted, police bullets winged through the air and the National Guard was called in to restore control.

Homes were also set ablaze in Vietnam. A whole village, Cam Ne, was torched by American marines ordered to search out and destroy the Viet Cong, 'their positions and their fortifications'. Villagers pleaded but were ignored. According to an American TV crew, who recorded the incident, no VC were found and innocent people were killed, maimed and made homeless. Their film was shown on CBS, but, as well as shocking millions, it also outraged many who thought it treacherous and a deliberate attempt to undermine support for America's operations.

CBS boss Frank Stanton was in bed when the phone shrilled.

"Frank, are you trying to fuck me?" yelled a voice.

"Who is this?"

"Frank, this is your president, and yesterday your boys shat on the American flag," spat Lyndon Johnson.

That same morning newspapers across the nation featured an Associated Press photograph of a Marine setting fire to a hut with a cigarette lighter. Amid all the claim and counter claim of that dreadful story ran a familiar theme. That the Press had slanted the truth. LBJ ordered investigators to see whether the TV crew had Communist links, or whether they had set it all up just to get an exclusive. Nothing was found to substantiate either line of enquiry.

The Marines remained adamant that they had not committed an atrocity. Cam Ne, they insisted, was a VC stronghold. Several Marines had been hit by rifle fire coming from the village. VC fighters, stationed in the village, had been killed and injured by American retaliation, but the Cong had retreated into the jungle, dragging their dead and maimed with them, leaving behind a series of lethal booby traps. CBS had seen, filmed and broadcast only half the picture.

The full truth remained veiled in the Vietnam jungle. What is clear is that this Search And Destroy (later known by the acronym SAD) was a forerunner of many such missions. Villagers were subjugated and used by the VC, then, when they withdrew, had their homes devastated by the Americans. Vietnam became the first 'Living Room War' with TV pictures beamed into millions of homes. But the fate of villages deep in the countryside was not always seen. My Lai-4, one of a series of hamlets, was the scene of a massacre in which at least 200, possibly as many as 700, men, women and children were gunned down, yet it took 12 months for the story to emerge.

Many of the soldiers in Vietnam were young, badly prepared and incompetently led. After the war, some 'vets' claimed they had been brutalised in training camps. One recounted: "It was taught to us, go into this 'Ville', and you have to blow everything away...they were not human beings." The mother of one My Lai-4 platoon member said: "I sent them a good boy and they made him a murderer."

All war is brutal and demonic, with atrocities on all sides, but Cam Ne was the first widely publicised black mark against America's involvement in Vietnam, and, while the CBS film provoked a patriotic backlash, it also sowed a seed of doubt. Sure, we're right behind you, boys. God is on our side. But, yeah, maybe they didn't have to torch the whole village, and those kids, best not to ask but, wonder what happened to those kids...

The victims, of course, were not always Vietnamese. From a military report:

BROWN, DONALD HUBERT JR.
Remains Returned 14 August 1985

Name: Donald Hubert Brown, Jr.
Rank/Branch: O2/US Navy
Unit: Attack Squadron 23, USS MIDWAY
Date of Birth: 22 August 1938
Home City of Record: Berkeley CA
Date of Loss: 12 August 1965
Country of Loss: North Vietnam
Loss Coordinates: 201159N 1053200E (WH557335)
Status (in 1973): Killed/Body Not Recovered
Category: 2
Aircraft/Vehicle/Ground: A4E
Refno: 0123
Other Personnel in Incident: (none missing)

Source: Compiled by Homecoming II Project 15 May 1990 from one or more of the following: raw data from U.S. Government agency sources, correspondence with POW/MIA families, published sources, interviews. Updated by the P.O.W. NETWORK 1998.

REMARKS: PROB SAM HIT - NO PARABEEP - J

On the night of August 12-13 1965 Brown's plane was hit by one of two SAMs (Surface To Air Missiles) while on a reconnaissance mission. Another plane was also hit, but limped back to their aircraft carrier. It was the first time an American jet had been destroyed by a SAM and, as the bombs rained down on them in the three years of Operation Rolling Thunder, the North Vietnamese fought back by developing a highly sophisticated ground defence network, supplied intensively by the Soviets and the Chinese. Donald Hubert Brown Jr was the first of many such casualties and the grief and anguish in his California home would have been as deep and as awful as that of any hut in Cam Ne or My Lai-4.

*****

PART of a journalist's training was a day release course at a college in Manchester where we sharpened up our shorthand and were taught law, local government and newspaper practice. After a while a couple of us got bored and spent longer and longer lunchtimes in the pub. There was the Old Vic, close to Granada TV's studio, where the Coronation Street cast gathered and Pat Phoenix, looking even more glamorous off stage than on it, knocked back glasses of red wine. And Sinclair's with its oysters and Guinness. Sometimes I set off by myself, ambling up Deansgate, turning right into Brazennose Street, past The Twisted Wheel, thinking how wonderful it would be to work in the city.

In August 1965 I wrote to the Sports Editor of the Manchester Evening News, asking for a job and listing my qualifications as: Nine months experience on a busy (ha! ha!) weekly newspaper covering Mid-Cheshire League soccer and Manchester Association cricket; shorthand (slow and incoherent) and typing (super quick); extensive knowledge of all sport including athletics (I was the Boys' Club's one mile walking race title-holder), boxing, darts, dominoes, rugby, swimming etc. I enclosed cuttings of my cricket reports for the MEN Pink, told him how ambitious and enthusiastic I was, and waited impatiently for the reply.

Dear Colin,
When you have finished your three years indentureship at the weekly, get two years of experience at one of the minor evening papers and then re-apply. Yours sincerely, Vernon Addison, Sports Editor.

A devastating blow. I had fancied myself writing about the latest feats of Statham and Best. I thought I could conjure the words to match their magic. I had dreamed of being a big time sports reporter since the age of 12, kneeling on the living room floor on Christmas Day morning, ignoring something sharp that was jabbing into my knee, reading in my first 'Football Book Of Champions' of how one national newspaper correspondent had travelled the world, writing about internationals and European Cup-ties.

I remembered my first trips to the two Old Traffords - being a child and not knowing any better I was then a United fan - watching Statham and Washbrook, Roger Byrne and Duncan Edwards, who was my favourite in the Busby Babes side. Not just because he was such a good player, but because, one night, after an FA Youth Cup game he came out of the red painted 'Staff' door, stopped and signed his autograph. We walked alongside him across the concreted area in front of the ground and down the road. He had been watching the match. He had to catch the bus home. Yes, United were going to win the title. See you...He wore a grey coat which quickly merged into the drizzle and gloom.

So it seemed the bright lights were not for me. One warm late afternoon, work for the day done, I stood in the office doorway, watching the quiet street. The sun shafted through alleyways and other gaps between the shops and pubs, laying golden bars across the road, and I wondered whether to pack it in, sling a bag over my shoulders and wander away. Something held me back, I wasn't sure what at the time, except it wasn't any journalistic ambition.

I understood more, 30 years on, after watching Brian Friel's play 'Dancing At Lughnasa', in which a household of unmarried sisters eke out an existence in their rural Ireland cottage, the poverty and tensions relieved by a spontaneous bout of dancing. As they jig and prance around the kitchen table, shouting and laughing, the women come together and, for a few glorious minutes, all their problems are forgotten, only for them to return, worse than ever, the moment the dance ends. Exhausted, they sink into their chairs before wearily resuming their daily chores. In the night two of them steal away, never to be seen again, although a report drifts back of destitution and death on the streets of London.

It seems, although I didn't know it as a young man, that, despite all the breakaway fever of my youth, continuity was important to me, that if there were to be change, it should be in a structured form with direction signs, inventories and memoranda, and that, if ties were to be cut, a lifeline should be first set up. And so I stayed, skating on the thin ice of family relationships, knowing that, if when it cracked beneath me, someone would throw out a rescuing hand. I suppose I just wanted to be there when someone said: 'Remember when we danced.'

*****

FROM Blackpool, after three ding-dong days against Warwickshire, Lancashire immediately travelled 250 miles to Bournemouth. They left Stanley Park in the early evening and arrived at the south coast close to midnight. The Dean Park ground, once privately owned and one of the oldest in the country, had marquees, wooden seating and only three permanent buildings, the pavilion and adjoining covered stand, players' dining room and Press/scorers' box. It was lined by trees and a tall hedge. Perfect for a cricket festival week. It rained.

When the teams did manage to get out, the cricket was hardly inspiring. Geoff Pullar made a century, but it took him four hours with only eight boundaries against the unrelenting seam attack of Derek Shackleton and the left arm spin of Peter Sainsbury. Bob Cottam, who had destroyed Lancashire at Old Trafford, was missing from the Hampshire attack.

Shackleton was 41 years old, yet he sent down 32 overs in Lancashire's first innings and, that summer, 1166 overs in all, taking 133 Championship wickets at 16.31 and carrying his career total past 2500. According to Wisden he was 'a master of movement, pace and flight'.

Desmond Eagar, secretary of Hampshire, had written earlier that the chance of seeing Shackleton bowling to Graveney would surely attract the fans, but Shackleton to Pullar? An interesting contest, yes, but only perhaps for the connoiseur. Pullar certainly got the best of it, shoring up Lancashire's total of 232-7 dec, but 'Shack' will always be remembered as one of England's top county cricketers.

John Arlott said he was 'shrewd, varied, and utterly accurate, beating down as unremittingly as February rain.' But he played only seven times for England. Even at his best (he was a Wisden Cricketer Of The Year in 1959), he could not push his way past the likes of Trueman and Statham. And, while he was able to exploit even the merest hint of help from the pitch, he became much less potent with the sun bearing down onto a flat track.

Derek Hodgson of The Independent said: "Those who have seen the grainy 1963 film of Shackleton's bowling against West Indies must have wondered how he came to be chosen. Here was a man opening the England bowling from a few easy strides, delivering at a pace best described as slow-medium. But by then he was approaching his 40th birthday, and any attempt at speed had been forgotten. Earlier in his career he had a faster ball sufficient to make his county keeper stand back."

Shackleton's 1963 appearance against the West Indies came at the expense of Statham, who was unusually dropped after a dreadful Test display, unhappily at Old Trafford, where he fluffed a catch off Trueman (a miss, which, said The Times, was as rare as spotting a great crested grebe in the middle of Manchester), and, even more unusually, finished with figures of 0-121. Shackleton bowled well in the second Test at Lord's and kept his place for the rest of that series. Statham's Test career was coming to a close, but it was two years later, near the end of the 1965 season, that he ended it in a style more fitting.

When the conditions were perfect for Shackleton he was almost unplayable. Against Somerset, at Weston-super-Mare in 1955, he took eight wickets for four runs and 14-29 in the match. Sussex, led by Ted Dexter, once decided to attack him: "We were caught off strange parts of the bat and Shack finished with 6-50, but in 12 overs instead of his usual 28."

A team-mate, Neville Rogers, remembered: "He didn't leave any footmarks. It was as though he bowled in slippers." Hampshire supported him with an expert close catching field – although 46 per cent of his victims were bowled or lbw – and such was his reliablity that his county captains were able to get away with some outrageous declarations, knowing that the eventual target could always be defended. His record places Shackleton alongside Wilfred Rhodes as the most consistent English bowler. Between 1948 and 1969 he took 2,857 wickets at an average of 18.65.

It was Shackleton's stamina and longevity which impressed me. When Hampshire won their first Championship in 1961 he bowled 1501 overs, taking 151 wickets at 19. In 1965 he appeared in all 28 Championship fixtures. He retired at 45.

A county cricketer's age was of no great concern in pre-fitness guru days. Somerset's Bill Alley headed the charts at 47. "Some of his shots were too ambitious for a man of his years," it was reported, "but he remained a dangerous man to bowl against." Alley, an uncomplicated Aussie who had boxed professionally and had played in Lancashire league cricket until making his county debut at 38, scored 842 runs, took 73 wickets and played in every game of 1965.

Worcestershire's average age was well over 30. Don Kenyon, the captain, was 41, Roy Booth 39, Graveney 38 and Flavell 36. D'Oliveira, said to be 31, was in fact 34. D'Olly and Flavell were ever-presents, Graveney missed one match, Booth three and Kenyon nine, several because of his duties as a Test selector.

Flavell had played in four Tests, all against the Aussies, once hitting Norman O'Neill so painfully with a vicious break-back that it made the batsman vomit. When Worcestershire met Yorkshire at New Road in his benefit game, Flavell was so badly hampered by an Achilles tendon injury that he could only bowl eight overs off a shortened run-up before retiring for treatment. Even with him out of action, Worcestershire made Yorkshire follow on, and in their second innings, he re-appeared to send down one token over. No run-up at all this time, just standing at the crease, turning his arm over. Unfortunately for Doug Padgett, the last delivery grubbed along the ground and bowled him for a duck. They went off the field together, Flavell limping badly and leaning on Padgett for support while the crowd convulsed.

Looking back at the days of the golden oldies, David Green said: "I've noticed in recent times an increasing tendency on the part of some current cricketers and younger commentators to cast doubt on the ability of their predecessors. In fairness, there has never been a time in cricket's long history when old men have not praised their contemporaries at the expense of the current crop, so a bit of reciprocal disdain is, perhaps, understandable.

"Nevertheless, the line regularly produced today when an old player's name crops up - 'Of course he wouldn't have survived in the modern game' - jars with those of us who treat cricket's past with respect. One reason for this negative attitude may be that cricketers these days hang up their boots comparatively early. A few, including Jack Simmons, have carried on well into their 40s, but many now retire in their early or mid 30s, not surprisingly considering the kamikaze approach to fielding.

"There were times when few retired much before 40, often in their mid 40s, and up until World War Two cricketers aged 50 plus were not thought of as too remarkable. Sidney Barnes was still confounding Test quality batsmen until his late 50s, and club batsmen well into his 60s. Arguably, he is the greatest of all English bowlers."

Subtly blending swing with leg-spin and off-spin, Barnes took 189 wickets at 16 each in 27 Tests between 1901 and 1914, routing the Aussies in 1911-12 with his new ball partner Frank Foster and claiming 49 wickets in four Tests in South Africa two years later. He could be a difficult customer, on and off the field. His brief career at Old Trafford ended after a contract dispute, and at the age of 47 negotiations for him to tour Australia broke down after he had insisted on his wife accompanying him. He had two years with Lancashire but played most of his cricket for Staffordshire and in the leagues. Even when 56 he was a force to be reckoned with. Playing for Minor Counties he demolished the South Africans with 8-41, bowling 32 overs unchanged, and soon afterwards he had the tourists in trouble again, when, appearing for Wales - he lived in Colwyn Bay - he returned match figures of 10-90. Nine years later, eligible for the old age pension, he was Bridgnorth's professional with 126 wickets at 6.94 apiece.

Green added: "I read in Cyril Washbrook's autobiography that he had found Barnes very difficult to bat against when Cyril was playing for Lancashire's 2nd X1. Barnes was then 60! I once talked to Cyril about it and the conversation went like this:

Green: "You played against him, didn't you? What did he bowl?"

Washbrook: "Off breaks and leg breaks, quite slow by then."

Green, innocently: "Did you give him some stick then?"

Washbrook, with feeling: "Did I fuck!"

"There is no concrete rebuttal nowadays to the argument that because today's athletes run faster and jump higher than in the past, today's cricketers must be better. However, because cricket is, as well as a game, an art, such arguments seem to be inadmissible. You might as well set Luciano Pavaroti above Enrico Caruso purely on the grounds that he was born later. For me,

I'm happy to praise good cricket when I see it, while still paying tribute to the heroes of my youth and to the great players of even earlier eras."

In August 1965, Barnes was back at home after, it was reported, a 'splendid recovery in Staffordshire Infirmary' after a fall at home in which he broke some ribs. 'He remains tall and upright and still retains his copper-plate handwriting.' He was 93 and died on Boxing Day 1966, aged 94.

Lancashire's game at Bournemouth was destined for deadlock, but the second game of the festival produced fireworks, with the controversial Colin Ingleby-Mackenzie's declaration which kept Worcestershire in the title hunt. Ingleby-Mackenzie signed off his Hampshire captaincy at the end of the season with a dig at Lancashire and other clubs who customised their pitches to blunt the opposition.

"I do thoroughly agree," he wrote, "with Micky Stewart (the Surrey captain) when he writes about those counties who deliberately produce 'hot' wickets to reduce the power of the opposition. If Trueman is in the 12 sent to the ground before a match, for instance, the groundsman removes the grass - and the pace. The reverse applies if there is a good spinner in the visiting side. Old Trafford last year fell between those two stools and roughed up all their wickets to get results. If they had the luck they would have a chance of winning. How wrong they were, and they soon realised it... Great batsmen and attacking bowlers win the crowds - and the matches. With these wickets, nothing is achieved."

ELEVEN

"FAST bowling is no job for old men in Test cricket these days," said Brian Statham as the debate mounted over England's scant attacking resources ahead of the third and final Test. He had not played for England for two years, and, despite his outstanding form for Lancashire, had already ruled himself out of the tour of Australia. Now he appeared to be admitting that his Test career was all over.

Statham knew, from bitter personal experience after his 1963 shocker at Old Trafford, that the step-up from three day county cricket to a five day Test, and against the young, lively South Africans at that, was a step too far for a veteran bowler. But as the selectors searched desperately for someone to plug the hole left by him and Fred Trueman, and as Statham's haul of county wickets continued to mount, they persuaded him to make a return. Maybe he could help to square the series.

Northants' David Larter was sidelined by injury, but England could have gone for any of the following: John Snow, Fred Rumsey, Jack Flavell, Len Coldwell or Jeff Jones. Statham, however, was in sparkling form. "He has bowled with a zest and conviction which a year ago he seemed to have lost," said The Guardian.

Statham's displays had made a nonsense of fears that he would be weighed down by the burden of captaincy. In fact, the new job had motivated him. As he linked up with the Test squad at The Oval, The Times dubbed him 'The Reluctant Hero'. He was noted as looking 'thinner and greyer' than for his last England appearance. Surprising, that. The Greyhound, as he was called early in his career, may have had a few more grey hairs, but 'thinner'? If he had lost weight, I don't know where it could have fallen from. Thirty years later, when President of Lancashire, he was greyer, no doubt, and still lean. There was the slightest thickening around the waistband, but you could hardly notice it.

"He was one of those blokes who could eat and drink what he wanted and not put on any great weight, whereas someone like me would pile it on," said David Green. "Of course, he wasn't going to put on too much, bowling the amount he did."

By the time of the third Test at The Oval, Statham had got through more than 700 overs. Other seamers had bowled more - the indefatigable Derek Shackleton was beyond the 1000 mark, as was Statham's Lancashire partner Ken Higgs. Statham, however, had taken 117 wickets, comfortably more than anyone else. Understandably, Statham was nervous on the morning of the match. Much rested on him, and the unhappy memory of his last England appearance niggled away at the back of his mind. "It had been two years and there was a lot of expectation," he said. "I did not want to tour again, and I knew this might be my last match. I wanted to bowl well and, no matter how experienced you are, you're bound to feel a bit jumpy. I felt a lot better when they told me that Higgs was going to play as well."

Higgs was to make his debut, coming in for Tom Cartwright, who had injured a thumb. Within a few overs on the first day they were bowling in tandem, and making inroads into the South African batting. Statham 'showing all his old virtues' finished with 5-40. Higgs, showing all his new promise, had 4-47 and South Africa were all out for 208.

England's batsmen also found it difficult, Peter Pollock claiming another five. Complaints were made of poor light; it was difficult to see the ball from the Vauxhall End, there was movement off the seam and swing, but, whatever the excuses, it made poor viewing for the crowd, not in keeping with the previous two games. But Colin Bland transformed it with a delightful century. Statham's age at last caught up with him, his second innings analysis was 29-1-105-2, and while Higgs continued to impress, taking his match collection to 8-143, England were left to chase a seemingly impossible target of 399. At the start of the last day, with six hours and nine wickets remaining, they needed another 335.

That Tuesday may well have entered into cricket history. Bookies were offering 100-1 against an England win, but when a downpour ended play, they were well on course at 308-4, with Colin Cowdrey eyeing a century and 70 minutes to go. South Africa had been reduced to delaying tactics, slowing the over rate to 14 an hour after taking the new ball.

So the Test summer ended on a dramatic, if entirely predictable, damp note. The reaction to The Oval encounter was intriguing. Praise for England's brave attempt and little criticism of South Africa's time-wasting. Many commentators expressed pleasure at the tourists' 1-0 series win. They played good cricket, in the main, and had the most entertaining players in the Pollock brothers, Bland and Eddie Barlow - a quartet who would grace a World XI. England, however, had taken them close, despite the handicap of losing Ted Dexter and John Edrich, whose blow to the head from Peter Pollock in the first Test at Lord's had sparked off an outcry against the use of the bouncer. That, coupled with the return of Statham, who hated to use them in any event, led to not one being delivered in the entire Oval clash.

During the match, Statham took his Test wickets to 252. His 250th was Tiger Lance. I have a black and white photograph of him, shouting an lbw appeal. Keeper Jim Parks looks on thoughtfully, Colin Cowdrey at slip seems to be doing a little jig.

*****

ONE of the spectators at The Oval was between jobs. Alec Douglas-Home, kicked out of 10 Downing Street in late 1964 by a pipe-smoking Northerner, had also been recently replaced as leader of the Conservative Party by a man who became one of the big stars of Spitting Image, Ted Heath. There seemed nowhere left for Alec, aka Lord Dunglass and the 17th Earl of Home, so, naturally, in 1966, he became President of the MCC.

Harold Wilson's smoke rings wreathed Heath's manic grin in the latest snapshot of the British political scene in mid 1965, with George Brown hovering over the PM's shoulder, waving a document headed The National Plan. A five year Plan, promising a new economic boom, as long as we were all prepared to keep our noses to the grindstone and churn out record productivity figures. They had plans like that in the USSR, but there they could control the workers, fiddle the books and silence the media. Brown's plan, not envisaging the devaluation of the pound and a few other matters, such as trade union intransigence, fell apart within two years.

Not that it stopped him enjoying himself. At one lingering luncheon he drunkenly ordered one of his Civil Service lackeys to 'Get me a woman'. When Wilson, worried about his right-hand man's worsening demeanour, approached the drinks-littered table, Brown turned to the Civil Servant and complained: "I ordered a woman and you've brought the Prime Minister!"

Douglas-Home was 'the first British Prime Minister to have played first-class cricket'. Wherever you see his name, this cricketing link suddenly pops up, as though of enduring importance. Lord Dunglass, as he was then known, played a few games of first-class status. Two were for Middlesex against Oxford University, the others were for the university and for a MCC side which toured Argentina in the late 1920s. An all-rounder, he was not considered good enough to have made a career of it. Wisely, he chose politics, and, though not considered good enough to have made a career of it, actually became Prime Minister. He must have wondered sometimes whether if he had stayed in county cricket, he might just have become captain of England.

Did it matter that the Prime Minister had played first class cricket? Yes, said Robert Mugabe. "Cricket civilises people and creates good gentlemen."

Douglas-Home had a gaunt, almost skeletal, washed-out appearance. Undergoing intense work from the make-up artist one evening as he prepared for a TV programme, he asked: "Can you make me look better than I do on television? I look rather scraggy, like a ghost."

Make-up girl: "No."

Douglas-Home: "Why not?"

Make-up girl: "Because you have a head like a skull."

Douglas-Home: "Doesn't everybody have a head like a skull?"
Make-up girl: "No."
Cricket loomed large in the life of the 17th Earl of Home. "My wife had an uncle," he said, "who could never walk down the nave of an abbey without wondering whether it would take spin."
Politics? Actually he was quite good at it. As Foreign Secretary in Harold Macmillan's Cabinet, he won friends with his honesty and aristocratic charm and, though a surprise choice to take over from SuperMac, he carried it off with a certain panache. However, by the time of the 1964 Election, the country had had 12 years of Tory rule and wanted a change. Douglas-Home, who had renounced his peerage to take a seat in the House of Commons, was kicked out of office. But he remained to the fore of British politics, acting as the MCC's front man in negotiations with South Africa's Prime Minister John Vorster in the D'Oliveira Affair, and then returning to government in Heath's Cabinet of 1970.

Wilson was enjoying a family holiday on the Isles of Scilly. He liked cricket, thought Trueman was the 'greatest living Yorkshireman' and could chat forever about his native county's cricketing history. But, coming to the end of his first full year as PM, he needed some relaxation and knew he would find it on St Mary's, the largest of the Scillies, that beautiful archipelago 27 miles into the Atlantic, off Land's End.

Wilson was a canny, manipulative operator. The more you read about him, the more disagreeable he becomes, yet to many he seemed an easy-going, approachable bloke who enjoyed a pipe, HP sauce and Huddersfield Town football club. A spin merchant could not have devised a more folksy image and some critics have tried to debunk it all as a myth. But, according to Labour's Gerald Kaufmann, it was all true, to the extent that Mrs Kaufmann complained that Wilson's pipe smoking would 'kipper' them all.

Wilson was buried in the graveyard at Old Town, St Mary's, looking out to sea. It's a simple resting place, easily by-passed. The granite church is simple, too, and so tiny that the nave definitely would not take spin.

Despite his relaxed, homely image, Wilson had worries. Britain's economic boom was about to burst, although only those in the lofty reaches of Whitehall and Downing Street and The City could have known that the devaluation of sterling was high on the agenda. Although the crash was imminent, for most it was still out of sight. Car sales grew, Concorde blasted through the sound barrier on its test flights, fashion, art and music spread their arms in an ever widening embrace.

More people had more spending power than ever before, buying fridges, electric cookers, stereograms and smart living room suites. They went for a Sunday ride in the car, calling in at a nice countryside pub to scoff scampi and chips in a basket, and went home for tea before settling down for ITV's

Sunday Night At The London Palladium variety show. It wasn't that the living was cheaper than today. A pint of Chester's Mild was 1s 8d, so a ten bob note would buy you a real sway. But that was five per cent of the average basic manual wage of £10 a week for an adult male. Five per cent of the average wage today (2008) would buy you at least the same amount of alcohol (and much stronger, if you so chose).

Other 1965 prices:

New Vauxhall Viva Super Luxury ('quieter, more distinctive').........
£628 inc purchase tax;
Hotpoint electric cooker................£48 6s;
English Electric washing machine..........£63 3s;
Radiogram ('the new inexpensive Decca')...... 44 guineas;

Electrical appliances were expensive. Kitting out a kitchen alone would cost possibly £150, 15 weeks of wages. Now, you can buy a mid-range fridge, cooker and washing machine for around £1,200, only three times the weekly wage. IKEA was only a dream. But, no matter what the cost, most articles were accessible, if you had a regular wage coming in, because everything could be bought on tick - hire purchase. The English Electric cooker can be yours, dear, for just £5 deposit, and 9s 6d a week - you can manage that, can't you? Sign here, oh yes, that 9s 6d a week, you understand it's for three years, don't you? Oh, and I bet you like Cliff, don't you luv? Why not have a new radiogram, play his records on stereo, only £4 12s 6d. Yes, dead cheap isn't it? Look good in the living room, will that, neighbours will be dead jealous. Sign here. So £4 12s 6d for the deposit and, after that, it's only 103 payments of 9s 7d a week and one of 11s 9d.

Throughout the decade, Britain's homes had filled up on credit, sparkling white in the kitchen, polished teak in the lounge, the buff coloured repayment books hidden away in the back of a drawer. But, even in times of real wealth, you can never eradicate poverty, and, late that summer, two London School of Economics academics were applying the finishing touches to a work which, according to their data, picked out what sociologist Mark Donnelly described as a 'disturbing underside to the gaudy materialism and credit fuelled affluence of the high sixties.'

The LSE whiz-kids, Brian Abel-Smith and Peter Townsend, headed their publication 'The Poor and The Poorest', having based their research on government figures of household spending and National Assistance scales. Among other findings, the statistics, superficially, indicated that millions of children were living in low-income families and needed state support.

Questions were raised about the methodology used. Poverty, said the critics, had been re-defined rather than re-discovered. But, doesn't poverty have to be constantly re-defined? One critic sniped: "What significance and value attach to the definition and measurement of poverty in the Western world and other advanced communities? Before long it will mean the non possession of a colour TV set." Whereas, he implied, in other parts of the world, it meant non-possession of a bowl of rice or loaf of bread. But whether re-defining or re-discovering the poor, Abel-Smith and Townsend had exposed some uncomfortable reading for this new look Britain.

The lukewarm response from the government was not quite that expected of Labour in power, but, then, few appreciated the dark, economic undertones seeping through the walls of 10 and 11 Downing Street. In mid summer, the Chancellor, Jim Callaghan, the man who had wrecked the political ambitions of Ted Dexter in the 1964 poll, had withheld £350million of investment earmarked for education, hospitals and other local authority projects. They were bringing in a Rent Act to help hard-up tenants who were having to pay through the nose for sub-standard accommodation, but as much of the bottom end inner city housing was occupied by newly arrived immigrants, scarcely aware of their rights, the legislation made little immediate impact on wily landlords. Rachmanism still flourished. But 'The Poor And The Poorest' struck a chord. The Quakers, for example, helped to set up the Child Poverty Action Group, which became a model for later pressure groups such as The Low Pay Unit and Shelter.

While writing this chapter in 2008, I take an afternoon off to walk through a local shopping precinct, politely turn down three offers of a Big Issue, spend £5 on a music mag, and then stroll back over the bridge ignoring one of the several silent, blanket-wrapped beggars who rotate the shifts, collecting tins at their sides, and spend the remainder of my money in Tesco's. Back home I switch on the news to hear of a protest march in London against child poverty.

Where we now live, there are more charity shops in the town than of any other type. It's a good re-cycling concept, offering the chance for some to get shut of their cast-offs, for others to buy at cheap prices, and for all concerned to give to charity. But some of the shops are so well-organised, so professional - one has an advert in the window for a full-time manager - that it's possible to forget their raison d'etre. I find it all rather strange.

Consumers in the Western world have shown they can force prices down, but we are deep into recession and there is massive world-wide debt. Stock Markets have crashed. Banking is in crisis. People in other parts of the world are close to starving. Where has all the money gone? It was never there, I suppose. I recall a daft shop sign from my youth: "Please don't ask for credit as a refusal can often result in a punch on the nose." While I was never sure who was most in jeopardy, the shopkeeper or the customer, it sort of made its point. Certainly, saying yes to credit has left society with a very bloody nose, and, if the Sixties can be blamed for anything, it is the belief that not only could you have virtually anything you want, but that you should have it, no matter what the cost.

Not that Dad, bless him, would have asked for credit. All he expected was a fair product at a fair price and to slap the cash on the counter. Although if he had said "Put it on the slate", the poor shopkeeper would have smiled weakly and hurriedly planted some cans of baked beans in front of that sign.

I know we were not The Poorest. But for some years we must have been on the fringes of The Poor. Otherwise why did we have the Co-op's own brown sauce, instead of HP, and in what cookery book did half a tomato, some lettuce leaves and a couple of slices of cucumber constitute a salad? Hell, I was thinner than Brian Statham. The TV set in the front room remained solidly black and grey, changing occasionally to black and white horizontal stripes, or a colourless fuzziness which forced Dad to take remedial action (a good whack on the top of the set to shake up the tube), and the suite came from a second-hand furniture store. But the house that we had moved into was nice. Roomy, with front and back rooms, decent-sized kitchen, upstairs bathroom, three bedrooms and gardens, a mansion compared to the previous house, and the rent was usually paid on time.

Dad had a good, solid job as a postman, and, in the summer, took on occasional work as a gardener. He was the most tireless worker I have ever seen. Even in his late 80s he enjoyed digging a trench for spuds. Clever with his spade-like hands, too. He built us some banquette seating around the kitchen table, fashioning odd bits of wood, with hammer, chisel and knife. Mum also part-timed, as a housekeeper in a big place on the posh side of town. I was working at the newspaper, £6 10s a week after deductions, giving Mum £2 for my keep, spending £2 10s and hiving away the remaining £2, secreted between two pairs of Y fronts in a wardrobe drawer. So life was better, yet still we always seemed to have just enough to get by on, never enough to have the best of anything. Not moaning, just wondering where the money went.

Many Brits who came into The Poor category were gobbling up the biggest bargain on the shelf, an assisted passage to a better life in the warm, wonderful and welcoming country on the other side of the world. Thankfully, we never considered emigrating to Australia - and you could for just £10 on an assisted passage, as long as you were of decent, white British stock ('No darkies, please, we've got enough of those Abos here already'). The migrants found life Down Under totally different from that promised in all the brochures. They complained bitterly about accommodation, lack of jobs, the flies and became known as 'whingeing Poms', but what they couldn't moan about was the amount, quality and cheapness of meat on offer. Steaks, chops, joints - Oz was paradise for British carnivores brought up on scrag ends.

Sometimes I yearned to dig my teeth into a real piece of cow. And one Saturday, after finishing the morning shift and without a cricket match to report, I dodged into the butcher's, the one where all the staff had developed a funny, shuffling gait to cope with the sloping floor, and bought a 12 ounce rump steak for my lunch. I had never before spent so much cash on one item of food. I had never had a whole steak for myself. And this was a big one, marbled with creamy fat, oozing blood. I could taste it all the way home. Imagined what it would look like under the grill of our White Diamond cooker, the fat starting to brown and curl, the juice dripping and sizzling. What it would smell like, that sweet, cloying, carnivorous smell. And waiting for it to cook through, not impatient because the anticipation would be so good, and then sliding it out onto a wide empty plate.

I thought everyone would be out. Dad gardening, Mum at the shops, sister and brother with friends, but Mum ambushed me in the kitchen, plucking at my sleeve, demanding to know what I was trying to hide under my jacket. "It's some meat, and it's mine."

It became a struggle, the survival of the fittest. Mum, a closet socialist, wanted me to share it with the others. The steak slid out of its brown paper wrapping and slapped onto the floor. We stared at it, Mum with a tinge of astonishment, me with rancour, as though the steak had betrayed me. Now I would give it what for. I picked it up, brushed it off, ignoring the specks of blood on the lino, and pulled out the grill pan.

"You can't have all that to yourself."

"Yes, I can. I've paid for it and I'm having it."

I grilled the steak, all anticipation deadened, plonked it on a plate and stomped into the front room to eat it in private. I heard Mum say: "I didn't think he could be so selfish." I'd like to say that I didn't enjoy that steak. But I did.

But where did the money go? Dad drank, but only cheap beer and only at weekends. He didn't gamble. He had given up cigarettes years previously after a bout of flu. Forty Woodbines a day, then finished, just like that. Strong-willed? That's akin to saying Diana Rigg looked rather fetching in a basque and high heels. To combat an ulcer, the doc advised him to eat nothing but steamed fish for six weeks. He ate nothing but steamed fish for six weeks and cured the ulcer. Downside was the lingering stench - no-one could be invited into the house for months. Mum's only vice - apart from bringing home cheap fruit from the market ('just cut out the bruised bits') - was the occasional packet of 20 Kensitas cigarettes. They had blue gift vouchers which she stacked up in a drawer. Sometimes she would ask me to count them, to see if there were enough to get something cheap and nasty out of the catalogue.

Mind you, compared to some of our ancestors we were extremely well off. Back in the 18th and 19th centuries, they were The Poorest, living in peasants' hovels in the Cheshire farming lands and in the bleak Wiltshire and Dorset landscapes where, in spring, young Tess danced with the other village girls and where you were buried 'in wool' if the price of a coffin was too much to bear. Others sought their fortunes in India. One was Thomas Avery, who rose from private in the Hon. East Indies Co. Army to Quarter-Master Sergeant in A Troop, Madras Artillery.

Quarter-Master Avery, my great, great, great grandfather, knew how to make money, and how to husband it. When he died in Bangalore, possibly of cholera, he left an amount of cash, closeted in the new Madras bank of Arbuthnot's, with a modern value of about £300,000. And, again, it's a mystery as to where the money went. He married three times, secondly to an Indian woman, perhaps a camp follower. Her grave is in a former military cemetery in Bangalore, southern India, and it is not a peasant's grave, nor a simple one. Dad never knew of the Indian connection, that, in fact, he had Indian blood. But he did proudly tell of how just after the First World War his Army stock parents had bought a farm, where the family lived well, perhaps ostentatiously, for a number of years, before running out of cash and beating a retreat to a more humble terrace cottage, with a back garden rambling down to the railway line, and from where I first saw the ageing slag heaps of south Wales, black and lichen green.

I don't know how to measure poverty nowadays. My wife and I have no debt. We buy what we can afford, no more. We have squirreled enough away to regularly visit our beloved India, where we use local buses and trains and stay in budget lodgings. In India we see immeasurable and, notwithstanding 'Slumdog Millionaire', inescapable poverty. You might not believe that, having seen Danny Boyle's fairy-tale, and having read about the multi-million pound auctions of the Indian Premier League and endlessly re-cycled garbage of India's economic boom. A boom which has not touched millions of people still fighting to survive in abject conditions. See the naked kids playing in the stench of the open sewage drains - and the women, old before their time, earning a few rupees a day by breaking stones, then you will ask, like us, where has the money gone?

*****

LEAGUE cricket in Lancashire was well worth watching in 1965 despite the poor weather. Nelson dominated the Lancashire League, completing a double, with their Pakistani Test star Saeed Ahmed setting an example to other pros. Ahmed hit 637 runs and claimed 99 wickets, but he also led the way in the field and in the way he encouraged the club's juniors.

Alan Wharton, the former Lancashire player, was back at his home town club Colne, scoring 720 runs to finish as the leading amateur batsman. Ken Grieves, for many years a team-mate of Wharton at Old Trafford, also scored prolifically for Accrington, but could not lift them from bottom place. Other big names were ex-England spinners Tony Lock and Johnny Wardle, at Ramsbottom and Rishton respectively, although the best overseas bowler was West Indian paceman Cec Wright, who took 109 wickets for Colne.

In the Central Lancashire League, the big draw was another West Indian fast bowler, the controversial and sometimes uncontrollable Roy Gilchrist, who had a penchant for bowling ferocious beamers from 18 yards when a batsman irritated him. Gilchrist was a terror, rated by some as the fastest of all the West Indies Test bowlers, and, universally, as the one most likely to break bones and spill blood. His turbulent Test career was over, but he remained a fearsome sight on a league ground.

In 1963, guesting for Darwen against a Commonwealth XI, he had a sensational scrap with Aussie batsman Lou Laza. It kicked off when Laza, hit on the glove and chest by a perfectly good delivery, caught the ball as it bounced off him and quickly threw it back to Gilchrist, who immediately appealed for a catch. After a frank exchange of views, Laza smacked Gilchrist over the head with his bat. In retaliation Gilchrist used a stump on Laza's head. Darwen fielders rushed in, fans invaded the pitch and the home team's captain Ted Friend was knocked over in the melee. Fortunately the two protagonists made it up during the tea interval.

But, as his side Crompton were battling for the 1965 Central Lancashire League title, Gilchrist exploded again, in a brush with another batsman, schoolteacher Derek Bickley of Radcliffe, who, slightly miffed by one ball which he thought whizzed a little too close to his skull for comfort, cheekily and foolishly invited the West Indian to put the next one on his chin. Which, never refusing a challenge, Gilchrist attempted to do. Not from the usual bowling distance, but from around six feet, having hurtled down the pitch, ball in hand, to chuck it with all his strength. Somehow it missed, but the row which followed caused the game to be abandoned only 20 minutes after it had started.

Gilchrist was suspended. In 1967 he lost his temper again, this time his victim was his wife, whom he attacked with an iron. Treating him leniently with probation, the judge said: "I hate to think that English sport has sunk so far that brutes will be tolerated because they are good at games." Born into poverty in Jamaica, Gilchrist was 5 feet nine inches tall, with a gigantic chip on his shoulder. I met him once after a court case in Manchester and, when I asked him for a comment for the paper, he glowered and ordered me to get out of the way. I didn't argue. He continued to play league cricket into the 1980s, but returned to Jamaica and died there after a long illness in 2001, aged 67.

*****

OVER in the States, The Beatles shaped up for the biggest date of their lives. They were staying in a rented house in the Coldwater Canyon area of Los Angeles, and, about 9pm, two limousines drew up to ferry them to Perugia Way in Bel Air. Arriving at their destination, a huge mansion, John Lennon noticed a Rolls Royce Phantom in the drive, just like his own, except he had had the chrome bits painted black. It was August 27, 1965 and they were seconds away from realising a dream. They were to meet Elvis Presley.

For once the Beatles were quiet and anxious. None of their usual Scouse jocularity. They were big stars in America as well as Britain, having just played in front of 55,000 fans at New York's Shea Stadium, where no-one could hear the music because of all the screaming. But still not quite as big as Elvis. Not yet.

The shrewd Colonel Parker, Elvis' manager, had leaked the rendezvous to the Press. Hundreds of fans dripped over the walls surrounding the property, some climbed trees to get a better view, reporters roamed, security men swarmed. No recordings were taken of what happened inside the house and the recollections of those involved sometimes fail to tally. But there was tension, that alone is clear. Elvis, dressed in red shirt, and black trousers and jerkin, was lounging on a sofa, watching TV with the sound turned down, when The Beatles entered the spacious, circular lounge which Priscilla Presley called the family room. Priscilla claimed: "He barely bothered to get up. This was a summit and the fact that Elvis greeted them with studied casualness didn't mean that he didn't care. He was simply re-affirming his role as Original King."

The Beatles had been well brought up, knew how to behave, how to show respect. For 30 minutes they barely spoke, sipping at Scotch and Coke or bourbon and Seven Up. Elvis kept his eye on the TV, leaning back on his couch. Others in the room averted the potential for embarrassing silences. Colonel Parker and The Beatles manager Brian Epstein chatting in a corner, Priscilla, wearing a gingham frock and a bow in her beehive hairstyle - Paul McCartney thought she looked like a Barbie doll - house staff, Elvis' motor bike mates, and so forth, but conversation between The Fab Four and The King was stilted, until he said: "If you guys are just going to sit around and look at me I'm going to bed."

Whether joking or serious, it broke the ice. Someone pulled out a roulette table, Elvis began plucking his bass guitar and Paul offered a few tips, electric guitars were suddenly produced for The Beatles and they began to jam, starting off with Cilla Black's 'You're My World', Ringo glumly tapping on the side of his chair because no drums were available.

"If only we'd had a tape running," groaned one of the guests later.

They strummed and sang for a couple of hours. Elvis Presley and The Beatles, with an audience of less than 20. He enjoyed their stuff like 'Michelle', 'Yesterday' and 'Hey Jude', although, later, he was dismissive of their more psychedelic ramblings. They had thrived on his good ol' rock 'n' roll, but Lennon, particularly, wasn't so struck with some of his soppy film hits. Neither was Lennon, the pacifist who had just enjoyed his first LSD trip, happy with Elvis's patriotic support for the Vietnam war. Some say that this get-together ended with bad feeling between the two, and eventually to a feud in which they never spoke to each other again. The party broke up around 2am. On the way out, Lennon put on a Peter Sellers voice, saying: "Tzanks for ze music Elvis and long live ze King." But there was a note of sarcasm in it.

Priscilla said: "Elvis respected that they had achieved their artistic freedom, but he was conscious of competitors and that generational idols come and go. He viewed this whole world of music coming from England - The Beatles, Stones, Dave Clarke Five - with tremendous interest, but he worried about losing popularity and in 1965 no-one was more popular than The Beatles."

*****

WHILE Brian Statham and Ken Higgs were involved in The Oval Test, Lancashire brought in Peter Lever and Ken Shuttleworth as their new ball attack for the Championship trip to Gloucestershire. Lever, we have discussed earlier. St Helens-born 'Shut' had made his debut the previous season at the age of 19. He was tall and slim yet, with a curtain of dark hair opening and closing on his forehead as he bounced in off a long run-up, there was a faint hint of Fred Trueman about him. Shuttleworth was quick. It seemed a long, successful career lay ahead, particularly when he took 5-47 in Brisbane when Ray Illingworth's side launched their Ashes winning tour. But that memorable debut was followed by a series of injuries and disappointments He played in only four more Tests. In 12 seasons with Lancashire he took 484 first-class wickets at 22.92.

Although Shuttleworth was four years younger than his partner, he and Lever were joined at the hip, making their England debuts against the Rest of the World in 1970, touring Australia together, and sharing in the successes of Lancashire's one-day side. Shuttleworth left in 1975 to play for Leicestershire and Lever quit playing a year later. I saw Shuttleworth bowl well a number of times for Lancashire in the early 1970s. But my fondest memory of him is in the breakfast room of a Blackpool hotel. I had never seen anyone putting so much salt onto their porridge. I was transfixed. He looked up, saw me staring, gave me a Gilchrist type glare and carried on shaking.

At Bristol, they grabbed the chance to show Lancashire the future, sending back nine Gloucestershire batsmen in the first innings. Sadly, Lancashire had already capsized to a dismal 105, the last seven wickets falling for 35.

Shuttleworth gave Lancashire a glimmer of hope with these figures, 26-8-38-5, and Lever had 4-60, but Gloucestershire took a lead of 133 and, even though Lancashire did better in their second attempt, thanks mainly to an entertaining knock of 70 from Lever, who punished John Mortimore for four sixes, the home side knocked off the runs with nine wickets to spare. David Green liked Bristol, admired Arthur Milton, who had played cricket and soccer at the highest level, and hugely respected Gloucestershire's captain Mortimore. If he were to play anywhere other than at Old Trafford, this would be the place for him.

The Championship was drawing to a close. As in 2008 rain spoiled much of the cricket but had helped to produce a thrilling finale to the title race. Worcestershire had won only three matches in the first half of the season, but now, with one game left, stood on the threshold of a remarkable success. All they had do was to dispose of Sussex at Hove - and, by lunch on the first day, they had it wrapped up. Or so it seemed. Jack Flavell, with 7-26, and Len Coldwell wreaked havoc on that first morning, bowling out Sussex for 72 in 31.4 overs. But it proved to be a nail-biter. The Nawab of Pataudi headed a batting fightback, and John Snow bowled brilliantly after Worcestershire had been left to score 132 for the Championship. Slumping to 36-4, they needed all but 11 of the 260 minutes available and all their nerve to dig themselves out of trouble and edge to victory.

Worcestershire's captain Don Kenyon praised their overall never-say-die effort, and picked out Flavell, Graveney and Basil D'Oliveira for special mention, adding: "The remarkable thing is that we won the Championship with only three batsmen scoring 1000 runs and one bowler taking 100 wickets. Despite that we won 10 out of our last 11 matches. It was a wonderful run, but just a bit wearing on the nerves." Mischievous critics pointed out that Kenyon's debut season as a Test selector might have also played a part in it - not one Worcestershire player was picked for England's seven games. But, as with the condemnation of their New Road pitch, it was a red herring. Worcestershire had their luck, particularly in Colin Ingleby-Mackenzie's cavalier declaration at Bournemouth, but they also had some outstanding performers and unflagging team spirit.

Lancashire signed off at Old Trafford with another powerful all-round performance from Lever against Kent. Again Statham and Higgs were absent, Pullar too, and Keith Goodwin stepped down to allow Geoffrey Hodgson his debut - and his farewell. The ex-Yorkshire wicketkeeper left the county with this first-class record: Matches 1, Inns 1, Runs 1, Ave 1, Ct 2, St 0. Green, Pilling and Lever hit half centuries, the first two sharing in an opening stand of 81, but, after most of the first day had been lost to rain, it was fairly subdued, end of season fare. Lever, though, took 5-36. Declarations set up a possible finish, only for Lancashire's campaign to end early after more rain.

There are no available records of the attendance for that game. Above average, I guess, because many members enjoy the last rites of a season, even if there is little to play for. When Lancashire were relegated in 2004, a decent crowd turned up for the last day's play against Gloucestershire and I chatted to a cross-section, asking whether they would be back the following year to watch second division cricket. Not one said no. Disappointed, yes. Concerned about the future, yes. But the overwhelming view was that they would pay for another year's membership without hesitation.

One lady from Bolton was accompanied by her 82 year old grandmother, watching a county match for the first time in her life. Both were wrapped up against the cold. "Oh yes, we'll be back," said the elderly but evergreen debutante. "I've loved every minute of it. And I could just imagine on a nice, sunny day sitting here with a glass of wine. Wonderful!"

I imagine the fans at that last day's play in 1965 were just as enthusiastic, despite the weather and Lancashire's lowly position in the table. They had seen improvements on and off the field, new faces making their presence felt in the committee room, new faces impressing on the pitch. And as that final Championship fixture fizzled to a draw, I bet there were groups of supporters huddled together, cold and damp, patiently waiting for the much delayed official announcement that it was all over, because to love cricket is to harbour the hope that it is never all over.

TWELVE

APOLOGIES if you thought it was all over, but David Green has another story to tell, and I couldn't let the summer of '65 end without giving you a final pillion ride on my, by now, badly dented, red, white and rust brown scooter. So if you are brave enough, hop on.

This trip is a short one, just a quick rev to a tree-lined avenue in our town, with large late Victorian and Edwardian houses, bay windows, porches, gravel drives shaded by rhododendrons. Substantial homes for substantial people, with substantial incomes. And some with more income than others. You can tell that from the tidier lawns, sharpened and shaped by a hired hand. Other front gardens are taking on an unloved appearance. During my schooldays I once had a job cutting the grass at one of these properties, each Saturday morning, two hours at 1s 3d an hour. I lasted 30 minutes, squeezing the throttle on the petrol mower too hard, losing control and letting it lurch like David Green's old car through a neatly planted rose bed. When the owner re-appeared, he gazed aghast at the crazy stripes on his once immaculate lawn and sighed: "Not quite like Wembley now is it?" He was a gentle soul. I left him quietly extricating from the blades of the mower remnants of the cardboard identification tags which had been tied around his beloved rose bushes.

No worries…that's a year ago and right now there's a party on just up the road, and that's where we pull in, cut the engine and leave the Capri alongside the Lambrettas and Vespas, at the side of the house. It's warm and damp, early September, with the sniff of a premature autumn. In the hall, two youths are fighting with ceremonial swords grabbed from hooks on the stair walls. Others are roaring them on. The combatants have obviously watched 'The Three Musketeers'. The clash of steel rings up the stairs and onto a middle landing. One fighter jars his wrist in defending a full-blooded slash, throws down the bottle of brown ale he was holding in his left hand, takes a two fisted grip on the sabre guard and charges full tilt, pushing his opponent back, through an open doorway leading off a second landing. They disappear but you hear the grunts of battle.

"Ron started it - I think he's on something," I'm informed. In a living room various characters sit on the floor, drinking, listening to a Dylan LP. One girl, long and lean, is full length on her stomach, kicking her heels up and down. "I'm swimming. Do you want to swim?" Fitz, a dark-haired lad in horn-rimmed glasses and once the subject of a nation-wide police search, pops his head up from behind an armchair, triumphantly holding up a used condom. "I had a bet I would use at least one tonight." I can see the girl's head, poking out from one side of the chair, and her bare feet from the other side. "I've got two left," says Fitz, sliding out of view.

On an oval, mahogany table is a large glass container, packed with multi-coloured bubblegum balls, which are freed with a shove penny slot mechanism. Something normally seen on the corners of sweet shop counters.

"We whipped it from Mundays," I'm informed.

"But how did you get it here, it must weigh a ton."

"Yeah got pissed off with lugging it. Tied it onto the pillion. Want a bubbly?"

As long as they haven't used the air pistol in the sweet shop heist, the long-barrelled air pistol which, in the last days of school life, had made the prefect suddenly clutch his backside, jump, twist and shout, the one which I hid under the gingham teacloth which covered the apple pie which Lesley of 5A had baked in domestic science, then I'm not too worried about this latest escapade. But, thinking of Fitz's disgusting rubber, stretched between thumb and forefinger, no I don't want a bubbly. Ever again. Upstairs, a scream. "You twat, you've cut me. Now it's for real." And the chandelier, dripping from the 10 foot high ceiling in this once elegant room, shakes.

I look around, open a door and find a double bed hosting four guests. Two are strangers to me, but I recognise instantly the other couple, my girlfriend who looks extremely comfortable apparently asleep, snuggled up to one of my mates. Jed is enjoying a post coital, I assume, smoke. He eyes me appreciatively. "You've got good taste," he says, patting her on the head. Never having been in that position with her, I wouldn't know. But I share the joke. Not to would be deemed unmanly.

K, in tight white jeans, ghosts towards me, offering ephedrine tablets. You can buy them cheap over the counter at Boots, yet he is able to sell them at a good profit. I've had them before. No buzz. So: "No thanks."

"Haven't got anything else."

"Don't want anything else."

One thing puzzles me. Whose place is this? No-one seems to know. The party stretches through the night, spells of languidness interrupted by spells of utter mayhem. The swimming girl keeps kicking me, gently with her heels. I sleep on cushions on the floor and am woken by my ex, black semi circles under her eyes, pale face, dishevelled blonde hair. He can have her.

"Want a coffee?"

"Sod off."

"Ooh, what's wrong with you, then?"

The morning is cool, damp, sunless. Ron nurses a deep gash on his hand. Few speak. There is a forlorn atmosphere about the place. I go outside and find the Capri wrecked, the clutch cable ripped out of its socket and dangling over the handlebar, the rear tyre punctured. Someone else has taken it for its final ride. Sad, but not surprised nor angry - live by the sword and all that - I'm wheeling it slowly away when a car, a Humber I think, pulls up; a couple get out, banging the doors shut, and the man, a tall, sporty-looking, 40-something type with open-necked shirt, exclaims: "What the bloody hell is going on" and strides towards the front door. He is holding some keys, but I could tell him he doesn't need them, the place is wide open.

*****

THE cricket season wasn't quite over, although the 28-match Championship programme had ended. Worcestershire were celebrating the title for the second year on the trot, but Yorkshire were to re-group and to dominate the title for the rest of the decade.

David Green still had the chance to show the South Africans his class, even though it was too late to win a place in the Ashes touring party. Lancashire's last game was against the tourists at Old Trafford, after which Green was to appear for TN Pearce's XI, also against the South Africans, at Scarborough.

Manchester's cricket lovers saw the Pollock brothers say farewell to England, the last time they played together on the tour, with Peter stepping down for the light-hearted shindig at Scarborough later in the week. Unfortunately Colin Bland was missing from the Old Trafford line-up, but the Pollocks said goodbye in style.

Ken Higgs underlined his new England status by sending back Denis Gamsy, Eddie Barlow and Ali Bacher in his first six overs for 11 runs and, perhaps, if Brian Statham had been at the other end, the South Africans would have been embarrassed. But Statham had earned a rest. The veteran put his feet up, allowing Peter Lever and Ken Shuttleworth to link up again, and, anyway, he would not have wanted to play, knowing that after 692 Championship overs and a full-on Test, he was too tired to give 100 per cent.

Green explained: "Unlike some England quick bowlers he never saved himself in the county game preceding a Test, nor took it easy in the match that followed. He felt that his club and his colleagues were entitled to his best at all times and he gave it unstintingly. His great stature as a cricketer never distanced him from less gifted players. Because he was chivalrous as well as tough and because he was highly competitive without rancour he was something more than a great cricketer; he adorned the game as few men have done."

After Higgs' new ball assault, Lancashire's seam attack faded, the wicket encouraging spin and batsmen who showed initiative. From 34-3 the tourists recovered to total 273, Graeme Pollock batting beautifully for 75, including 20 off David Lloyd's opening over. Peter Pollock contributed six fours in a free-hitting 51, for once his batting overshadowing his bowling as the two off-spinners Norman Crookes and Broomfield were to share the Lancashire wickets.

Green also batted well for 46 and, with Harry Pilling rising to the challenge, Peter Pollock's 17 overs earned him a modest 2-42. But the other batsmen struggled against the slower bowlers. With a lead of 114, the South Africans went for their shots in the second innings, Graeme Pollock heading it up with 40 and, taking advantage of their carefree attitude, the young Lloyd claimed three late wickets with his left-arm spin. As he also produced a defiant innings on the last day, going in at 40-4 and sticking it out for 85 minutes before being last man out for 42, he was to remember the game with some pride.

He said: "I ended that first half season of Championship cricket with 202 runs and 17 wickets, but my best performance was in that game. Four wickets in the match came as a relief after some initially rough treatment from a tall left-hander who I didn't know. I had watched him from the field during the first morning and thought he looked vulnerable around leg stump. When David Green brought me on for the mandatory single over of spin before lunch, I duly attacked that area and saw my plan exploded as this chap - utterly unknown to me - hit every ball to the square leg boundary. As I trailed off with the figures of 1-0-24-0, I asked one of our senior players who this batsman was. The reply was: 'He's Graeme Pollock. He'll never make a decent player. Much too free.'

"On the last day of the match, as we were bowled out for 117 I was last out for 42. I was no longer just a promising bowler. I had taken my first tentative steps as a county player. I was engaged to be married and I owned my first car, a Mini with 48,000 miles on the clock. In all senses I was on the road."

If you think the Pollock story should be well salted, remember Lloyd was just a naïve kid in county cricket terms and had never met Pollock until that game. He did not remember seeing him on TV during the Test series, so the only visual clues as to his identity would have come from newspaper and magazine photos. Anyway it's a good story. And as The Aviator, Howard Hughes, told his movie company researchers: "Never check an interesting fact."

Next day, after Lancashire's 166 run defeat, Green lined up in a powerful TN Pearce's XI, including current Test stars Bob Barber, Colin Cowdrey, Peter Parfitt, Mike Smith and Fred Titmus. Also involved were Trevor Bailey and the country's top all-rounder in the 1965 season, Barry Knight of Essex, wicketkeeper John Murray, and pacemen Derek White and Fred Rumsey.

Peter Pollock dropped out, but Bland returned. Scarborough could sell it, with justification, as a contest of international status and 5000 fans rolled up.

But the South Africans were demob happy. At lunch, after 29 overs, the scoreboard read 164-4. Fifty one balls into the afternoon session it read South Africa 207 all out! Barber and Green fell quickly to the new ball, but solid middle-order batting gave the home side a 34 run lead. Again the crowd were treated to some wonderful entertainment in a second South African spree, Richard Dumbrill twice hitting 18 in an over off Titmus during a knock of 64 in 37 minutes, but their Festival spirit cost them the game. TN Pearce's XI cruised home by eight wickets late on the second day, thanks to an unbroken stand of 136 between Cowdrey and Parfitt. Green made 24. The sides stayed on to fill the vacant third day with a one-dayer, and again TN Pearces's XI won, this time by 13 runs.

Green completed the season top of the Lancashire batting chart with 1784 Championship runs from 53 innings at an average of 34.4. He played in all 28 matches. His overall first-class record was: Innings 63; Runs 2037; Highest Score 85; Average 32.85. He finished 20th in the national list of first-class averages.

England's Top 20
(+ denotes left-hander, * denotes not out)

	Inns	NO	Runs	HS	Ave
M C Cowdrey (Kent)	43	10	2093	196*	63.42
J H Edrich (Surrey)+	44	7	2319	310*	62.67
P H Parfitt (Middlesex)+	44	9	1774	128	50.68
T W Graveney (Worcs)	45	9	1768	126	49.11
M D Willett (Surrey)	9	3	271	83*	45.16
B D'Oliveira (Worcs)	45	6	1691	163	43.35
E R Dexter (Sussex)	19	3	676	98	42.25
B L Reed (Hampshire)	9	1	334	79	41.75
W E Russell (Middlesex)	54	5	1930	156	39.38
W J Stewart (Warwicks)	39	8	1187	102	38.29
J M Parks (Sussex)	39	7	1212	106*	37.87
K F Barrington (Surrey)	41	4	1384	163	37.40
J A Ormrod (Worcs)	26	9	634	66*	37.29
A Jones (Glamorgan)+	57	7	1837	142	36.74
G Boycott (Yorkshire)	44	3	1447	95	35.29
H Horton (Hampshire)	55	9	1596	107*	34.69
J Pressdee (Glamorgan)	46	12	1179	150*	34.67
D Gibson (Surrey)	40	11	996	98	34.34
C T Radley (Middlesex)	26	8	612	138	34.00
D M Green (Lancashire)	63	1	2037	85	32.85

Sixty six batsmen passed 1000 runs. Forty averaged 30 or more, which, in those days, indicated a decent season. Alan Ormrod, later to serve Lancashire as a player and manager, played 17 Championship innings for title-winners Worcestershire and took third place in their averages.

The South Africans went home happy, with a profit of £15,000 and a vault of good memories, and presumably not too bothered that their final scheduled game, a one-dayer against the Gillette Cup winners Yorkshire, was rained off. The Wisden Editor was one of their many admirers: "If there was any question whether their representative matches should be labelled Tests since their enforced withdrawal from The Imperial Cricket Conference *(which, in 1965, became The International Cricket Conference)* in 1961 the excellence of their cricket definitely settled the matter.

"The most heartening feature of the tour was the willingness of these gay young men to hit the ball. Their enterprising methods were in marked contrast to those of the teams of 1951, 1955 and 1960. Much of the credit for that transformation must go to RA McLean, who fought a lone battle for initiative in those far off days. McLean moulded the new Springboks when he brought the Fezela side to England in 1961. Under his direction they played positive cricket and among them were six of the present team, van der Merwe, Barlow, Lindsay, Bland, PM Pollock and Botten.

"....One of the reasons for the South Africans' success was their excellent team spirit. They were never involved in unpleasant controversies and the presence of anti-apartheid demonstrators in some places left them unperturbed."

Only four South Africans averaged 30 or more, Graeme Pollock leading the way with 57.35, followed by Ali Bacher (40.32), Eddie Barlow (38.84) and Colin Bland (37.75). Peter Pollock was the top wicket-taker with 50 at 17.02. Early on he raised eyebrows with his use of the bouncer, but adapted quickly to English pitches and claimed six 'five-fers'. Off-spinner Crookes had success against the county sides, taking 47 at 19.44. Often they found the pitches too slow for their liking and, as a result, the big-hitting Bland was regularly caught in the deep, but they made no complaints about the conditions, and captain van der Merwe, diplomatic and upstanding, went out of his way to praise the umpiring after the last Test.

South Africa were on the up, ready to tackle the Aussies and the West Indies, and, many believed, were capable of beating them. England, despite question marks against their pace attack, had good reason to be confident as they prepared for their winter Ashes challenge. World-wide, cricket had a lot going for it.

The county game, however, hesitated at its crossroads, occasionally edging over the white line, then drawing back as the traffic of modern life roared past. Perhaps that did not matter to the diehard supporter, who resented change - remember the fuss over the introduction of coloured kit and then Twenty20 when phrases like 'the pyjama game' and 'Mickey Mouse cricket' were bandied around? But change had to come. The success of the Gillette Cup was perhaps the biggest factor. Other potential sponsors wanted a slice of one-day cricket, but Gillette were firmly ensconced so further possibilities were considered, leading to the revolutionary concept of a one-day county league. Perhaps the 1965 Gillette Cup final between Yorkshire and Surrey proved the popularity and value of limited overs competition. Over 25,000 at Lord's - 21,000 paying - watched Geoff Boycott's startling match-winning innings of 146, with three sixes and 15 fours, as Yorkshire powered to 317-4. With Fred Trueman grabbing three wickets in four balls, Surrey never got close.

Boycott showed how a cautious Test opener, criticised and punished for slow scoring, could blossom in the one-day environment. The Gillette Cup was then a 65 over contest, giving a player like him time to get his eye in, then open up, although Brian Close, his captain, who shared a stand of 192, alleged that Boycott also needed a verbal kick up the backside. Whatever the motivation, Boycott's display and the fans' response rammed home the virtues of one day cricket as never before.

*****

AS for Lancashire there remained the annual inquest, which in recent years had taken on a funereal air, but this time contained a whiff of optimism.

REPORT OF THE COMMITTEE

'Once again the County's final place in the Championship table was most disappointing but, on the other hand, there were signs of better things to come from quite a number of the younger players. In his first year as Captain, Brian Statham's leadership and personal performance were beyond praise, and in order to show their appreciation of his efforts, the Committee took the unusual step of inviting him, as early as September, to be captain again next season, an invitation, it is pleasing to report, which has been accepted.'

Statham, then, had eradicated all the misgivings. Higgs, said the report, had bowled consistently and economically. Green had had a 'splendid season' and Harry Pilling, Keith Goodwin and Peter Lever had been awarded first XI caps. The coach Charlie Hallows, who had been helped by Ralph Alderson, was to have a new assistant in Buddy Oldfield for 1966 and all the players, apart from Sonny Ramadhin and a member of the 2nd XI, Nigel Wood, were re-engaged. Mac Taylor, the scorer, had raised £1312 from his benefit year, extensions and improvements had been made to the Tyldesley Suite and the Indoor School, and two salaried organisers had been put in charge of the fund-raising Supporters' Association.

The club's Year Book carried an 'independent review' by an un-named contributor, who waxed lyrical about Statham: "It would be difficult to find in the countless pages of cricket history the equivalent of a pace bowler captain dominating the scene so late in a career of international brilliance, with the one object in view of stemming the declining prestige of his native County. Well might he have been unanimously and almost instantly invited to undertake the task again and, under his efficient, unassuming leadership, the near future...could not be in better hands."

The committee could afford to bask in the reflected glory of Statham's success. Few outside the confines of the committee room knew just how close they had been to handing the job first to AC Smith and then to Freddie Millett. Green, the vice-captain, had also played a part in the leadership stakes, taking over as skipper from the absent Statham on six occasions. Green was 26 and viewed as a Lancashire captain of the near future, despite showing disapproval of some committee decisions. But within two years it had all gone badly wrong. The 1968 Lancashire Year Book told a terse story.

D. M. GREEN

'David Green has left the County and will be playing for Gloucestershire in future. He was born on November 10th 1939, first played for Lancashire in 1959, and was awarded his county cap in 1962. He was awarded his Blue at Oxford University in 1959, 1960 and 1961. At his best he was a most attractive and hard-hitting opening batsman and also a useful medium-pace bowler.'

Green had scored 1180 runs at 22.65 in 1966 and, crippled by a leg injury, only 222 in 13 innings in 1967. Lancashire wanted him to have an operation, he refused, insisting, justifiably as it turned out, that rest and physio would do the trick. But it wasn't just the injury and lack of form which concerned Lancashire. He was his own man, and sometimes - in the opinion of some - difficult to handle. There was also a report of tomfoolery in a Cheltenham hotel, unfortunately for Green's sake, witnessed by a man close to the committee.

Green, fit and happier at Bristol, responded with the best cricket of his life in 1968, hitting 2137 runs at 40.32, including a career best of 233 at Hove, and earning the accolade of one of Wisden's Five Cricketers Of The Year. He worked well with the coaches George Emmett and Jack Crapp, the former captain John Mortimer helped him to cope better with spin, and batting with Arthur Milton was an 'education'.

The Wisden citation said: "With Gloucestershire, Green is regarded as a batsman with the ability to restore some of the lustre of Hammond and Barnett of old by his bold and venturesome brand of batsmanship and reliable change bowling. In Lancashire there is general regret that yet another fine cricketer 'got away'. Certainly the powers that be at Old Trafford gave a fine strokeplayer little opportunity to make a lasting recovery from a leg injury that specialists said required surgery. Green did not think this necessary…he has been proved right and Gloucestershire have gained a tremendous asset in the signing of a cricketer whose zest for life is embodied in his cricket."

After leaving Old Trafford, Green burned his Lancashire blazer. "I had a bonfire in the garden and just put the blazer on it. I had been angry with them over a number of issues, but this was more about getting rid of something I didn't need. I was a Gloucestershire player, not a Lancashire player, simple as that."

Three decades later, Green, working as a freelance cricket writer for The Daily Telegraph, was in the Old Trafford Press Box and was invited into the committee room. He must have thought: "What the hell have I done wrong now?" But there was his old mate, Brian Statham, President of the club, offering him a new blazer. They had a laugh about it. The blazer Statham produced actually belonged to Jack Simmons. They didn't have a new one which fitted Green - would send him one in the post.

It's 2008, and I'm chatting to Green at his Bristol home. He has cooked for me breakfast, sausage, bacon and egg, and then a lunch of grilled trout, potatoes and peas. "Got a mate who fishes for trout, brings me back one now and again. As for the chef bit, that's no problem. When I packed the game in I worked for a big catering firm and got to know the tricks of the trade.

"Anyway," he continues, "they promise to send me the blazer, and a package arrives and, well, I've got to show you. Hang on. It's in a cupboard. I've never actually worn it, you'll see why."

Green vanishes for a few minutes and re-appears through the lounge doorway. I collapse. For a bloke, who even in his playing days was 'heavily built, tending towards rotundity', they have picked out a garment more suitable for Harry Pilling. Somehow he has squeezed it on, the cuffs just reaching the tops of his wrists, the hem barely touching his trouser belt. It's so tight he can't move his shoulders. He's laughing so much he's got tears in his eyes.

"Fucking thing…have you ever seen anything like it? Not that I'm ungrateful or anything."

He gave up cricket in 1971 without ever making a great deal of money out of it. He is 69, still full of fun, still passionate about the game, still blisteringly hot on his history, still revelling in life. I only wish I had known him that summer.

*****

STILL, it had been quite a summer, not one which, even looking back from this range, I would readily change.

Dad, suited and pale-faced, standing at the bar of the Oaks, had spotted me sneaking into the best room with a couple of pals. I was still a month short of legality. He laughed and sent over a pint. He could see I was one of the lads and, maybe, one Sunday lunchtime, he and I would walk through the estate together and push the tap-room door open with a flourish and he would order two pints, one mild, one bitter, and wink at the barman and say: "He's with me." And that would be a big moment, a man's moment, like Dylan Thomas bumping into his newspaper's chief reporter in the wet-tiled office toilet, where blood smeared one of the basins, and arranging to go out with him that Saturday night in Swansea town.

I would be 18 in a month, and the summer was maturing, too. Its last throw of youthfulness came in the middle of September. We watched ITV's 'Ready Steady Go' - "The Weekend Starts Here"- on Friday night, with Cathy McGowan spouting how 'super' and 'smashing' everything was. She was called The Mod Queen, but most Mods were sick of her silliness by now. Neither did they think much of her urbane co-presenter Keith Fordyce, nor Jimmy Savile on BBC's 'Top Of The Pops'. My preference was for Brian Matthews, who hosted BBC Radio's 'Saturday Club'. He never made too big a play of anything. Always sounded relaxed and knowledgeable. And, of course, he didn't have to act up for the cameras. I still switch him on now, although his show has been re-named 'Sounds Of The Sixties'.

Saturday, September 11 was the last night of the Brazennose Street Twisted Wheel. John Mayall And The Blues Breakers, such a significant part of the club's history, were to apply the last rites. Although The Wheel was to re-open just across the city centre in Whitworth Street, and was to enjoy another era of success, we knew this was the end. Others felt similarly. Phil Scott claims in the book Central 1179 that the final six months, i.e. March-September 1965, was the best period of its celebrated history.

DJ Roger Eagle reckoned that most of the Brazennose Street regulars moved to the new premises without demur. But there's no doubt the Mod scene was changing rapidly. Keith Fordyce had talked on RSG late in 1964 of the trend for long hair, to the disgust of Mods whose hairstyle even then was actually getting shorter and shorter, and while the Faces still sported their Italian mohair suits, there were more Levi's jeans and Ben Sherman shirts on view. Scooter sales were declining.

My Capri was rotting on the refuse tip, dumped on its side, surrounded by the town's household rubbish, a ripped Kellogg's Corn Flakes box resting against its kick-start. I never even considered saving up to buy a replacement. A 1965 summer scooter, nothing more.

Mayall played at The Wheel. I've no idea what. The last night, but I can't recall it in detail. I assume there was a feeling of something lost, mixed with talk of what the new Wheel would be like, but I don't know. I know I went in and came out an hour or so later. I can remember walking through Albert Square to Central Station (now G-Mex) in light drizzle, and, with 20 minutes to wait before the last train home, ordering a pint of Guinness at the desolate waiting room bar. The station lights burned a mucky yellow, a train shunted, and the barmaid asked why a young bloke like me looked so fed up.

"Winter's coming," I said, nodding at the tears streaming down the outside of the black windows.

"Yes, and what a summer we've never had. Awful."

"Yeah, awful."